D0205454

Mythology
in the Modern Novel

Mythology
in the Modern Novel

A Study of Prefigurative Techniques

BY *JOHN J. WHITE*

PRINCETON UNIVERSITY PRESS

1971

Publication of this book has been aided by
the Whitney Darrow Publication Reserve Fund
of Princeton University Press

This book has been composed in Caledonia
Printed in the United States of America
by Princeton University Press
Princeton, New Jersey

For Ann

Contents

Preface

This study has two principal aims: to consider the main problems of interpretation raised by the use of myths in fiction, and to examine in detail various patterns of correspondences that contemporary novelists have chosen to establish between their subjects and classical prefigurations. The common goal of these two undertakings is a new way of looking at the role of mythology in the novel.

Although *Mythology in the Modern Novel* is intended to be an essay in comparative literature, it betrays a quantitative bias towards American, English and German novels; and this is not by accident. As an Englishman working mainly in the field of German literature, I naturally find this study's emphases reflecting my own particular interests, but I hope that there is more to my selection of material than this. Much has been written in recent years about the marked predilection of certain countries for mythology. "The Germans," Harry Levin once observed, "have tended to be a nation of mythopoets, or—at least—mythophiles; whereas . . . the French are a nation of mythoclasts."[1] And such nationally different attitudes are reflected in literature not only in the mood in which mythology is handled, but also by the sheer number of mythological novels produced. There are far more mythological novels in English or German literature than in French. Hence my process of select-

[1] "Some Meanings of Myth," *Daedalus: Journal of the American Academy of Arts and Sciences,* Spring, 1959, p. 228.

ing novels from various literatures as illustrations to my argument involved more than a mere question of personal inclinations; it was intended to mirror national attitudes.

Extracts from two earlier articles I wrote on this subject have been included in Chapters Four and Five, and I wish to thank the editors of the *Germanic Review* and *Mosaic* for permission to use this material in revised form. I am also very much indebted to a number of friends and colleagues who helped me with my work on mythological literature. Miss Marie-Luise Waldeck and Mr. Richard Beckley, both of London University, read and criticized different versions, and I am most grateful to them and to my editor, Miss Mary Laing, of Princeton University Press, for the revisions they suggested. I should like to record the assistance I received from Professor Eric Herd, of the University of Otago, Mr. Peter Hutchinson, Dr. Alan Marshall and Mr. Edward Thomson, all of London University, and Professor Theodore Ziolkowski, of Princeton University. I owe a particular debt to two scholars. Professor Elizabeth M. Wilkinson, of University College London, not only supervised those parts of this study which were originally presented as a doctoral thesis for London University, but has also aided and encouraged me with this work in many ways since then; and Professor Siegbert Prawer, of Oxford University, has given me a host of helpful suggestions over a number of years. However, it is a particular pleasure for me to admit that I owe most to the help, criticism and encouragement which I have received from my wife Ann.

Westfield College, London   J. J. W.
February 1971

Acknowledgments

Quotations from the following works appear with the kind permission of the publishers:

From *A World Elsewhere* by John Bowen
  Copyright © 1965 by John Bowen
  Reprinted by permission of Faber and Faber Ltd. and Coward-McCann, Inc.

From *Der Tod des Vergil* by Hermann Broch
  Copyright © 1958 by Rhein-Verlag A.G.
  Reprinted by permission of Suhrkamp Verlag

From Hermann Broch, *The Death of Vergil*, translated by Jean Starr Untermeyer
  Copyright © 1945 by Pantheon Books
  Reprinted by permission of Pantheon Books

From *Die Schuldlosen* by Hermann Broch, edited by Hermann J. Weigand
  Copyright © 1950 by Rhein-Verlag A.G.
  Reprinted by permission of Suhrkamp Verlag

From Hermann Broch, *Briefe*, edited by Robert Pick
  Copyright © 1957 by Rhein-Verlag A.G.
  Reprinted by permission of Suhrkamp Verlag

From *L'Emploi du Temps* by Michel Butor
  Copyright © 1957 by Les Editions de Minuit
  Reprinted by permission of Les Editions de Minuit

From *Trepleff* by Macdonald Harris
  Copyright © 1968 by Macdonald Harris
  Reprinted by permission of Holt, Rinehart and Winston, Inc. and Victor Gollancz, Ltd.

ACKNOWLEDGMENTS

From *Doktor Faustus* by Thomas Mann
  Copyright © 1947 by Thomas Mann
  Reprinted by permission of S. Fischer Verlag
From Thomas Mann, *Doctor Faustus*, translated by H. T.
  Lowe-Porter
  Copyright © 1948 by Alfred A. Knopf, Inc.
  Reprinted by permission of Alfred A. Knopf, Inc. and
  Martin Secker and Warburg Ltd.
From *Adel des Geistes* by Thomas Mann
  Copyright © 1945 by Bermann-Fischer Verlag, A.B.,
  Stockholm
  Reprinted by permission of S. Fischer Verlag
From Thomas Mann, *Essays of Three Decades*, translated
  by H. T. Lowe-Porter
  Copyright © 1947 by Alfred A. Knopf, Inc.
  Reprinted by permission of Alfred A. Knopf, Inc. and
  Martin Secker and Warburg Ltd.
From *Il Disprezzo* by Alberto Moravia
  Copyright © 1955 by Valentino Bompiani & C.
  Reprinted by permission of Valentino Bompiani & C.
From Alberto Moravia, *A Ghost at Noon*, translated by An-
  gus Davidson
  Copyright © 1955 by Valentino Bompiani & C.
  Reprinted by permission of Farrar, Straus and Giroux,
  Inc. and Martin Secker and Warburg Ltd.
From *Nekyia* by Hans Erich Nossack
  Copyright © 1961 by Suhrkamp Verlag
  Reprinted by permission of Suhrkamp Verlag
From *Interview mit dem Tode* by Hans Erich Nossack
  Copyright © 1948 by Wolfgang Krüger Verlag, G.m.b.H.
  Reprinted by permission of Suhrkamp Verlag

For permission to quote from a dissertation entitled *Das
Hermesmotiv in der Dichtung Thomas Manns* (Kiel, 1961),
I am indebted to the author, Dr. Jürgen Plöger.

Mythology
in the Modern Novel

Chapter One

Myth and the Modern Novel

The Return to Myth

"The Mythical Age" was the name the German novelist Hermann Broch gave to the twentieth century.[1] It is a view which would at least seem to be corroborated by the preoccupations of many writers and critics of today. Yet although a common denominator of much modern literature, myth can assume as many shapes as Proteus himself, and the attribute "mythical" may conceal a variety of cultural phenomena. Anyone consulting the relevant critical literature on the importance of myth for recent writers or on the particular role of mythology in contemporary fiction will find himself confronted by a plethora of general statements about the survival, revival and creation of myth. The recurrent idea of a "return to myth,"[2] for example, betrays decidedly Rousseauistic overtones and needs much careful delineation if it is to be profitably applied in the modern context. In practice, one is often left uncertain whether the notion denotes a return to specific mythologies, such as Greek, Roman or Sumerian, or whether it refers to the revival of certain archaically mythical qualities in modern literature. For Broch, the return meant only "a return to myth in its ancient forms (even when they are so modern-

[1] "The Style of the Mythical Age," *Dichten und Erkennen: Essays,* I, ed. Hannah Arendt, Zürich, 1955, p. 249.
[2] Broch, *op.cit.*, p. 262. See also the works by Baisette, Fischler, Jouan and Kahler listed in the bibliography. (Abbreviated references given in footnotes are to works entered in detail in the bibliography on the subject of mythology and literature.)

3

ized as in Joyce), and so far it is not a new myth, not *the* new myth."[3] Yet the "return to myth" is not always so precisely defined; the reader is often left wondering which kind of myth is being reanimated.

The ambiguity of the word "myth" does not help the reader in search of guidance. Indeed, it induces many critics to operate with a misleadingly shifting set of ideas or a rather private interpretation of the concept. Hence, while Northrop Frye can state that "in literary criticism myth means ultimately *mythos*, a structural organizing principle of literary form"[4] and Frank Kermode rejoins that Frye "arrives at myth through archetypes,"[5] the uninitiated may have difficulty in tuning in to these different semantic wavelengths: the one aesthetic, the other psychoanalytical. In *Quest for Myth*—a work whose very title exploits this central ambiguity—Richard Chase asserts that "an interest in the creative literature of our century forces upon us an interest in myth."[6] Yet he undertakes to substantiate this point by using a blanket terminology, sometimes referring to myths as myth and at other times as poetic images of a different order. And to write of the survival of myth—"das Fortleben des Mythos"—as Erich Kahler does in *Die Verantwortung des Geistes*, may sound equally ambiguous. Being a particular kind of image-making, myth has always existed as one of the categories of perception and of the imagination. "Myth making is a permanent activity of all men," Eliseo Vivas writes;[7] "all men can do is to abandon one myth for the sake of another."[8] To write of its survival as such would be to wax too dramatic. What Kahler in fact examines, quite legitimately, is the way in which particular

---

[3] *op.cit.*, p. 262.   [4] *Anatomy of Criticism*, p. 341.
[5] *Puzzles and Epiphanies*, p. 72.   [6] Introduction, p. v.
[7] "Myth: Some Philosophical Problems," p. 89.
[8] *op.cit.*, p. 92.

myths have lived on in our literatures. By using the apparently generic word "Mythos," he implies, as Chase does, that these myths are necessarily identical with the archaic power of myth: that they survive *as myth.* Yet need a return to the use of specific myths inevitably entail a return to myth in the other sense? And have both kinds of return to myth manifested themselves jointly in modern literature? According to C. S. Lewis:

> Certain stories, which are not myths in the anthropological sense, having been invented by individuals in fully civilized periods, have what [one can] call the "mythical quality." Such are the plots of *Dr. Jekyll and Mr. Hyde,* Wells's *The Door in the Wall* or Kafka's *The Castle.*[9]

Many modern novels also leave one in little doubt that there has been a comparable return to the use of particular myths from traditional sources. Such titles as *Ulysses, Proserpina, The Centaur, The Labours of Hercules* and *Gilgamesch* all serve, in a limited sense, to show that modern novelists still use material from old mythologies in their works. So there may have been a return to myth in more ways than one.

The "return to myth" is often assumed to be a particular feature of the Modernist movement in the early part of this century. It appears in some writings on the subject as a product of the influence of depth-psychology on certain novelists. One reviewer refers to such a use of mythology as "that old wayside halt for tired novelists in our post-Freudian age."[10] An impression may be given that this method is rather a thing of the past: that any contemporary novel which still incorporates myths should be assigned as a throwback to the context of an earlier epoch. Hence the elegiac ring to many of Thomas Mann's pronouncements on

[9] "On Myth," p. 42.
[10] *TLS,* 9 September 1965, p. 769.

5

the subject, in the forties. For instance, in a letter to Karl Kerényi, he remarks:

> Um jene "Rückkehr des europäischen Geistes zu den höchsten, den mythischen Realitäten" . . . ist es wahrhaftig eine geistesgeschichtlich große und gute Sache, und ich darf mich rühmen, in meinem Werke gewissermaßen Teil daran zu haben.[11]

Although many writers of the Modernist era, including Eliot, Joyce, Kazantzakis, Pound and Yeats, were certainly preoccupied with myths, such an interest is to be found with equal richness, and at times with a far greater intricacy of expression, in much subsequent twentieth-century literature. Therefore it cannot be assumed to be a distinguishing feature primarily of earlier decades or (worse still) to be derivative of them in an eclectic sense.

A study of the preoccupation with myth in the twentieth century would be a vast undertaking. Fortunately much of the groundwork has been carried out. Studies such as Hugh Dickinson's *Myth on the Stage* and Gilbert Highet's *The Classical Tradition* have surveyed large areas. In turning my attention to another aspect of the subject, the modern predilection for mythological motifs in fiction, I am partly responding to an evident lacuna. But the choice represents more than this. Among numerous possible features characterizing the contemporary interest in myths (including the dramatization of myths, modern poems on mythological subjects, anecdotal versions and variations on myths), the novel employing motifs from traditional mythologies remains the most frequently misunderstood example of the presence and function of mythology in modern literature.

---

[11] *Gespräch in Briefen*, p. 42. "As for that 'return of the European spirit to the highest, to the mythical realities' . . . it is, from a cultural point of view, a truly great and good thing, and I may praise myself for to some extent taking part in it in my work." (Translations, unless otherwise indicated, are my own.)

It is as much to consider certain problems of methodology as to fill a gap in critical literature on the subject that the following study has been undertaken.

James Joyce's *Ulysses* is the best-known illustration of this type of novel with mythological motifs which, for the sake of brevity, I shall henceforth refer to as the "mythological novel."[12] The two fundamental characteristics of such works are: first, that the mythological parallel is suggested as an analogy or contrast to the contemporary world in which the main events of the novel occur; and second, that the parallel is an extended one and could be described as a motif. This characterization excludes novels such as Cesare Pavese's *Dialoghi con Leucò*, Thomas Mann's Joseph tetralogy and Jean Giono's *Naissance de l'Odyssée*; for such works remain in the world of myths, even if the narrative tone is a modern one, occasionally tinged with irony or what Mann once called the spirit of Voltaire. Whereas the role of mythological motifs is analogical, describing the modern world in the light of a readily available set of models, works that are mythical do not offer myths as analogies, but make them their principal subject-matter or structural principle.

Distinguishing Myths from Mythological Motifs

The need to differentiate mythological allusions and motifs from myth proper accounts for some of the terminology used in this study. Throughout, the phrase "mythological motifs" will be preferred to the simpler form "mythical motifs." "Mythological" here signifies no more than "embodying a scheme of references to mythology." (Usually this will be to Greek mythology, but the increase in anthropological studies has meant that a modern writer now has quantitatively more myths to choose from and qualitatively

---

[12] A list of such novels is given in the first part of the bibliography.

7

a greater understanding of them, and can turn to more recondite mythologies, when Greek images have become clichés.) By using the word "mythological," one can avoid the assumption which so readily presents itself: that a work containing substantial elements from old mythologies creates, or is even necessarily intended to generate, myth. "Mythical," the usual adjective in critical discussions, remains too indiscriminate a word for this purpose; it is commonly associated with a dynamic quality, a *mana* seldom present in works that are here described as mythological.

Any attempt at demonstrating the mythical, rather than the mythological elements in literature,[13] would draw substantially upon Romantic theory and upon such modern theoretical classics as Sir James Frazer's *The Golden Bough*, Ernst Cassirer's *Philosophy of Symbolic Forms*, Claude Lévi-Strauss's *Mythologiques* and the studies in this field by Mircea Eliade, Susanne Langer and Eliseo Vivas. We have, however, no reason to suppose that a work of literature is necessarily constructed to create or resuscitate myth, just because it includes mythological motifs.[14] Indeed, one finds that most of the writers who are generally acknowledged nowadays as successful creators of such new myths, amongst them Borges, Faulkner, Giono, Kafka and Pavese,[15] have all noticeably refrained from constructing

[13] There has already been a number of studies with this purpose; cf. the works by Andres, Frye, Kermode (1967), Mühlher and Schmidt-Henkel listed in the bibliography.

[14] This in turn does not mean that certain writers may not at times have been seeking to create a new myth out of old ones. Joyce's *Finnegans Wake* and Malcolm Lowry's *Under the Volcano* have this mythical quality. And Broch once declared the goal of his literary endeavors to be a modern counterpart to the *Epic of Gilgamesh*: "ein Mythos . . . , der es wieder mit dem Gilgamesch wird aufnehmen können" (*Briefe*, Zürich, 1957, p. 186).

[15] For representative, rather than isolated, opinions concerning the mythical quality of works by these writers, see: Carter Wheelock, *The Mythmaker: A Study of Motif and Symbol in the Short Stories of Jorge Luis Borges*, Austin and London, 1969; Oto Bihalji-Merin, "William Faulkner: Mythos der Zeit," *Sinn und Form*, XVI, 1964, pp.

them with bricks taken from older mythologies. E. W. Herd has even argued that in the work of Broch, Joyce and Mann "the creation of 'new myth' is frustrated . . . by the return to traditional myth-material."[16] Hence, the conclusion which suggests itself is that mythological motifs are in fact different from myths, from both old and new myths alike.

If the concept of a motif is to prove a viable one in this context, it will be helpful to exclude solitary similes and metaphors borrowed from classical mythologies and placed in isolation in modern novels. One can clearly observe the difference between isolated allusions to myths and a more organized mythological motif in Elisabeth Langgässer's *Märkische Argonautenfahrt*, a symbolic quest-novel which appeared in Germany after the Second World War.

The narrator almost works through the whole Greek pantheon before the novel has ended, yet despite numerous references to classical mythology[17]—to which a host of biblical images could be added, there is only one mythological motif in the whole of the novel: that of the Argonauts' voyage mentioned in the title. The narrator reminds readers of it towards the end of the story: "so hat seiner Fabel das alte Modell der heiligen Argo zugrunde gelegen."[18] Where-

---

752-770; Antoinette Francine, *Le Mythe de la Provence dans les premiers romans de Jean Giono*, Aix-en-Provence, 1961, esp. pp. 9-11; Wilhelm Emrich, "Die Bilderwelt Franz Kafkas," *Protest und Verheißung*, Frankfurt a.M., 1960, pp. 262f.; John Freccero, "Mythos and Logos," *Italian Quarterly*, iv, 1961, pp. 3-16.

[16] "Myth Criticism: Limitations and Possibilities," pp. 74f.

[17] Comparisons are duly made between modern characters and Proserpina (p. 19), Endymion (p. 27), Diana (p. 28), Pan and Nausicaa (p. 38), the Gorgon (p. 45), the Medusa (p. 52), Vulcan (p. 54), Orion and Andromeda (p. 57), Hera, Apollo, Hermes and Aphrodite (p. 58), Hercules (p. 65), Pan (p. 91), Tartarus (p. 126), Dionysos (p. 130), Artemis (p. 135), Eurydice (p. 141), Prometheus (p. 221), Venus (p. 222), Atreus (p. 227), Charon (p. 237), Chronos (p. 239), Achilles (p. 240), Odysseus (p. 241), Persephone (p. 247), Demeter and Kore (p. 272), Aeneas (p. 328) and Niobe (p. 339).

[18] p. 399; "and so the old model of the sacred Argo acted as foundation to the tale."

as the biblical references and the allusions to Greek gods appear haphazardly throughout *Märkische Argonautenfahrt*, the Argonaut motif reveals a definite pattern in its appearances. As might be expected, the narrator stresses the importance of this mythological quest motif at the point where the main characters set out in search of the Golden Fleece: the convent at Anastasiendorf, their goal during a pilgrimage after the *tabula rasa* of the Second World War. On the second page of the novel appears the description of a photograph showing the assembled travelers. It bears the inscription: "DIE ARGONAUTEN MIT IHREN DAMEN AUF DEM WEG ZU DEM GOLDENEN VLIESS."[19] The motif signaled here once more plays an important role as the adventurers approach their goal. Their desire to compare themselves with the Argonauts allows these travelers to see their spiritual quest in very concrete, and perhaps more optimistic, terms. The title of the novel, above all, has ensured that we see the whole journey in the light of the Greek analogy. Such a calculated use of allusions for a pattern of dramatic effect and objectivization marks the main difference between references to mythology rather preciously scattered through the narrative and the motif of the quest for the Golden Fleece. It would be difficult to avoid mentioning the Argonaut motif in any interpretation of *Märkische Argonautenfahrt* (just as one could not discuss Joyce's *Ulysses* without reference to the Homeric parallels), whereas only a detailed examination of the novel's imagery would require reference to most of the other allusions.

The noticeable patterning, rather than simply the frequency, of allusions is one measure of their function within a motif-structure. Other useful criteria for assessing the relative importance of allusions include their position in the narrative and the kind of mythological figure involved. At

---

[19] "The Argonauts with their ladies *en route* to the Golden Fleece."

times a single word is enough to establish a motif, if it appears in a novel's title, as it does for example in *Ulysses*. Yet if it occurs in isolation elsewhere in a work, as the Greek allusions do so often in Elisabeth Langgässer's novel, one might see it as an incidental reference only and not as part of a motif. It is clear, too, that even frequent allusions to certain mythological figures and events, such as Eros, Mars or Venus, or the Odyssey, do not always produce a mythological motif. It would, for instance, be difficult to make out a case for Anthony Powell's *Venusberg* or Rachilde's *Monsieur Vénus* as mythological works. Venus is one of those mythological figures who have a general, almost allegorical connotation that does not readily lend itself to the creation of a motif linked with specific events or characters. Furthermore, it follows that if the chosen tale is not fairly straightforward, it cannot provide a clear-cut pattern. It is generally agreed, for example, that the Greek mythological figure Hermes is used as a symbol in Thomas Mann's *Felix Krull*. Yet Hermes has so many associations that one cannot really speak of a mythological motif giving any real pattern to our reading of this novel. To lend itself to creating a mythological motif, the analogy has to be well defined, clearly indicated to the reader and presented at significant points in the development of the narrative.

Myths as Literary Prefigurations

Rather than being viewed in isolation, mythological motifs will be related to the more general technique of prefiguration, a literary device which embraces both this and other kinds of patterning in the presentation of character and plot. A myth introduced by a modern novelist into his work can prefigure and hence anticipate the plot in a number of ways. Although an awareness of sources is declining, the ideal reader can still be expected to be familiar with most prefigurations beforehand, just as the novelist himself was

11

when he wrote the work. And because it is better known than the new work, the myth will offer the novelist a shorthand system of symbolic comment on modern events. "Prefiguration" is a useful word to describe this relationship, since it suggests "coming before" and hence offering a comparison with a whole configuration of actions or figures.

Although now frequent in literary criticism, the word "prefiguration" is of religious origin, a translation of the Latin technical term *figura* used to describe the scheme by which "the persons and events of the Old Testament were prefigurations of the New Testament and its history of Salvation."[20] One of the classic examples of prefiguration in this sense is the prophetic relationship between Abraham's preparation to sacrifice his son Isaac and the Crucifixion. In St. Augustine's time, the word *praefiguratio* was used instead of *figura*[21] and since then the term has been secularized and adapted to many other contexts. Obviously, when used in the secular sense, the idea of prefiguration loses its original prophetic connotation. In the literary context, Homer's *Odyssey* can hardly be interpreted as a joyous or foreboding prophecy that Joyce's *Ulysses* was to come.

One merit of the term "prefiguration" in its secularized sense is its latitude of meaning. With it, one can enlarge the scope of an investigation of such symbolic correspondences, to avoid certain misconceptions, by treating not only motifs taken from old mythologies, but also those using legends. For example, the legendary motif of Faust and the devil in John Hersey's *Too Far to Walk* is structurally very similar to many mythological motifs. A wider term also makes it possible to compare mythological motifs with literary plot-

[20] Erich Auerbach, "*Figura* in the Phenomenal Prophecy of the Church Fathers," *Scenes from the Drama of European Literature*, New York, 1959, p. 30.
[21] Auerbach, *op.cit.*, p. 39, gives the example of Noah's Ark being described as a prefiguration of the Church: "praefiguratio ecclesiae" in St. Augustine's *De civitate dei*, XIV, 27.

prefigurations, such as the use of Shakespeare's plays in Aldous Huxley's *Brave New World* or of Chekhov's *The Seagull* in Macdonald Harris's *Trepleff*. And prefigurations, can, of course, come from other, less dignified sources. Echoing some lines from Walt Whitman's *Song of the Exposition*,[22] Leslie Fiedler recently suggested that we "must cancel out those long overdue accounts to Greece and Rome. . . . The new mythology must come out of pop songs and comic books."[23] A recent German pop-novel, Heinz von Cramer's *Der Paralleldenker*—aptly sub-titled *Zombies Roman*—chooses its analogies from among cinema and cartoon characters.[24] These too I would see as prefigurations. For, despite the wide range of sources for literary motifs, all these patterns bear close resemblances to many mythological prefigurations usually discussed in splendid isolation. These devices need to be compared and occasionally contrasted with one another, if this type of authorial comment is really to be understood. By concentrating, nevertheless, primarily on the *mythological* motif, I hope to pinpoint certain important features of the presence of mythology in the novel and to give less treatment to other aspects, such as the use of isolated allusions, metaphors and similes— techniques which have not changed fundamentally in recent times. Interpreting the mythological motif as an in-

[22] Come Muse migrate from Greece and Ionia,
   Cross out please those immensely overpaid accounts,
   That matter of Troy and Achilles' wrath, and Aeneas,' Odysseus' wanderings,
   Placard "Removed" and "To Let" on the rocks of your snowy Parnassus . . .
   For know a better, fresher, busier sphere, a wide, untried domain awaits, demands you.
[23] Quoted by Ann Banks in her report, "Symposium Sidelights," *Novel*, III, 1970, pp. 208-209.
[24] Zombie, the hero of this novel published in Hamburg in 1968, is compared with Jean-Paul Belmondo (p. 23), Sean Connery (p. 24), and Batman's friend Robin (p. 212), while his mistress of the moment is prefigured by Jeanne Moreau, Brigitte Bardot and Anna Karina (pp. 23f.).

13

stance of *secularized* prefiguration serves at the same time to highlight its role as an analogical system of comment and precludes certain essentially Romantic views of myths in fiction as the prerequisite of mythical fiction. To use the term "prefiguration" instead of "myth" entails, it is true, a mere semantic substitution, itself solving none of the problems I shall outline later. But semantic substitutions can have a heuristic value at times; they can clear away some of the misconceptions and prejudices contaminating the traditional vocabulary of the subject. And when the central word has the almost magical associations that "myth" bears, such liberation can be a useful step towards looking at the topic from a new perspective.

Historical Background

If mythology appeared in the novel in earlier times, it was not generally presented in an organized motif-pattern. There are, for instance, Virgilian overtones to Fielding's *Amelia*, but they do not pattern our reading of the novel any more than do the classical epithets of the heroic epic. It seems quite clear from surveys such as Douglas Bush's *Mythology and the Romantic Tradition in English Poetry* and Henri Peyre's *L'Influence des Littératures antiques sur la Littérature française moderne* that Romantic Hellenism in England and France found its home mainly in poetry rather than in the novel. In Germany, on the other hand, as Strich's *Die Mythologie in der deutschen Dichtung* reveals, there was both an interest in old mythologies and in the creation of a new mythology,[25] and these preoccupations did leave some mark on fiction.[26] But the German Romantics

[25] An outline of the Romantic idea of the "new mythology" can be found in the first chapter of Kenneth Negus's *E.T.A. Hoffmann's "Other World": The Romantic Author and his "New Mythology,"* Philadelphia, 1965.
[26] Hölderlin's *Hyperion*, Novalis' *Heinrich von Ofterdingen* and much of E.T.A. Hoffmann's work include mythological material.

tended to identify mythology with the notion of a success-ful poetic cosmogony and generally thought of this as the goal of all great literature.[27] Even if traditional mythologies were used with this end in mind, such a general interpreta-tion of literature as the sister of mythology is not conducive, in novel writing, to the production of strictly organized mythological motifs. As a rule, motifs are limited to one or two myths, whereas such a view is essentially polytheistic. In creating his mythological motif, the twentieth-century novelist usually borrows a single myth, or at least draws upon a limited body of mythological material, and offers this as comment on part of the modern plot. His aim is most frequently to *use* myths, not to create a whole mythology, be it new or old. In contrast, the quasi-religious Romantic quest for all-embracing mythologies would require a whole mythological pantheon to do justice to its aspirations. Ad-mittedly, a number of vaguely mythical figures may still be emphasized in relative isolation in some Romantic works. The Titanic gods are often espoused by the Romantics (even, for example, in the mythological Gothic of Mrs. Shel-ley's *Frankenstein or The Modern Prometheus*), but such figures are largely left as unexploited, heroic embodiments of a vague spirit of vitalism. In Hölderlin's *Hyperion*, the eponymous hero, the one figure who might have introduced a detailed prefiguration to modern events, is not treated in such a way. In short, detailed prefigurations are rare in the novel before the twentieth century.

[27] In his "Rede über die Mythologie," Friedrich Schlegel, the leading theoretician of German Romanticism, defines mythology as a hiero-glyphic expression of nature around us, transformed by the imagina-tion and love: "ein hieroglyphischer Ausdruck der umgebenden Natur in [der] Verklärung von Fantasie und Liebe" (*Charakteristen und Kritiken 1 (1796-1801)*, Munich, Paderborn and Vienna, 1967, p. 318). Modern literature, he suggests, should seek to attain this quality once more. Similarly, Herder's "Vom Gebrauch der neuern Mythologie," Schelling's "Kunstphilosophie" and the theories of Creuzer, Görres and Hülsen all equate mythology primarily with cosmogony.

Besides a difference in attitudes to mythology, dividing a Romantic age, either feeling the lures of Hellenism or seeking cosmogonies of a personal kind, from a later epoch of increased psychological fragmentation and introspection (where the name of a myth becomes the label for a complex), one also finds another reason for the late arrival of the mythological motif in the novel. A poetological sense of the innate appropriateness of certain themes to specific genres decreed for a long time that the place of the gods, even gods who were no longer believed in, was in drama or poetry, but not in such an unheroic, bourgeois form as the novel. In this century, when the novel—not necessarily the low-mimetic form it was in the nineteenth century—has achieved a more poetic status and is no longer considered a poor relative of the other genres, symbolic gods may enter fiction freely without any taboos being broken. Granted, however, that in this age certain changes in attitude to the novel have made it easier for mythology to play a significant role in its imagery, one still has to consider why a modern writer should ever want to include such anachronisms in his work.

One of the basic assumptions underlying the following approach is that mythological motifs, together with other prefigurative devices, form a part of what is nowadays usually known as the rhetoric of fiction. They emerged at a point in the historical development of the novel when theorists of the genre observed (and some even prescribed) a constraint upon more direct forms of authorial comment and characterization. Yet despite this striking chronological link between the device's appearance and the observable change in narrative fashions, most critical accounts of mythological literature which have successfully avoided Romantic misconceptions concerning some inherent mythogenic power in such devices, take as their Archimedean Point the findings of psychoanalysis. Freud and Jung have certainly given a great impetus to the subject. In Chase's words: "the psychoanalysts make the salutary suggestion that mythology is not primarily concerned with natural phenomena [as the Romantics assumed it to be] but with human nature,"[28] a point which the novelists themselves were soon embodying in their works. Depth-psychology marks a watershed in literature; it has been argued, for instance, that "l'interprétation du mythe d'Orphée est marquée par l'optimisme avant Freud, et par le pessimisme ensuite."[29] Nevertheless, although much of our knowledge of mythological novels derives from current findings about myths themselves, it can also benefit from our changing theories of fiction. Such books as Wayne Booth's important study of *The Rhetoric of Fiction,* Herman Meyer's *The Poetics of Quotation in the European Novel,* and, more recently, Frank Kermode's account of patterns in *The Sense of an Ending,* and work on the novel by Malcolm Bradbury and David Lodge have played as decisive a role in influencing my approach to the function of mythology in the modern novel as the anthropological and psychological perspectives offered by Eliade, Freud, Jung, Kerényi and Lévi-Strauss. While previous work on the subject often stressed the impetus from depth-psychology during the first part of this century, it failed to consider other factors. Two questions have to be answered: why *mythology* should make such a striking appearance in much modern fiction, and why *the modern novel* should have recourse to mythology for much of its symbolism. Why mythology?—and why the novel?

Non-Aesthetic Theories

An underestimation of the rhetorical uses of mythology has led to an anachronistic image of many novels. This can be

28 *Quest for Myth,* p. 94.
29 Eva Kushner, *Le Mythe d'Orphée,* p. 24.

17

seen in the way the relationship between modern character and mythological analogy has been expressed. The modern character has sometimes been regarded as a *reincarnation* of the appropriate god, as *playing the role* of a mythological figure, or as engaging in an *imitation* of him. Yet such approaches beg a lot of questions. When told that the idea of imitation is the main structural principle underlying Mann's *Doktor Faustus*,[30] are we, for example, to assume that the hero Adrian Leverkühn is imitating Faust from the cradle—which would give him a new dimension of precociousness —and that his father is also part of the act? Furthermore, does such an interpretation imply that we can conclude with Leslie Miller that an early event like "the Leverkühn-Hetäre Esmeralda episode in *Doktor Faustus* . . . is an act of imitation on the part of Leverkühn,"[31] without wanting to modify this statement in any way? And do we assume likewise that everyone else in the novel also plays an appropriate role in conscious imitation of the well-known legend? If this were true, why should a group of fictional characters be made to behave in such a strange way?

Of course, it is deliberately perverse to pose the questions in this way, for two kinds of imitation are implied: the author's imitation of a traditional theme in a new work, and the conscious copying of some prefiguration by characters in the work (a secularized version of the *imitatio Christi*). The latter is described at some length in Mann's influential essay "Freud und die Zukunft":

> Das antike Ich und sein Bewußtsein von sich war ein anderes als das unsere, weniger ausschließlich, weniger scharf umgrenzt. Es stand gleichsam nach hin-

---

[30] "die Idee der imitatio [ist] das bestimmende Gestaltprinzip des Romans" (Jürgen Plöger, *Das Hermesmotiv in der Dichtung Thomas Manns*, p. 232).

[31] "Myth and Morality: Reflections on Mann's *Doktor Faustus*," p. 206.

ten offen und nahm vom Gewesenen vieles mit auf, was es gegenwärtig wiederholte, und was mit ihm "wieder da" war. Der spanische Kulturphilosoph Ortega y Gasset drückt das so aus, daß der antike Mensch, ehe er etwas tue, einen Schritt zurück trete, gleich dem Torero, der zum Todesstoß aushole. Er suche in der Vergangenheit ein Vorbild, in das er wie in eine Taucherglocke schlüpfe, um sich so, zugleich geschützt und entstellt, in das gegenwärtige Problem hineinzustürzen. Darum sei sein Leben in gewisser Weise ein Beleben, ein archaisierendes Verhalten.— Aber eben dies Leben als Beleben, Wiederbeleben ist das Leben im Mythus. Alexander ging in den Spuren des Miltiades, und von Caesar waren seine antiken Biographen mit Recht oder Unrecht überzeugt, er wolle den Alexander nachahmen. Dies "Nachahmen" aber ist weit mehr, als heut in dem Wort liegt; es ist die mythische Identifikation, die der Antike besonders vertraut war, aber weit in die neue Zeit hineinspielt *und seelisch jederzeit möglich bleibt.* Das antike Gepräge der Gestalt Napoleons ist oft betont worden. Er bedauerte, daß die moderne Bewußtseinslage ihm nicht gestattete, sich für den Sohn Jupiter-Amons auszugeben, wie Alexander. Aber daß er sich, zur Zeit seines orientalischen Unternehmens, wenigstens mit Alexander mythisch verwechselt hat, braucht man nicht zu bezweifeln, und später, als er sich fürs Abendland entschieden hatte, erklärte er:"Ich *bin* Karl der Grosse." Wohl gemerkt—nicht etwa: "Ich erinnere an ihn"; nicht:"Meine Stellung ist der seinen ähnlich." Auch nicht: "Ich bin wie er"; sondern einfach:"Ich *bin's.*" Das ist die Formel des Mythus.

Das Leben, jedenfalls das bedeutende Leben, war also in antiken Zeiten die Wiederherstellung des Mythus in Fleisch und Blut; es bezog und berief sich auf ihn; durch ihn erst, durch die Bezugnahme aufs Vergangene wies er sich als echtes und bedeutendes Leben aus. Der Mythus ist die Legitimation des Lebens; erst durch ihn und in ihm findet es sein Selbstbewußtsein, seine Rechtfertigung und Weihe. Bis in den Tod führte Kleopatra ihre aphroditische Charakterrolle weihevoll durch, — und kann man bedeutender,

kann man würdiger leben und sterben, als indem man
den Mythus zelebriert?[32]

This notion of imitation, which owes much to Freud, depends on the character's own self-awareness. As I shall
argue later, it seldom helps to account satisfactorily for a
mythological motif's full effect. And it is too often applied
metaphorically to novels where the protagonist is not consciously modeling his life on a forerunner's. At times, the
metaphor means little more than that the modern novelist

---

[32] *Adel des Geistes: Sechzehn Versuche zum Problem der Humani-
tät*, Stockholm, 1948, pp. 581f. H. T. Lowe-Porter's translation of this
passage reads: "The ego of antiquity and its consciousness of itself
were different from our own, less exclusive, less sharply defined. It
was, as it were, open behind; it received much from the past and by
repeating it gave it presentness again. The Spanish scholar Ortega y
Gasset puts it that the man of antiquity, before he did anything, took a
step backwards, like the bullfighter who leaps back to deliver the
mortal thrust. He searched the past for a pattern into which he might
slip as into a diving-bell, and being thus at once disguised and pro-
tected might rush upon his present problem. Thus his life was in a
sense a reanimation, an archaizing attitude. But it is just this life as
reanimation that is the life as myth. Alexander walked in the footsteps
of Miltiades; the ancient biographers of Caesar were convinced, rightly
or wrongly, that he took Alexander as his prototype. But such "imitation" means far more than we mean by the word today. It was a
mythical identification, peculiarly familiar to antiquity; but it is operative far into modern times, *and at all times is psychically possible.*
How often have we not been told that the figure of Napoleon was
cast in the antique mold! He regretted that the mentality of the time
forbade him to give himself out for the son of Jupiter Ammon, in
imitation of Alexander. But we need not doubt that—at least at the
period of his Eastern exploits—he mythically confounded himself with
Alexander; while after he turned his face westwards he is said to
have declared: "I am Charlemagne." Note that: not "I am like
Charlemagne" or "My situation is like Charlemagne's," but quite
simply: "I am he." That is the formulation of the myth. Life, then—at
any rate, significant life—was in ancient times the reconstitution of
the myth in flesh and blood; it referred to and appealed to the myth;
only through it, through reference to the past, could it approve itself
as genuine and significant. The myth is the legitimization of life; only
through and in it does life find self-awareness, sanction, consecration.
Cleopatra fulfilled her Aphrodite character even unto death—and
can one live and die more significantly or worthily than in the cele-
bration of the myth?" ("Freud and the Future," *Essays of Three
Decades*, New York, 1968, pp. 424f.; my italics).

has based his plot on—and hence is in that sense imitating —a well-known theme.

Metaphors of imitation and reincarnation misrepresent the relationship between myths and modernity, confusing half-truths with fuller statements about the function of prefigurative motifs. The main criticism of them is not that they are metaphors—metaphors can be very helpful for critical illumination—but that critics who use them tend to forget that they retain the essentially distorting quality of all metaphorical utterances. Such images frequently preclude the fundamental consideration of why the aesthetic device in question is used at all. On the other hand, the alternative image of a mythological figure as a prefiguration, in the secularized sense, does not so readily discourage the necessary further examination of aesthetic function, since prefigurations (in any sense) are a kind of message.

Metaphorical descriptions have a tendency—especially because of the type of metaphor used—to overstress the role of the novel's mythological "prototype,"[33] implying that the events narrated in the modern context are only comprehensible as a version of the myth. The contention that a character is imitating a myth, or lives under the aegis of a mythological deity, makes the myth sound far more important for the novel than it usually is; the myth is simply being used in most cases to offer some kind of looser analogy. (The assumption underlying the metaphorical approach appears to be that there is only one myth per novel, which is not always the case.) In most mythological novels, the myths do not offer a scaffold upon which the modern story has been erected. Nor can one usually read the modern

---

[33] This term, used by Richard Ellmann in *James Joyce* (London, 1966, p. 200), has the advantage of suggesting that the myth and the work are separate entities; but the idea of a prototype puts too much stress on the myth as source. A product is usually more derivative of its prototype than the novel of its prefiguration.

21

story as a straightforward attempt at revitalizing an old myth by putting it into a modern setting. These suggestions make the novels apparently depend too deterministically on myths. They derive largely from a jejune school of comparative literature which was content to analyze works in terms of their sources. In fact, within the system of hierarchical structures implanted in such a novel, the myth is not the major component.[34]

To set the later discussion in perspective, I should like to suggest three main reasons why we find so many interpreters of modern mythological novels attributing a preeminent position to the mythological component.

One factor, considered in greater detail in the next chapter, is a shifting terminology which leads to a confusion of mythological elements and real myths at the purely taxonomic level. When using words which have such imprecise areas of meaning as "myth" and its cognates undoubtedly possess, the critic often becomes the unwitting victim of his own vocabulary: general and specific senses of the word can easily be elided.

A second reason, an inheritance from both Renaissance and Romantic Hellenism, is the idea that mythology, with its associations as a primitive cultic form of literature and expression, must be more significant than other elements, even when appearing in an apparently ancillary position in modern works of fiction. There is the corollary supposition, also resting on the assumption that myths are *per se* of the greatest importance: that if myth and modernity are counterpointed in fiction, the myth is bound to be set up as the norm against which our age should measure itself. For

[34] In the original religious context of prefiguration, the earlier event was subordinate to the latter, since it merely prophesied the greater thing to come. This sense of subordination—making the earlier less important than the later phenomenon, be it work of literature or coming of a Messiah—can be transferred to the secularized connotation of prefiguration.

example, Alexander Fischler talks of a "general myth revival" in literature which he takes to be "prompted by the continuing search for new values founded on the old."[35] This view, with its stress on myths as the vessels of pristine values, seems especially suspect, since Fischler takes the myth of Narcissus in all its ambiguity to make the point.

In many cases, this sense of value attributed to old myths leads to the abandonment of one of the cardinal principles of literary criticism: that context is more important than source. As a result, a twentieth-century novel (say, Robbe-Grillet's *Les Gommes*), set in contemporary society but with a mythological motif running through it, can become so distorted that the modern tale is interpreted allegorically as a veiled myth. It would be misleading to contend that such modern novelists as Broch, Butor, Moravia, Robbe-Grillet and Updike are indulging in the whimsical practice of putting classical myths into modern garb or even "returning" to myth as if to some avatar. In this sense, the back-to-myth movement was largely curtailed after 1945. It makes more sense and enriches our experience of these writers to appreciate how many modern novels are inviting their readers to *interpret* new experiences in the light of traditional sources of archetypal patterns. Rather than offer his reader new myths or revitalized old ones, the mythological novelist presents a modern situation and refers the reader to a familiar analogy.

A third reason for the distorted image of mythological fiction is a procrustean desire to establish a simple identity between modern novel and myth because of the importance attached at the present time to imagery, which is after all the leading source of motifs. "What we often do in practice is to exaggerate the symbolic relevance" of any pattern of images we locate, Barbara Hardy argues. By applying our "Jamesian standards of cross-reference and total rele-

[35] "Recent Visitors to the Fountain of Narcissus," p. 149.

23

vance"[36] to the modern psychological novel—standards which, according to her, make us over-emphasize image-patterns, we are prone to schematize and hence overrate the mythological component. As a result of this tendency, which Malcolm Bradbury sees as an attempt to transfer the New Critics' techniques from poetry criticism to that of fiction,[37] occasional parallels and scattered allusions to specific myths are forced into an exaggerated system offered to the reader as the key to the whole work rather than just a limited set of analogical comments on the plot or on a given character. Thus contrived, the pattern is elaborated to suggest a novel modeled totally on an old myth or even identical with it.

Myths in Drama and Myths in Fiction

I have already talked of myths being put into modern garb. It is an idea that sometimes occurs in discussions of mythology as an alienating device.[38] In fact, the notion of "putting into modern garb" suggests theatre; and "imitation" and "playing the role" of a god, the two metaphors most recurrently used to describe mythological fiction, are also borrowed from the stage. Criticism of mythological novels and the manner in which they function has quite often suffered from certain ideas being transferred, with insufficient modification, from our experience of mythology in drama. A comparison between the role of myths in the two genres soon shows, however, that modern fiction and modern drama are two very different contexts and that the mythological element in each of them has its own idiosyncrasies.

[36] *The Appropriate Form: An Essay on the Novel*, London, 1964, p. 13.

[37] "Towards a Poetics of Fiction: 1. An Approach through Structure," *Novel*, I, Fall 1967, pp. 45f.

[38] Hans Erich Nossack, for example, talks of myths in modern literature being used "als Kostüm für heutige Probleme" (*Die schwache Position der Literatur: Reden und Aufsätze*, Frankfurt a.M., 1966, p. 75).

Modern novels tend not to narrate myths straightforwardly in their traditional settings. Certainly, there are exceptions to this generalization: Thomas Mann's *Joseph und seine Brüder* and *Die vertauschten Köpfe*, Jean Giono's *Naissance de l'Odyssée* and J. C. Powys's epics, for instance. And contemporary readers might also cite such works as Mary Renault's Greek novels and Michael Ayrton's recent interpretations of the Daedalus myth in *The Testament of Daedalus* and *The Maze-maker*. However, most people could probably count on their fingers the works of this kind they know. In contrast, it would take more than these digits to enumerate even the names alone of the principal modern playwrights who have dramatized myths. Anouilh, Claudel, Cocteau, D'Annunzio, Gide, Giraudoux, Hauptmann, Hofmannsthal, Kaiser, O'Neill, Sartre, Werfel and Wilder are but the most prominent exponents of the technique.[39] This pattern of distribution, revealing complete myths often in drama but seldom in fiction, is reflected in the fact that dramatic adaptations of myths have received more attention from critics than any other aspect of mythology in literature.[40]

In fact, the nature of the two genres partly accounts for the distribution of motifs in fiction and drama. A myth, as the Greek implied, is little more really than the equivalent of a simple plot, albeit a plot traditionally related to the action of gods or heroes. Its essential quality is that of a basic configuration of actions. For this reason, the poet Howard Nemerov defines myth as:

> an equation, or drama, repeated cyclically until it gathers around itself in the memory of man a residuum,

---

[39] Another list of (somewhat different) mythological dramatists can be found on the first page of Hugh Dickinson's *Myth on the Stage*.

[40] Cf. the general works by Aler, Asenbaum, Dietrich, Dickinson, Hamburger, Highet, Hunger, Jouan, Maulnier and Reichert listed in the bibliography. There are also numerous more limited studies in this area.

abstracted from its various diverse repetitions, which residuum or accretion is independent of time.[41]

This approximate identification of myth with drama and hence plot, calling to mind Aristotle's contention that plot is the essence of drama, explains why myth so often appears on the stage rather than emerging as a motif to a modern plot.[42] (Such plays as *Les Mouches*, *Mourning Becomes Electra*, *Pygmalion* and Brecht's version of *Edward II*, with its motif from the Trojan War, are exceptions to this general pattern.) The modern novel, on the other hand, adheres less rigidly to the skeletal structure of plot, though it still of course maintains a "story line" in most cases. It meanders, devoting its attention more to undramatic incidentals and to the depiction of multi-faceted characters and milieux, matters independent of the direct exigencies of the plot in most cases. And—a more obvious point—it is usually much longer than a play, both in narrative and narrated time; it assumes the proportions of biography rather than being limited to a single dramatic event or plot which could easily be compared with a traditional myth. In the light of the general distribution mentioned above, it is not surprising that there have been numerous studies of myths in drama and that these have exerted a strong influence on theories about the role of mythology in fiction.

The most comprehensive surveys of the presence of ancient myths in modern literature are to be found in the 1939 edition of the *Cahiers du Sud*, dedicated "aux mythes, et surtout à leur valeur d'inspiration littéraire";[43] in Luis Díez del Corral's monograph *La función del mito clásico en la literatura contemporánea*; in a collection of essays by

---

[41] *The Quester Hero*, p. 3.

[42] In "Myth in Modern French Literature" (pp. 78ff.), R. G. Stone points persuasively to the element of ritual as the link between myth and drama. Ritual and plot are undoubtedly closely connected in this respect.

[43] Etienne Fuzellier, "Les Mythes," *CdS*, xlx, 1939, p. 1.

Dutch scholars edited by Jan Aler under the title *De Mythe in de Literatuur*; in the Spring 1959 issue of *Daedalus*; and in the University of Otago lectures on *Myth and the Modern Imagination* edited by Margaret Dalziel. With the exception of this last study, such contributions make no more than passing reference to the place of traditional mythologies in the modern novel. Admittedly, Díez del Corral's introductory chapter mentions Thomas Mann and James Joyce briefly, but the book then goes on to concentrate on poetry and drama, dealing at some length with the Symbolists, with Rilke, Eliot, Nietzsche, Anouilh and the Existentialists, a representative sample of the writers usually treated by works on this general subject. Classicists' surveys of mythology's place in literature are remarkably reticent about modern fiction: Grant's *Myths of the Greeks and Romans*, Highet's *The Classical Tradition* and Hunger's *Lexikon der griechischen und römischen Mythologie*, all, despite their stated aim of considering mythology's influence on later literatures, mention very few novels. Yet certain ways of handling mythological material are peculiar to recent fiction. Hence, any study which, either because of its date of publication or its chosen perspective, concentrates too much on drama or on novels written before 1945, inevitably gives a distorted and limited image of the subject.

Towards a Methodology: Practical Considerations

In his distinction between the adaptation of specific myths and the literary embodiment of archetypal patterns, Theodore Ziolkowski points out that archetypal patterns differ from other prefigurative motifs "inasmuch as they are not necessarily associated with a specific name or figure or concatenation of events."[44] For, more than any structural similarity between a modern plot and a classical myth, this act of naming or alluding unmistakably to a given myth is the

[44] *The Novels of Hermann Hesse*, p. 119.

27

main feature of the mythological novel. It is this, above all else, which lifts it out of a vague archetypal similarity with many myths and puts it in the referential framework of a specific mythology. (It will be necessary later to look at many of the ways in which such direct references can be made to ensure that the reader notices the analogies offered to him.) Yet an even more important factor than this wide range of techniques at the novelist's disposal is the decisive effect of presenting the appropriate analogy at a certain, carefully chosen point in the action. Patterns of expectation and innuendo can become more relevant than the simple models of cognition so often put forward by critics beholding in every mythological motif an Ariadne's thread to guide the reader through a labyrinth of fragmented modern reality. The sequence of ideas is crucial, although it is a factor to which little consideration has been given hitherto. In *The Classical Temper*,[45] S. L. Goldberg shows convincingly that one must distinguish between major and marginal references to mythology in Joyce's *Ulysses* (in a way that certain industrious allusion-hunters had signally failed to do). We can see, for example—to apply the point elsewhere—that the title of Thomas Mann's *Doktor Faustus* is a fundamental reference to the novel's main prefiguration. In contrast, the fact that a pledge between nations, which in Mann's German is talked of as a "Faustpfand," is mentioned by the narrator in the twenty-sixth chapter (i.e. immediately after the pact scene) remains an allusion of a lesser order. But what makes them different kinds of allusion, too, is their position in the work, not simply the fact that one is a direct statement of prefigurative motif whereas the other is merely a play on words. To demonstrate how important the sequence of references can be, I shall offer an approach to mythological fiction which relates the information given by allusions to the point in the work at which it is offered.

---

[45] Especially pp. 145-150.

Then, in my final chapter, other patterns of motifs will be described; with these, sequence is of less importance, the effect being largely achieved by overlapping motifs.

It would be impracticable to undertake a comprehensive survey of the modern mythological novel, nor indeed would any such *catalogue raisonné* be a feasible or worthwhile undertaking while the more fundamental questions of how the mythological elements in novels can be unmistakably recognized, how they operate and in what context they occur, remain unanswered. A certain amount of compromise is involved in striking a balance between a structural analysis and a diachronic approach to the subject. But it is a necessary compromise; for to ignore such features as the quality of a mythological novel and its historical context would be to misrepresent the subject. However, if I have felt obliged to compromise with a bias in either direction, it has certainly been in favor of the formal analysis of specific structures and to the relative detriment of historical perspectives. This has been necessary because the scales have until now been weighted too restrictively on the side of historical accounts of the metamorphosis of a given myth or the development of a particular novelist's attitude to mythology. Since the use of prefigurative motifs is to be found in all kinds of modern fiction, both good and bad, Modernist and post-war, my examples are intended to counteract the usual impression that only a small number of novelists, including Broch, Joyce, Mann and certain *nouveaux romanciers,* used the device. I have therefore examined both works by novelists who are not internationally well-known, amongst them John Bowen, Macdonald Harris and Hans Erich Nossack, as well as the more familiar exponents, and have even included novels which have proved rather infelicitous in their handling of the device. (I would put Guido Bachmann's *Gilgamesch* and Heinrich Mann's *Die Göttinnen* in the rogues' gallery.) Although trying not to tread over-familiar paths by avoiding too many subsequent illustrations from Joyce's *Ulysses* or Thomas Mann's mythological fiction, I have at times felt compelled to fall back on such classics to make some point. In general, the selection is intended to be representative of the wide range of modern prefigurative novels in various literatures. For mythological novels do not occur in isolation in any one literature, despite the well-documented "tyranny of Greece over Germany" or the classical heritage of certain Mediterranean countries. Almost all modern literatures show an interest in mythology in the novel (although, as I have already indicated, not necessarily to the same extent). Joyce could write to his brother Stanislaus from Paris in 1920:

> *Odyssey* very much in the air here. Anatole France is writing *Le Cyclope*, G. Fauré, the musician, an opera *Pénélope*, Giraudoux has written *Elpénor* . . . Guillaume Apollinaire *Les Mamelles de Tirésias*. . . . Madame Circe advances regally toward her completion.[46]

In fact, mythology is still very much "in the air," though not specifically in the Parisian air. For this reason, I have included novels from American, English, French, German, Italian and Russian literature in order to give the topic a wider treatment than it has hitherto received.

Certainly, a study of mythology in the modern novel, no matter how confined its scope, cannot avoid considering James Joyce's *Ulysses*, the archetypal mythological novel, as it was once rightly called.[47] Above all, Joyce's *Ulysses* affords the practical advantage of being the most generally known mythological work. It also illustrates, as Goldberg has shown, a large number of devices connected with the technique of prefiguration and has been analyzed as a novel

[46] Quoted by Ellmann, *op.cit.*, p. 504.
[47] "Der Urtyp des mythischen Romans in unserer Zeit" (Gunilla Bergsten, *Thomas Manns "Doktor Faustus,"* p. 195).

containing mythology more often than any other novel of this kind. Admittedly, a certain methodological danger nevertheless arises here, as I shall need to show later; for at times one may be tempted to transfer certain formal principles observed in Joyce's novel to the interpretation of other works on the mistaken assumption that they operate in the same way. But, this problem aside, studies of Joyce's work by such astute critics as Hugh Kenner and S. L. Goldberg have done much to increase our general understanding of the role of mythology specifically in modern novels. In contrast, French and German scholarship in this field has been variously influenced by Thomas Mann's thoughts on mythical imitation, by the ghost of neo-classicism and by the Jungian notion of a collective unconscious (if not by even more sinister ideas concerning mythology that arose in Fascist Europe during this century). Theorists are inclined to concentrate too much on myth *per se* and not enough on its role in fiction. But in general, English criticism has not been hampered by any large corpus of statements of intention (such as French and German novelists have enjoyed providing)[48] and has viewed many theories concerning mythology with a sceptical mind. And this freedom from abstract pronouncements seems to have been an asset.

[48] Apart from his remarks in "Freud und die Zukunft," Mann refers frequently to mythology in his lecture on *Joseph und seine Brüder*, in his correspondence with Karl Kerényi and in *Die Entstehung des "Doktor Faustus." Roman eines Romans*, Frankfurt a.M., 1949. As Helen Watson-Williams has shown (*André Gide and the Greek Myth*, pp. 84ff.), Gide's "Considérations sur la Mythologie grècque: Fragments du *Traité des Dioscures*" are of great importance for an appreciation of much of his work. In *Dichten und Erkennen*, Hermann Broch has three essays on the subject of myth and literature: "James Joyce und die Gegenwart," "Die mythische Erbschaft der Dichtung" and "The Style of the Mythical Age." In *Repertoire 2*, Paris, 1963, Michel Butor refers to the subject in a much-cited essay entitled "Le Roman et la Poésie."

Chapter Two

Terms and Distinctions

Myth Criticism and the Meanings of "Myth"

The hazard of employing such words as "myth," "mythical" and "mythological" is not so much that they refer to a single, ill-defined "area of meaning," as Wellek and Warren once suggested,[1] but that they can imply various, almost distinct connotations, largely dependent upon the user. While elasticity can sometimes be a definite asset, in the case of words which possess such different associations as "myth" can have in various contexts, it at times becomes the critic's worst enemy. To illustrate this point, I shall first review some definitions and widespread uses of basic vocabulary associated with myths in literature, including the words "myth," "archetype" and their various cognates. This critical examination of terms also covers a number of foreign words which either lack direct English equivalents, such as the Greek word *mythos* (used by various modern critics) and the German words "Mythe" and "Mythologem." An excursus into international semantics is necessary in order to perceive how nebulous usage of such terms has frequently led to misinterpretations of the mythological novel. Whenever possible, the emphasis will lie on the current meanings of these words. Attempts at explaining them etymologically, arriving at the awe-inspiring Greek morpheme μυ which Liddell and Scott define as "a muttering

[1] *Theory of Literature*, p. 181.

32

sound made with the lips"[2] usually bear little relevance to the role these concepts play in contemporary criticism.[3] To avoid the pitfalls of the etymological method, I shall present examples of usage in modern criticism and establish a set of definitions that coincides, wherever possible, with current usage. Only in the case of terms which are inevitably ambiguous shall I resort to any *ad hoc* definitions.

Although dealing with the importance of mythology for an understanding of certain modern novels, I shall not be embarking on the popular venture commonly known as myth criticism. This usually signifies something more in keeping with the search for archetypal patterns in literature undertaken in our century by Maud Bodkin, Joseph Campbell, Gilbert Murray and above all by Northrop Frye. To quote Frye: "In myth criticism, when we examine the theme or total design of a fiction, we must isolate that aspect of the fiction which is conventional and held in common with all other works of the same category."[4] This is a method to which weighty objections have been raised.[5] In a review of Claire Rosenfeld's *Paradise of Snakes: An Archetypal Analysis of Conrad's Political Novels*, Tony Tanner points to one of the method's main weaknesses:

[2] H. G. Liddell and R. Scott, *A Greek-English Lexicon*, Oxford, 1929, p. 982.

[3] In "Das Fortleben des Mythos," Erich Kahler contends that the word "Mythos" can only be understood in present contexts, if we know its etymology. He continues: "seine Wurzel ist aller etymologischen Wahrscheinlichkeit nach ein Urlaut, ein Laut vor dem Wort . . . ein elementarer und animalischer Laut, wie er im Brüllen des Rindes und des Löwen oder im kosmischen Donner ertönt" (*Die Verantwortung des Geistes*, p. 201). But all this remains rather remote from most present-day usages.

[4] *Fables of Identity*, p. 34.

[5] Joseph Blotner's "Myth Patterns in *To the Lighthouse*," Northrop Frye's *Fables of Identity* and Honor Matthews's *The Hard Journey: The Myth of Man's Rebirth* represent the kind of approach under discussion, although E. W. Herd has since questioned whether one can usefully talk of a school of myth critics; cf. "Myth Criticism: Limitations and Possibilities," p. 69.

uniqueness of novelistic detail is lost by reference back to certain rudimentary shapes or outlines which in their generality can subsume the most heterogeneous material if the critic so wishes. A man can scarcely get into a boat but he will find himself engaged in a repetition of "a night-sea journey into an ambiguous region either in the dark interior of the earth or below the waters of the sea."[6]

In *Concepts of Criticism*, René Wellek describes myth criticism in this sense as one of the six major critical approaches that modern scholars have adopted to literature. But he rightly remains highly critical of the way in which "whole groups of critics have tried to discover the original myths of mankind behind all literature."[7] Paraphrasing such an approach, Wellek suggests that "Huck Finn floating down the Mississippi is a myth."[8] (Perhaps in all fairness to Frye, if not to all of his emulators, one should remember that he refers to his practice as "a kind of literary anthropology"[9] and holds that "literature is a reconstructed mythology."[10])

The adjective "mythical" can have this archetypal connotation, too. Calling a work "mythical," a writer may wish to express its affinity with myth in the wider sense, as Gilbert Durand did when he entitled a recent study *Le Décor mythique de la Chartreuse de Parme*.[11] Here again, the connotation is essentially that of the Jungian archetype. A reviewer of this book was able to conclude (as no one could solely from the ambiguous adjective "mythique" in the title):

> Gilbert Durand veut appliquer la théorie de Jung selon laquelle les archétypes psychologiques seraient la base de la mythologie et de la littérature. Le héros de roman suivrait le schéma des mythes: double naissance

---

[6] *Modern Language Review*, LXV, 1970, p. 407.
[7] p. 360.   [8] *op.cit.*, p. 335.
[9] *Fables of Identity*, p. 12.   [10] *op.cit.*, p. 38.
[11] Paris, 1965.

comme Hercule, prophéties et oracles, obstacles sous forme de dragon, or ou de femme, deux types de femme: Dalila ou amazone, conversion du héros, souvent dans un labyrinthe.[12]

Yet this Jungian, archetypal sense is only one way in which the idea of myth can be relevant to the interpretation of modern literature. The proverbial "return to myth," as I have already suggested, can also refer to a revival of specific mythologies.

The two adjectives "mythical" and "mythic" share the root noun's quality of being a "term . . . not easy to fix."[13] These words also involve a further complication of meaning. Almost all dictionaries define the adjective "mythic" as synonymous with "mythical," yet any speaker of modern English knows that this is only sometimes the case. The epithet "mythical" has two basic meanings. First, there is the pejorative one of "fanciful" which it often receives in everyday parlance and invariably in journalism. When the husband in James Thurber's short story "The Unicorn" goes up to the bedroom to tell his wife that he has seen a live unicorn in the garden, he is soon put in his place. " 'The unicorn is a mythical beast,' she said, and turned her back on him."[14] In contrast, there is the more positive meaning that the adjective enjoys when employed to endow something with the status of an archetype. The adjective "mythic" rarely has the everyday negative meaning that "mythical" can have. It comes closer to the meaning of the German word "mythisch"—invariably a positive epithet—and is most frequently used by scholars who have worked within the Central European tradition of *Mythenforschung*.[15] A further problem with the adjective "mythical"

---

[12] "Notices bibliographiques," *Orbis litterarum*, xx, 1965, p. 234.

[13] René Wellek and Austin Warren, *Theory of Literature*, p. 181.

[14] *The Thurber Carnival*, Harmondsworth, 1959, p. 230.

[15] Cf. its use in two passages from the *Theory of Literature*: "Niebuhr speaks of Christian eschatology as mythic" (p. 180); and "if the

is that dictionaries usually telescope two of its principal meanings into one composite definition. Such a compound lexical account of the word as: "Of the nature of, consisting of, or based on a myth or myths"[16] reflects the present ambiguities of the word. Although something that is "based on" myth need not any longer be "of the nature of" myth— except in a very loose and almost meaningless sense—these meanings are given as one of the connotations of "mythical" rather than separate definitions. Yet these are the very two meanings that often need to be kept distinct.

The terminology used in French criticism seems to correspond generally to the English, except that one encounters a predilection for the adjective "mythologique" rather than "mythique." Michel Leiris writes of "Le Réalisme mythologique de Michel Butor" and by this he means archetypal patterns (not the mythology of Greece that Marion Grant discusses in her examination of "The Function of Myth in the Novels of Michel Butor"). Similarly, Maurice Blanchot's essay entitled "Romans mythologiques" is about novels which have a certain vague archetypal quality, not works which introduce material from specific mythologies. In his book on Butor, Jean Roudaut argues that "l'intention romanesque de Butor est celle de la pensée mythique"[17] and he quotes frequently from Lévi-Strauss to support this view. Yet in fact he appears to use the terms "mythique" and "mythologique" synonymously. Right at the beginning of his section on "La Mythologie," he distinguishes his archetypal meaning of the word from other possible nuances:

mythic has as its contrary either science or philosophy, it opposes the picturable intuitive concrete to the rational abstract" (pp. 180f.). For an illustration from literary criticism, see Alice P. Kenney's "The Mythic History of *The Severed Head*," MFS, xv, 1969, pp. 387-401.

[16] This is the *OED* definition, but Murray and Webster give similarly elliptical ones.

[17] *Michel Butor ou le Livre futur*, p. 200.

Cette société imaginaire n'est rien d'autre qu'une mythologie. Il y a encore deux mensonges complémentaires à éviter: traiter le monde moderne selon le schéma mythologique antique, ou introduire dans l'univers d'aujourd'hui des souvenirs mythologiques.[18]

But French, like English, has usually preferred not to resuscitate the Greek word *mythos*.

In modern German, the words "Mythos" and "mythisch" have enjoyed great popularity, but at the same time engendered ambiguity. Whereas a dissertation by D. Reichert, for example, bears the title *Der griechische Mythos im modernen deutschen und österreichischen Drama*, W. Asenbaum calls his work on a similar subject *Die griechische Mythologie im modernen französischen Drama*. One might well wonder whether or not there is, in these two dissertations written for the same faculty of the same university, a contrast of meanings between the words "Mythos" and "Mythologie." Does Asenbaum merely claim that material from Greek mythology is to be found in modern French drama (which would not be an evaluation), and is Reichert, in contrast, suggesting that German and Austrian drama not only embodies elements from Greek mythology but even achieves the original religious power—*mythos* in the dynamic sense—that the Greek myths possessed for the ancients? Certainly both make the first point: that there is mythological material in the dramas under discussion. They may well be tacitly proposing the second thesis too; but the drawback with vocabulary of this kind is that it is often difficult for the reader, and sometimes even for the critic, to realize exactly how much is meant. Because of its ambiguity, Karl Kerényi has attacked the German noun "Mythos" as a nebulous modern concept.[19] Unfortunately,

---

[18] *op.cit.*, pp. 195-196.
[19] "einen verschwommenen modernen Begriff" (*Gespräch in Briefen*, p. 21).

few critics have shared Kerényi's misgivings about the dangers of the word.

What is lacking is some generally acceptable, differentiated terminology for distinguishing two fundamental meanings of myth: first, some primitive or typical, recurrent pattern of human behavior, found both in literature and life, and second, a more specific form, linked with a particular culture and dealing with named characters and locations, and transmitted to us nowadays primarily through the medium of literature. Since I have chosen to use the word "mythology" to signify a set of myths bound to one particular society, "archetype" will be used to denote the other, more general meaning so often given to the word "myth"; this covers the exploits of such figures as the Fire-bringer, the Divine Child or the Voyager to the Under-world, and may even embrace certain stylistic features.[20] It will also imply such recurrent patterns as temporal cycles and common ritual events. At no point in my subsequent argument will the word "myth" be used without either a definite or an indefinite article, except in quotation or paraphrase of other critics, since in this form it is synonymous with my use of "archetype." When the word "myth" occurs, it is intended to refer to a particular myth, such as the myth of Orpheus and Eurydice.

The vagueness of terms indicated above has not always existed. Symptomatically it arose at the same time as the return to myth in this century. "Fable" was the usual word for individual myths in both English and French writings prior to the nineteenth century.[21] And the German word "Mythos" is, as Kerényi remarked, a modern innovation;[22]

[20] On the question of a possibly mythical style, see Gerhard Schmidt-Henkel's *Mythos und Dichtung* and my critical review of it in *GLL*, xxiii, 1970, pp. 374-375.

[21] Cf. Richard Chase, *Quest for Myth*, p. 134.

[22] "Mythus," the Latin form of the word, is preferred by some writers and critics, including Thomas Mann.

or, to be more precise, it is an old word which recent writ-ers have chosen to revive. Grimm lists only "Mythe";[23] Brockhaus, on the other hand, accepts only the word "Mythos"—perhaps somewhat apodictically censuring the use of "Mythe" in modern German as bad style.[24] Yet de-spite the apparently mutual exclusiveness of these two words, at one point during the interval of time between the 1880s and the 1950s when the word "Mythe" was disappear-ing from circulation and the more ambiguous noun "Mythos" came into almost exclusive use, a very sensible attempt was made to differentiate linguistically between the two ideas by using different terms. This was in André Jolles's *Einfache Formen* where the author explains in the section on "Mythe" the reasons for his distinction:

Ich muß . . . hervorheben, daß ich . . . einen Unter-schied mache zwischen der Einfachen Form als solcher und ihrer Vergegenwärtigung. Ich tue das, indem ich Mythe und Mythus trenne: Mythe heißt die sich aus unserer Geistesbeschäftigung ergebende Einfache Form, dagegen, ist die Form, in der sie vereinzelt jedesmal vor uns liegt, Mythus oder ein Mythus.[25]

[23] J.U.W. Grimm, *Deutsches Wörterbuch*, vi, Leipzig, 1885, p. 2847. André Jolles (*Einfache Formen*, pp. 91f.) doubts the complete-ness of Grimm at this point, suggesting, tongue in cheek, that the compilers were tired when they got to the end of the "M" section and rashly decided to call it a day.

[24] *Der Große Brockhaus*, viii, Wiesbaden, 1955, p. 237. The question is whether the instances of the word "Mythe" one still finds in modern German are all special cases or not. Certainly Gottfried Benn's pun "Die Mythe log" ("Verlorenes Ich," *Gesammelte Ge-dichte*, Wiesbaden and Zürich, 1956, p. 229) could well employ the old term for the sake of a play on words. But does one in turn have to indulge in either censure or special pleading when coming upon in-stances of the word in Elisabeth Langgässer's *Märkische Argonauten-fahrt* and *Proserpina: Eine Kindheitsmythe?* It seems more probable that the contributor to Brockhaus has observed a tendency and is try-ing to make a rule on the basis of it.

[25] p. 100. "I must emphasize that I am making a distinction between the 'simple form' as such and its concretization. I do this by differen-tiating between *Mythe* and *Mythus*: *Mythe* is the simple form which

This distinction between "Mythe," the simple form, and "Mythus," the individual embodiment of it, is very much the same as the contrast between archetypes and myths, for the "Einfache Formen" that Jolles describes are really literature's equivalents of archetypes. Jolles here shows an appreciation of the fact that it helps to have two terms to distinguish two ideas with any success.

Despite Northrop Frye's use of *mythos* and "myth," about which more will be said later, contemporary English on the whole offers no simple contrast between two terms. Critics who have tried to make a distinction have perforce arrived at different means to express this difference. Consider the following statements:

> Some scholars and critics have customarily assumed that a poem becomes mythological by referring to a mythology of the past. English poetry has of course repeatedly invoked the Greek gods, but to suppose that a poem becomes mythological by mentioning Zeus or Daphne is certainly misleading.[26]

> In every epoch there are the old myths of the past haunting the present like a fixation of childhood, and the new myths struggling to be born. It is a mistake not to be able to tell them apart.[27]

> Classical mythology was introduced into European poetry centuries ago. The vogue even reached a height in the eighteenth century. The poetry of the period teems with gods and goddesses. . . . However, there is no trace of the mythical in all these mythological ornaments. They are cleverly handled, but the true atmosphere is lacking.[28]

---

results from our mental processes, on the other hand the form in which it appears in isolation each time is *Mythus* or a *Mythus.*"

[26] Chase, *Quest for Myth*, p. 112.

[27] William Troy, "A Further Note on Myth," p. 100.

[28] Jan Aler, "Mythical Consciousness in Modern German Poetry," p. 189.

Poems "referring to a mythology" are contrasted in the first passage with "mythological" works; in the second, "old myths" are distinguished from "new myths"; and in the final passage—in direct contrast to the terminology of the first—the "mythical" quality is denied to many "mythological ornaments." As E.M.W. Tillyard once lamented: "The words *myth, mythical, mythology* and *mythological* have been dreadfully overworked in recent years and have a distressingly large range of significance." Nevertheless, Tillyard's conclusion—that "there exist no synonyms for these words"[29] and that we have to make do with them alone—does not necessarily hold in all contexts. One of the disadvantages of these words is that they are all derivatives of the noun "myth" and their sound implies comparison with rather than contrast to myth. This is why I have chosen the word "archetype": to make a contrast more evident. It might be objected that this removes the suggestion of mythical power from the very aspect of my subject which may still sometimes be dynamically mythical in the anthropological sense. But the word "archetype" at least draws attention to the non-religious system of categorization that myth now represents for most of us.

The Archetype

Within literary criticism, Maud Bodkin uses the term "archetype" with much the same connotation. In her introduction to *Archetypal Patterns in Poetry*, where she acknowledges an indebtedness to Jung, these archetypes are described as:

> themes having a particular form or pattern which points, amid variation from age to age, and which corresponds to, a pattern or configuration of emotional tendencies in the minds of those who are stirred by them.[30]

[29] *Myth and the English Mind*, p. 11.   [30] p. 4.

41

CHAPTER TWO

In actual practice, if not in her terminology, Maud Bodkin
maintains the contrast between mythology and the timeless
pattern of the archetypes to which her study is primarily
devoted. When she writes of "the *Prometheus* or *Faust*
figure, passionate for experience, adventure, knowledge,
defiant of human limitations,"[31] she cites two specific mythological figures, but remains more concerned with the
general archetypes they represent. Jung adopts the same
approach in his interpretation of Joyce's *Ulysses*: "Man ahnt
zwar archetypische Hintergründe," he writes. "Hinter
Daedalus [sic] und *Bloom* stehen wohl die ewigen Figuren
des geistigen und des sinnlichen Menschen."[32] The characters need not have been portrayed with the help of mythological motifs for such archetypal patterns to be visible;
these motifs merely underscore them.

The problem of ambiguity does not arise so often for
critics who employ the term "archetype," whether they are
discussing the archetypes or archetypal patterns in mythological works or their presence in all literature. In general,
the concept of the archetype acts as a generic abstraction
in tacit or explicit contrast to either a specific myth or a particular situation. Myth is, to quote Jung, the expression of
the archetype: "Ausdruck des Archetypus."[33] Although he
seems to handle the terms more loosely in *Fables of Identity*, Frye offers a useful distinction between myths and
archetypes in the glossary to his *Anatomy of Criticism*:

> ARCHETYPE: A symbol, usually an image, which recurs
> often enough in literature to be recognizable as an ele-
> ment of one's literary experience as a whole.
> MYTH: A narrative in which some characters are super-

[31] *op.cit.*, p. 192.
[32] *"Ulysses": Wirklichkeit der Seele: Anwendungen und Fortschritte
der neueren Psychologie*, Zürich, 1934, p. 156. "One senses archetypal
backgrounds. Behind Dedalus and Bloom stand the eternal figures
of the spiritual man and the sensual man."
[33] *Von den Wurzeln des Bewußtseins*, Zürich, 1954, p. 6.

42

human beings who do things that "happen only in stories"; hence a conventional or stylized narrative not fully adapted to plausibility or "realism."[34]

Admittedly, one can take issue with certain assumptions in Frye's definitions which only apply to his own study and lack greater applicability[35]—hence the need for a gloss to the book. Yet Frye's definitions do nevertheless mark a recognition of the need for discriminating between two levels of myth.

To be sure, even the word "archetype" is not without its modicum of ambiguity. One meaning which the word has at times acquired is never intended in the following pages: "archetype" has occasionally been used to refer to the original version or prototype of a myth. Accordingly, ripe old age, more than any other quality, seems to sanctify a myth; the older the version, the purer the form, would seem to be the formula. Writing of the mythological hero, W. B. Stanford states that his evolution as a subject in the literature of subsequent ages "will depend on his definitive portrait."[36] Using "archetype" in this sense, he refers to the "archetypal Ulysses,"[37] meaning specifically Homer's Odysseus. Yet the very openness of myth seems to conflict with the idea of a definitive portrait in most mythology.

[34] pp. 365f. The glossary also contains a definition of "mythos" which seems (to this reader, at least) unhelpful: "MYTHOS: (1) The narrative of a work of literature, considered as the grammar or order of words (literal narrative), plot or 'argument' (descriptive narrative), secondary imitation of action (formal narrative), imitation of generic and recurrent action or ritual (archetypal narrative), or imitation of the total conceivable action of an omnipotent god or human society (anagogic narrative). (2) One of the four archetypal narratives, classified as comic, romantic, tragic and ironic" (pp. 366f.). In *Fables of Identity*, the notion of *mythos* appears to have been simplified to the "sequence of events which holds our attention" (p. 25).

[35] For example, archetypes are not necessarily confined to one's literary experience. Furthermore, we find no attempt here to link myths with any specific culture.

[36] *The Ulysses Theme*, p. 5.

[37] *op.cit.*, p. 6.

Outside literary criticism, and most psychological nomenclature, this idea of archetype as primal form would be a more acceptable usage, for the non-technical dictionary definition is "the original from which copies are made" (*OED*). However, within some specialized fields, this becomes a most misleading reading. It presupposes the presence of an archetype in one given concretization, whereas in the technical sense the archetype remains an abstraction. No particular myth can present us with the archetype itself, since it denotes the configuration or discernible pattern of attributes common to a number of paradigmatic myths. Far from being historical, the archetype, as used in the accepted technical sense in anthropology, literary criticism and certain schools of analytic psychology, signifies something timeless: a kind of scientific category derived from comparative mythology. Specific myths become recognized as belonging to a certain class of archetypes because of a number of common denominators. Having posited an archetype, we can certainly isolate elements of it in many myths and works of literature; and this is what anyone is doing when he calls a literary work mythical.

"Archetype," in the above-mentioned sense, is close to the idea of "monomyth" employed by Joseph Campbell in his influential *Hero with a Thousand Faces*.[38] And "Mythologem," a word used by Jung and Kerényi in their *Einführung in das Wesen der Mythologie*, is also a near-synonym of "archetype" in the sense attributed to it. For this reason, the terms "monomyth" and "Mythologem" are redundant within my scheme of distinctions and I shall

[38] Campbell writes on p. 30 of *The Hero with a Thousand Faces* that he takes the word "monomyth" from Joyce's *Finnegans Wake* (New York, 1939, p. 581). As might be expected, it is not easy to discover from this context what the term means. The passage runs: "And their bivouac! And his monomyth! Ah ho! Say no more about it!"; Joyce does not, nor is the word given in the *OED*. It seems to be Campbell's borrowing from a Joycean neologism.

take them to mean no more than a configuration of archetypal qualities.

Illustrations

So far, the task of establishing a basic vocabulary, a set of terms to account for the various levels of significance, has been pursued somewhat in a vacuum. So to support the claim that a differentiated set of terms is necessary to describe mythological works, or even to recognize them at times, some illustrations follow. These will be taken both from critics who have mistakenly claimed that novels contain mythological motifs (for the simple reason that they lacked the critical apparatus to detect the *non sequitur* in their interpretations), and from critics who, using a more viable set of distinctions, avoid this pitfall. It should, of course, be stressed in advance that these illustrations are put forward primarily as a reflection of the general inadequacy of terminology in this area rather than in any deliberately polemical spirit.

The most common mistake in this field is the substitution of a particular myth for an archetype. In his *Anatomy of Criticism*, Frye has suggested that one finds a single quest myth common to all literature;[39] he even argues that "it is part of the critic's business to show how all literary genres are derived from the quest-myth."[40] Unfortunately, a number of critics have preferred to hypostatize the general archetype by naming a particular myth. Howard Nemerov, for example, writes of "the legend with which we of the West are most familiar under the name of Faust, and of which Mann's more epic protagonists are all the hero."[41] In like manner, the ubiquitous quest is seen by others as Orpheus' searchings for Eurydice, as the eternal wanderings of Ahasverus or as a search for some new kind of Grail.

---

[39] p. 215.   [40] *Fables of Identity*, p. 17.
[41] *The Quester Hero*, p. 18.

Nemerov carefully argues that "the most important common denominators between Mann, Goethe and the Grail cycles is found, *when abstracted*, to be the presence of the figure best described as the 'Quester,' after the earlier form of the three, and it is by this title that I shall designate Perceval, Gawain, Faust, Wilhelm Meister, Hans Castorp and Joseph."[42] In a reference to Nemerov's work, Mann notes: "ob er nun Gawain, Galahad oder Perceval heißt, ist [der Held] eben der Quester."[43] Mann then goes on to call Castorp a seeker after the Grail ("ein Gralsucher"), which overspecifies the quest image. There is a substantial contrast between the archetypal significance of the Grail for *Der Zauberberg* and its role, say, in Bernard Malamud's *The Natural*. In Malamud's baseball story the Grail quest is actually employed as a literary prefiguration.[44]

There are many times when our understanding of a work is not only kept at an inappropriate level of generality by such descriptions which have lost their metaphorical quality, but where these accounts of quests for grails or golden fleeces, of odysseys or journeys to the underworld even more seriously impair our image of a novel. In an article on "Hermann Broch und der moderne Mythos," Alexander Gosztonyi describes the archetypal pattern behind all literature as Orpheus' quest for Eurydice in the underworld. "Der Urmythos aller Dichtung," he claims, "ist der Mythos von Orpheus." Therefore, "jede große Dichtung gestaltet den Orpheus-Mythos in einer Abwandlung."[45] True, such

[42] *op.cit.*, p. 19. My italics.

[43] "Einführung in den Zauberberg: Für Studenten der Universität Princeton," *Der Zauberberg*, Berlin and Frankfurt a.M., 1964, p. xiv; "whether he is called Gawain, Galahad or Perceval, [the hero] is still the quester."

[44] See the discussion of this novel in my "Myths and Patterns in the Modern Novel," p. 49.

[45] *op.cit.*, p. 214. "The primal myth of all poetry is the myth of Orpheus . . . all great poetry recreates the myth of Orpheus in some variation."

recurrent literary themes as the search for a loved one, the path to self-realization or the attainment of some symbolic paradise lost—whether physical or spiritual—could all be related *mutatis mutandis* to the Orpheus myth. On the other hand, when Gosztonyi proceeds to observe that in Broch's *Der Tod des Vergil* "der antike Mythos, der im Hintergrund von Brochs Werk steht, ist ein Urmythos . . . der Mythos von Orpheus,"[46] he has obscured a valid point by his earlier remarks. The Orpheus myth is without doubt, as we shall see later, a motif in this novel; but this observation, applicable to the specific case of *Der Tod des Vergil* and not to all literature in the same way, is obfuscated by Gosztonyi's rhetorical introductory comments about the relevance to all literature of this particular quest myth. The similarity of his two pivotal terms ("Mythos"/"Urmythos") soon leads Gosztonyi to blur the semantic distinction between them.

The substitution of a particular myth for an archetypal pattern is a commonplace in psychoanalysis and has also been adopted in daily parlance. Oedipus, Electra,[47] Narcissus and Clytemnestra[48] have all been pressed into service as labels for patterns of typical behavior which could be called archetypal. It is when this *pars pro toto* approach is transferred from the methodology of psychoanalysis to lit-

[46] *ibid.*; "the classical myth which stands in the background of Broch's work is a primal myth . . . the myth of Orpheus."

[47] Cf. Sigmund Freud, *Vorlesungen zur Einführung in die Psychoanalyse, Gesammelte Werke*, ed. Anna Freud *et al.*, London, 1948, XI, esp. p. 211 and pp. 343ff., for the use of Oedipus and Electra in this way.

[48] For example, Hans Erich Nossack gives the two levels of meaning telescoped by this method in a remark to Horst Bienek: "Ich habe einen Komplex, den Klytemnästra- oder Anti-Mutter-Komplex" (*Werkstattgespräche mit Schriftstellern*, Munich, 1962, p. 79). Even this remark has been incorporated into an interpretation of Nossack as mythmaker in Hans Bänziger's "*Der Neugierige*: Zu Hans Erich Nossacks Anteil an der Mythenbildung," *Wirkendes Wort*, XX, 1970, pp. 183-189.

erary criticism that misconceptions can arise. There is another probable influence upon this kind of labeling, apart from post-Freudian psychoanalytic terminology. In *Die Geburt der Tragödie aus dem Geiste der Musik*, Friedrich Nietzsche, a great force amongst the mythomaniacs, uses the same approach. Apollo and Dionysos are employed as personifications of qualities found both in art and life. In the first paragraph of Nietzsche's essay we are told:

> Diese Namen entlehnen wir von den Griechen, welche die tiefsinnigen Geheimlehren ihrer Kunstanschauung zwar nicht in Begriffen, aber in den eindringlich deutlichen Gestalten ihrer Götterwelt dem Einsichtigen vernehmbar machen.[49]

In *Der Tod in Venedig*, Thomas Mann structures his imagery in direct allusion to these two mythological hypostatizations. Yet while it would be possible to apply the Apollo-Dionysos dialectic to various aspects of life and literature,[50] this would—in contrast—be at the archetypal level. In *Der Tod in Venedig*, there are allusions to a specifically Greek world, including identifiable attributes of Dionysos and Apollo, and not just examples of the conceptual dialectic.

In his essay on *Hamlet*, Ernest Jones concludes that what

---

[49] *Werke in drei Bänden*, ed. Karl Schlechta, Munich, 1960, i, p. 21. "We borrow these names from the Greeks who make their profound mysterious teachings about their view of art comprehensible not through concepts, but evident to the initiated in the penetratingly clear figures of their world of gods."

[50] The anthropologist Ruth Benedict has applied this dialectic to the Indians of North America: "The Southwest Pueblos are Apollonian. Not all of Nietzsche's discussion of the contrast between the Apollonian and the Dionysian applies to the contrast between the Pueblos and the surrounding peoples [but the] categories bring clearly to the fore the major qualities that differentiate Pueblo culture from other American Indians" (*Patterns of Culture*, London, 1935, p. 79). N. Joseph Calarco's study, *Tragic Being: Apollo and Dionysus in Western Drama* (Minneapolis, 1968), uses the dialectic archetypally, examples of it being found in such unmythological plays as *King Lear, The Master Builder* and *Mutter Courage*.

he has been unearthing "is at all events the mechanism of the Oedipus-complex that is actually found in the real Hamlets that are investigated psychologically."[51] Here, two characters—Oedipus and Hamlet—both function as generic labels for a common archetype, but the reader is told quite definitely by the word "complex" that this is not literary allusion or intentional prefiguration. The confusion of archetype with myth becomes most misleading in other instances, when the particular is substituted for the general: not consciously, as a generic label for a complex, but as a mistakenly adduced set of literary allusions. In a work where mythological motifs are directly named, either in the title or elsewhere, there can be no doubt about the relevance of mythology as well as archetypal patterns for its interpretation. However, certain novels invite the reader to assume the role of detective so often imposed on him by modern literature, in order to discover for himself a covert mythological motif. The prefiguration may never in fact be mentioned in the novel; instead the reader can be supplied with a number of clues, such as mythological attributes or anagrams, to direct his attention to the myth underlying the work.

Thomas Mann is notorious for hiding veiled allusions in his novels.[52] His mythological motifs often seem rather like

[51] "The Problem of Hamlet and the Oedipus-Complex," in William Shakespeare, *Hamlet: With a Psychoanalytic Study by Ernest Jones*, London, 1947, p. 16.

[52] For instance, he once wrote with reference to one of the chapters of *Joseph und seine Brüder*: "Ich warte auf den Kritiker, der als Erster merkt, woher ich das Kapital 'Die Hündin' im dritten Josephbande habe. Einmal muß er doch kommen" (*Gespräch in Briefen*, p. 79). Jürgen Plöger (*Das Hermesmotiv in der Dichtung Thomas Manns*, p. 79) suggests that the chapter in question relates to the Egyptian god Anup. But knowing Mann's technique of very definite allusion, well demonstrated in Herman Meyer's reading of *Der Zauberberg*, one suspects that Mann had a specific source of prefiguration. The comment to Kerényi certainly reveals the game of hide-and-seek the mythological novelist is at times tempted to play with his readers.

icebergs with, initially, only a small part of the prefiguration revealed to the reader; but the more he looks below the surface of the work, the more he finds of the concealed analogy. Such games of hide-and-seek also occur, rather characteristically, in a French *nouveau roman*: Alain Robbe-Grillet's *Les Gommes*. (Here, detection is both the theme of the novel and the way in which much of it has to be deciphered.) In "Oedipe ou le cercle fermé," Bruce Morrissette has exposed the latent mythological motif so persuasively that, after reading his interpretation, one cannot doubt that the Oedipus story forms an inherent part of the novel's structure and is not just the fabrication of what James Joyce once called "the ideal reader with ideal insomnia." Given the knowledge that such a mythological work can exist as a kind of palimpsest,[53] critics may be encouraged to attribute hidden mythological motifs to novels where they do not really occur or cannot be shown definitely to be of much import to the work in question. The following passage on Butor's *L'Emploi du Temps* shows the kind of temptations that novels of this sort put in the path of their critics:

> The year he [Jacques Revel] spends there is divided into two unequal periods; the seven months from the first of October when he arrives, and the five months from the first of May when he begins to write his book. These are five months that can be placed under the sign of Apollo, the bringer of light and harmony, and it is pertinent to remember also that Maia herself was the mother of Hermes, the god of eloquence. These mythological parallels are not as forced as they may

[53] Some of Bernard Malamud's works offer further examples of these elusive patterns. With the title of the short story "The First Seven Years" (*The Magic Barrel*, London, 1960, pp. 7-16), the author allows Jacob's seven-year service for the hand of Rachel to prefigure a modern wooing. Apart from the title, no further indication is given of this prefiguration in the work. Similarly, *The Natural* is prefigured by the Grail quest, though with little actual reference to the motif.

seem, because Butor is never a man to exclude support of this kind for the structures of his novels. . . .[54]

Such speculations, possibly resulting in the mythological allegorization of novels, take place when it is suggested a certain myth is latent in a text, although in fact all that has been located is an extraneous myth with an archetypal pattern in common with the novel in question. This alone cannot furnish satisfactory evidence to vouchsafe the presence of a covert mythological motif.

Categories of Mythological Fiction

There are only certain kinds of mythological fiction where a motif could be adduced. To put this more into perspective, it may help to sub-divide such novels into four categories. And since this is not the first attempt at such a typology, an indication is given of where the scheme set out below differs from others.

Theodore Ziolkowski hints at a bi-partite division of such novels, describing one approach as "the retelling of classical and medieval myths from a contemporary point of view" and pointing out that "the other face of the same coin, of course, is the modern story that is cast in the mold of traditional myths."[55] But to make the contrasts I shall wish to operate with later, further distinctions become desirable. One critic has attempted to posit a greater number of types. In "Myth Criticism: Limitations and Possibilities," E. W. Herd sub-divides mythological fiction into five groups: I. "the novel which assuredly sets out to retell an acknowledged myth"; II. "works in which the author uses myth as a means of literary allusion, intended to attract the attention of the reader and to add significance to a theme or situation by means of illustration or parallel"; III. "con-

---

[54] John Sturrock, *The French New Novel: Claude Simon, Michel Butor, Alain Robbe-Grillet*, London, 1969, pp. 117-118.
[55] *The Novels of Hermann Hesse*, p. 118.

scious use [of myth] as a structural element"; IV. "a mythical structure . . . within the novel without conscious development by the author"; and, finally, v. "the situation of an author who claims himself, or who is claimed by critics, to be creating a new myth."[56] In this typology, type one is clearly defined and agreed upon by most critics. Types two and three need not be mutually exclusive, of course, but the dilemma arises in distinguishing between three and five— and even between four and five. In many cases, I have found, this system proves too differentiated to be practical. Its other disadvantage is that it works largely with impressionistic factors such as whether or not the mythical structure has been *consciously* used by the author, whether or not he has achieved the nebulous "new myth." Frank Kermode once rightly questioned the concept of "the newly created myth" as "the kind critics talk of when they wish to confer upon a fiction some of the prestige of . . . regular myths."[57] In contrast to these drawbacks, the typology outlined below offers specific criteria, possibly at the risk of being positivistic and pedestrian in its distinctions.

The first two types listed below *must* name their myths; the two others *can* contain veiled allusions to mythology as part of their motif-structure (but these too can specify the myths, if the novelist wishes them to be unambiguous). The four types are:

1. *The complete renarration of a classical myth.*
With this method the author inevitably names his chosen mythological characters and settings, so the myths involved are not the subject of doubt. (A number of such novels was mentioned in Chapter One.)

2. *A juxtaposition of sections narrating a myth and others concerned with the contemporary world.*
John Bowen's *A World Elsewhere* and David Stacton's

[56] *op.cit.,* pp. 70ff.
[57] *Puzzles and Epiphanies,* p. 35.

Kaliyuga belong to this group. One problem with this kind of novel lies in deciding which is the dominant sphere—the mythological or the contemporary—for this is, after all, my decisive criterion for distinguishing between motif and main theme. Hence the novel which offers such juxtapositions stands closest to the typological dividing-line between the kind of work that I have chosen to examine and the traditional renarration of myths. The mythological chapters, at least, still offer comment on the others, and in most novels of this kind there is a distinct concentration of interest on the "modern chapters."[58] This results both from their length and their occurrence at nodal points in the work.

The main feature of the two methods mentioned so far is that they both deal explicitly, either wholly or in part, with a world of mythology; they present it, not in motif form, but as the setting for some ancient myth. Since they concentrate on specific, named mythological figures and events, there will be little doubt about the myths involved. In contrast, the following two methods may, but need not, help the reader this much.

3. *A novel, set in the modern world, which contains a pattern of references to mythology running through the work.*
The best-known works of this kind are Joyce's *Ulysses*, Mann's *Doktor Faustus* and Updike's *The Centaur*. The titles of these already indicate quite explicitly to the reader which myth or prefiguration is employed. In other novels, such as Alain Robbe-Grillet's *Les Gommes* and Bernard Malamud's *The Natural,* a more covert system of correspondences is employed in a similarly extended pattern.

[58] Apart from the works by Bowen and Stacton, the structure is to be found to a greater or lesser extent in Hermann Broch's *Die Schuldlosen*, Mikhail Bulgakov's *The Master and Margarita*, Alfred Döblin's *Hamlet oder Die lange Nacht nimmt ein Ende* and Hans Erich Nossack's *Interview mit dem Tode*. On the theme/motif distinction, see p. 122.

4. A novel in which a mythological motif prefigures a part of the narrative (a single event, a character or a limited group of people), but without running consistently through the whole narrative, as in Type 3.

A viable distinction between mythology and archetypes becomes crucial to any interpretation of a work of fiction ostensibly belonging to the second pair of types described here. In such cases, it may be difficult to ascertain whether a veiled motif from a particular myth is embodied in the novel or whether it merely shares an archetypal pattern of events or character structure with an otherwise completely unrelated myth, or any number of similar myths belonging to the same archetypal group. The dangers involved can be seen in the following illustrations of allusions—as one critic puts it—"existing more in the minds of ingenious critics than in the intentions of the author, the reactions of the reader or the reality of the fiction."[59]

In the case of the third type, there have admittedly been few attempts at positing a complete system of mythological correspondences hidden in a novel, of discovering the sort of recondite pattern that would have existed if Joyce had called his novel "Dublin" instead of *Ulysses* and Stuart Gilbert had then written his study divulging the author's elaborate scheme of veiled allusions to the *Odyssey*. But even this approach has been tried.

Mythological Allegorizations and Levels of Generality

George Schoolfield's article "Broch's Sleepwalkers: Aeneas and the Apostles" typifies such an approach. Here it is suggested that "the story of the *Aeneid* is told four times in Hermann Broch's *Die Schlafwandler*, once in each of the novel's three sections and again by joining the parts of the

[59] Theodore Ziolkowski, "The Odysseus Theme in Recent German Fiction," p. 227.

trilogy together."[60] Schoolfield begins his interpretation by adumbrating a series of correspondences between the role of certain characters in *Die Schlafwandler* and the function of comparable figures in Virgil's *Aeneid*. We are told, for example, that "Aeneas is Joachim von Pasenow, who must carry out the mission of his family and his class, the landed gentry. His father . . . is Anchises."[61] Analogously, both Ruzena and Mutter Hentjen become Dido, for the simple reason that the respective heroes of *Pasenow oder die Romantik* and *Esch oder die Anarchie*, already taken to be Aeneas, fall in love with them.[62]

The problem one is faced with here is whether these, and further allusions, are made by Broch himself or whether they are merely metaphors invented by an over-imaginative critic. When presented in quick succession, these putative allusions seem to corroborate each other. Yet once the original assumption that there is any reference to the *Aeneid* is questioned, the whole system becomes suspect as an over-ingenious induction. The way in which the critic presents such analogies often offers a clue to their validity or non-existence as aesthetically relevant factors. Myths and historical personages can be used as generic labels in a number of contexts: one may say that people are little Napoleons, that this man is a Romeo or that man a Machiavelli. The grammatical point about such a usage is that the words occur with an indefinite article or in the plural when used generically, whereas with a literary allusion to a specific prefiguration this is not the case. Critics who have isolated an allusion or a motif are more correct to express this discovery by saying, for instance, that Alberto Moravia's hero Molteni (in *Il disprezzo*) resembles Ulysses *in some respects* or that Blazes Boylan, in Joyce's *Ulysses*, is compared with Don Juan. Far from being *a* Ulysses or *a*

---

[60] p. 21.   [61] p. 22.   [62] pp. 22ff.

Don Juan, these characters represent allusions to *the* Ulysses of antiquity and to *the* legendary Don Juan.[63]. A predilection for indefinite articles in presenting motifs probably indicates an archetypal similarity rather than a specific prefiguration. When Schoolfield can talk of "a Turnus" and "a Lavinia" without singling out allusions, there is reason for suspecting mere prosopopoeia.

As the system of parallels subsequently breaks down, this is interpreted as the intention of both the author and even of his characters. Hence the inadequacy of the Aeneas analogy at a certain point in the novel is accounted for, apparently, by saying that Mutter Hentjen "forces Esch to abandon the role of Aeneas."[64] At another juncture, we are told: "now that the path to Rome is open, Esch puts down the burden of Aeneas."[65] Elsewhere, "Bertrand has deduced that the avenger [Esch] is not entirely happy as Aeneas— that he would like to free himself from the necessity of murder,"[66] as he in fact then does. But it is the system of superimposed mythological correspondences which really breaks down here, not the characters' willingness to conform to any mythological molds they themselves may perceive or create. Schoolfield lacks a differentiated set of terms which would permit him to question whether he is dealing with a valid allusion or an archetypal similarity. But so do his critics. Ziolkowski rejects the suggested motif, pointing out that a series of parallels to Homer's *Odyssey*, not the *Aeneid*, was once planned for the novel but eventually almost all were removed.[67] But although Ziolkowski

---

[63] This is, of course, a conscious reversal of Mann's observations about Napoleon and Charlemagne, discussed in Chapter One.

[64] p. 25.

[65] p. 26.

[66] p. 27.

[67] "Eben weil die Odyssee-Parallele in den beiden ersten Fassungen so ausdrücklich betont ist, muß ich das Hauptthema der geistreichen Arbeit G. C. Schoolfields . . . ablehnen" ("Zur Entstehung und Struktur von Hermann Brochs *Schlafwandlern*," *DVjS*, xxxviii, 1962, p. 46).

is able in this instance to use external, genetic evidence to refute the main hypothesis of Schoolfield's interpretation, it would be possible, bearing in mind certain stylistic features common to most generic metaphors of this kind, to question the internal mechanics of the above view. An awareness of these principles would also reveal that the novel contains both mythological[68] and other prefigurations.[69]

Schoolfield's reading is probably one instance where a knowledge of *Ulysses'* motif-structure led a critic to assume that all other mythological novels would conform to—perhaps even imitate—the pattern of Joyce's epoch-making work.

With the inductive method described above, any critic well versed in mythology might appear to have boundless opportunities for elaborating parallels between fiction and myths. No doubt the reason why there have nevertheless been few examples of the mistaken assumption that a whole novel contains a consistent system of ordered mythological

[68] In *"The Sleepwalkers": Elucidations of Hermann Broch's Trilogy* (The Hague and Paris, 1966), Dorrit Cohn has since argued that "the presence of the [Ahasverus] poem is the mythical double of Bertrand" (pp. 71f. and p. 108).

[69] In *Erkenntnistheorie und Prophetie: Hermann Brochs Romantrilogie "Die Schlafwandler"* (Tübingen, 1966), Leo Kreutzer has drawn attention to an archetypal process of generalization which operates linguistically with the same kind of label found in Schoolfield's attempt at positing an *Aeneid* motif. One of the characters, named Nentwig, who maligns Esch at the beginning of the second book and becomes a symbolic figure for Esch as his persecution complex grows, is used generically. The hero sees "hinter jeder Tür einen Nentwig, lauter Nentwigs" (*Die Schlafwandler*, Zürich, 1952, p. 233). As Kreutzer observes: "im Grunde bedeutet dieser Plural—'lauter Nentwigs'—ja schon das unbestimmte 'ein Nentwig,' eine Ablösung von dem bestimmten Individuum . . . vom Privaten ins Allgemeine" (*op.cit.*, p. 130). This technique of internal prefiguration, allowing a character to appear early in the work and prefigure others who appear later, is well known to readers of *Tonio Kröger*. In this *Novelle*, the first dance acts as a prefiguration of the second one in Denmark. Hans and Inge are prefigurations of the Danish couple: "Sie waren es nicht so sehr vermöge einzelner Merkmale und der Ähnlichkeit der Kleidung, als kraft der Gleichheit der Rasse und des Typus" (Thomas Mann, *Gesammelte Werke*, VIII, Frankfurt a.M., 1960, p. 331).

correspondences is the sheer improbability that a work of two hundred or more pages will possess an extensive pattern of archetypal configurations. A work of this length is hardly likely to be close in detail to the sequence of a specific myth, to the point of looking like a deliberate prefiguration. But in the more limited case of single characters —rather than whole myths—the specific is more often confused with the archetypal. This may just be a case of mistaken identity or loose expression, as in the following examples.

Ronald Grimsley draws attention to a confusion of this kind when he criticizes Leo Weinstein's *The Metamorphosis of Don Juan* because "the chapter on 'Don Juan in the Eighteenth Century' appears to be more concerned with the 'art of seduction' than with the Don Juan theme as such."[70] Weinstein, he concludes, is failing to distinguish Don Juans from Don Juan himself. Nevertheless, there is still a noticeable difference between this and Schoolfield's method of interpreting *Die Schlafwandler*. To speak of "a Don Juan" is to have recourse to a commonly accepted metaphor; on the other hand, to talk of "a Dido" or "a Lavinia" represents more of an innovation and a misleading one at that.

In some cases, the metaphorical nature of such expressions seems to be recognized. For Michael Grant "the maniacally brilliant Captain Ahab, in *Moby Dick*, is a latter-day Prometheus in the isolating Pacific wastes."[71] Yet the reader is aware that this is a figure of speech, just as he is when he reads the title of André Maurois's biography, *Prométhée ou la Vie de Balzac*.[72] In other cases, metaphor may have given way to interpretation. There is a possible case of misconstrued role-identity in Joseph Brennan's *Three Philosophical Novelists*:

[70] *Revue de la littérature comparée*, xxx, 1961, p. 683.
[71] *Myths of the Greeks and Romans*, p. 211.
[72] Paris, 1965.

archetypes are found as common themes in all the mythologies and religions of the world—the Fall, the burial and resurrection of the god, the Great Mother, the World Tree, Prometheus, Hercules, the Mage and so on.[73]

In actual fact, unlike the Great Mother and the Mage, Hercules and Prometheus do not figure in all mythologies; they belong quite specifically to classical Greek mythology. The archetypes to which they should really be assigned could be designated the Strong Man and the Fire-bringer. In some contexts this distinction may not be very important. It may even seem churlish to press for it; but in much literary criticism, as my next examples show, discrimination between the general and the particular is often crucial.

Denis de Rougemont's approach to *Doctor Zhivago, Der Mann ohne Eigenschaften* and *Lolita,* in his *The Myths of Love,* shows how unintentionally misleading critical statements can be without such safeguards. For these "three major works in which the Tristan archetype appears,"[74] de Rougemont conjures up a picture of various "Tristans separated from an Iseult" and "forbidden by a King Mark"[75] to meet their loves. (The method of presentation, including indefinite articles and names in the plural,[76] has much in common with Schoolfield's reading of *Die Schlafwandler.*) Later, we discover that these "three Tristanian novels"[77] are not the only things to which de Rougemont is ready to apply the Tristan metaphor. It is also used to depict Pasternak's predicament in the U.S.S.R.: the Soviet regime is

[73] New York, 1964, p. 33.   [74] pp. 43f.
[75] p. 46.
[76] As John Updike once remarked about de Rougemont's method here: "the effect is less to make myths real than to make men unreal," and in the case of one other figure: "to make of Nietzsche a 'Don Juan of knowledge' who 'wanted to *violate* the secret of each idea' . . . is to confuse a metaphor with an influence" (*Assorted Prose,* London, 1965, p. 193).
[77] p. 73.

59

to Pasternak what King Mark is to Tristan—the major obstacle in the pursuit of his beloved Russia: "Everything is happening as if this man were kept in his country by a secret and forbidden passion. . . . But what can be the nature of this inaccessible Iseult, whose Tristan he seems to be?"[78] It is his motherland, and King Mark is the official Soviet oligarchy! This is really a psychoanalyst's way of expressing types, and it has found its way into literary criticism. Using such figures of speech, de Rougemont completely fails to point out that Tristan is in fact used as a prefiguration in Musil's novel.[79] Nevertheless, the reviewer who taxed de Rougemont with "sniffing out mythic influence in unlikely places"[80] has missed the point: de Rougemont was almost certainly not implying influence or prefiguration. Yet in failing to state his terms in exposition, he lays himself open to the accusation that he could have seen the archetype in question in so many other novels. And, more important, he misses the passage in Musil's work to which this image is relevant.

A more complex example of this undifferentiated labeling concerns the suggested Telesphoros motif in Mann's Joseph tetralogy and Hermann Broch's *Der Tod des Vergil*. In his correspondence with Kerényi, Thomas Mann writes of one of the characters in *Joseph in Ägypten*:

> Es kann nach dieser Abschweifung nicht schaden, wenn ich noch einmal des unbeschreiblichen Reizes gedenke, den Ihre Studie über die Gestalt des kleinen Telesphoros mit "cucullus" und Buchrolle auf mich ausübte. Welche zauberhafte Figur, dieser kleine Totengott! Und im Besonderen: Welch ein Zauber geht aus von der Geschichte des Kapuzenmantels durch die

[78] p. 69.
[79] Musil's narrator talks of "das sehnsüchtige Paktieren mit dem Tod, das uns ergreift, wenn wir die Tristanmusik hören" (*Der Mann ohne Eigenschaften*, Hamburg, 1960, p. 914). And Clarisse and her brother are presented in Wagnerian terms throughout the novel.
[80] *TLS*, 9 September 1965, p. 767.

Jahrtausende hin. Sonderbar! Ich hatte keine Ahnung
von diesen Dingen, und doch habe ich meinen Joseph,
nach seiner Auferstehung aus dem Brunnen, als die
Ismaeliter ihn durch Aegypten führen, mit einem
Kapuzenmantel und einer Schriftrolle ausgestattet. Das
sind geheimnisvolle Spiele des Geistes, die beweisen,
daß Sympathie für gelehrtes Wissen bis zu einem
gewissen Grade aufkommen kann.[81]

In a letter to Karl August Horst, Hermann Broch describes
a similar hindsight recognition of what might seem to be an
allusion to the same mythological figure, this time in his
own *Der Tod des Vergil*:

. . . ich habe den *Vergil* während einer gewissen Zeit
nicht für Veröffentlichung geschrieben, doch als ich
ihn später zu einem richtigen Buch umgestaltete, hat
die Trance der Arbeit—eine richtige Trance—nicht
nachgelassen; dabei stellte sich heraus, daß eine
kontrapunktische Knabengestalt eingefügt werden
mußte, und das geschah mit der Person des Lysanias.
Hier in Yale erfuhr ich nun von meinem Kollegen
Faber du Faur, daß dieser Lysanias bis ins kleinste Detail die Attribute des Knabengottes Telesphoros (aus
dem Kreis des Äskulap) trägt, einer für mich bis dahin
völlig unbekannten Götter-gestalt. Solche Dinge kann
man bloß als Richtigkeitsbeweise hinnehmen.[82]

[81] *Gespräch in Briefen*, pp. 42f. "After this digression, it can do no
harm to remember once more the indescribable pleasure which your
study of the figure of little Telesphoros with his 'cucullus' [cloak] and
scroll gave to me. What an enchanting figure, this little god of death!
And in particular: what magic radiates through the centuries from
the story of the hooded cloak. Strange! I knew nothing of these
things, and yet I equipped my Joseph with a hooded cloak and a
scroll after his resurrection from the well, when the Ishmaelites lead
him through Egypt. These are mysterious games of the intellect which
prove that one can come to sympathize to a certain extent with
academic learning."
[82] *Briefe*, Zürich, 1957, p. 419; ". . . during a certain period I did
not write *Vergil* with publication in mind, but later, when I changed
it into a proper book, the trance of the work—a real trance—did not
weaken; it became evident that a contrapuntal boy-figure had to be
inserted, and this was done with the character Lysanias. Here in Yale
I now learnt from my colleague Faber du Faur that this Lysanias bore

Mann and Broch, at least, were both aware that the similarity between their creations and Telesphoros lay at the archetypal level only.[83] And in "Der Seelenhüter in Hermann Brochs *Der Tod des Vergil*" Curt von Faber du Faur examines the similarity between Lysanias and Telesphoros; but, like Jung in his account of *Ulysses*, he is more concerned with pointing out certain affinities between literature and mythology than with literary criticism proper. Despite the excitement of the two novelists' retrospective insights into the archetypal nature of their creations, it would be erroneous to see this as being of direct concern to a literary exegesis, either of *Der Tod des Vergil* or of *Joseph in Ägypten*. Although archetypal kinship occurs so frequently that it can hardly yield much insight into the peculiarities of any single novel, a number of critics have reiterated these remarks about Telesphoros and Lysanias without stressing the archetypal quality of the relationship. On reading such statements, one is often left with the impression of further examples of mythological motifs. E. W. Herd notes that Lysanias "is the counterpart of the boy-god Telesphoros, the bringer of health."[84] The description "counterpart" may be true, as far as it goes, but it needs further clarification to stress that this remains an archetypal similarity and does not constitute a specifically intentional prefiguration. Without such a rider, the critic has a great deal of leeway for suggesting analogies as if they were

---

right down to the smallest detail the attributes of the boy-god Telesphoros (from the circle of Aesculapius), a divine figure which was until then completely unknown to me. Such things can only be taken as proof of how right one was."

[83] "Es sind eben archetypische Vorgänge," Broch notes (*loc.cit.*); many years after his original letter on the subject to Kerényi, Mann refers to "der Erweis archetypischer Übereinstimmungen zwischen Mythologie und Romandichtung (Fall Cucullatus)" (*Gespräch in Briefen*, p. 133).

[84] *Hermann Broch: Short Stories*, ed. E. W. Herd, Oxford, 1966, p. 153.

motifs. (There are always enough possibly mythological attributes to facilitate comparable hypotheses.) The dilemma here is, in a sense, part of a much wider problem raised by any recondite allusion: the question of how much resonance the allusions can be expected to find in the average reader. Some will find overtones of mythology in all novels; others will want to ignore such reverberations, even in works where they are worthy of consideration.[85] Admittedly, it is not always possible to make a clear-cut distinction between allusions forming an integral part of a novel and fortuitous analogies that occur to certain readers. (Can one, for example, say with certainty whether there is an Oedipus motif in David Storey's *Graceless Go I*, even though Oedipus is mentioned in this account of growing mental aberration?) A number of clearly recognizable and interdependent allusions must have been established in the reader's mind before one can justifiably talk of a motif. Then, a work will have to be interpreted with reference to mythology as well as in terms of general archetypes. For one must bear in mind, as Frederick J. Hoffman puts it, that:

[85] It is clearly fashionable at the moment, at least in popular criticism—and possibly in English criticism in particular—to ignore or belittle such motifs. One often comes across statements of the following kind: "fortunately the [mythological] allusions are never obtrusive and can be ignored" (review of James Merrill's *The (Diblos) Notebook*, *TLS*, 9 September 1965, p. 769). A reviewer of Anthony Burgess's *The Eve of Saint Venus* is pleased to find that the majority of characters in the novel ignore the mythological aspects of the plot: "Only the vicar, who knows his Latin, seems to take things seriously" (*The Times*, 13 April 1968). Similarly, Bernard Dort (*Les Temps Modernes*, January 1964, p. 1335) claims that one should ignore all the correspondences in Robbe-Grillet's *Les Gommes*, and a critic writing upon the parallels between Macdonald Harris's *Trepleff* and Chekhov's *The Seagull* concludes: "The idea of shuffling the Chekhovian roles, then letting the characters take over, is an interesting one, but tends to leave the reader burrowing beneath the surface while the story goes on without him; the narrative permutations are endless. Back on the surface, though, there is more to enjoy" (*TLS*, 28 November 1968, p. 1346).

there is a great difference between a tradition of the ritual observance of a fixed symbolic and mythical pattern and the direct, knowledgeable, ingenious, overt *use* of myth in modern literature. To explain present literary circumstance by reference to archetypal patterns is to ignore the peculiarities of present practice and need.[86]

To do this would be like disingenuously mining for gold at Fort Knox, Stanley Edgar Hyman suggests elsewhere.[87] However, the real danger usually involves the converse: assuming that one must be mining at Fort Knox every time one comes across gold—that is, interpreting every archetypal similarity with a myth as an intentionally concealed allusion to it.

If the modern novel and the myth posited display only slight affinities, the critic may be tempted to resort to unintentional subterfuge by introducing the idea of parody into the argument. In "Job and Joseph K.: Myth in Kafka's *The Trial*," Donald Kartiganer thus argues that there is a "conscious parallel to the *Book of Job*" in *Der Prozess*.[88] He goes on to call Job "the archetypal image of the apparently innocent sufferer at the hands of the father."[89] But, like Brennan, Grant, de Rougemont and Weinstein, Kartiganer is using a specific myth as a label for an underlying archetype. One may conclude that if Job is standing for an archetype, this will probably not be a prefigurative motif at all, unless there are distinct attributes to suggest that he is being referred to unequivocally. Kartiganer, however, weakens his thesis substantially with the suggestion that *Der Prozess* is a parody of the Book of Job,[90] since it makes the supposed links between Joseph K. and Job even more tenu-

[86] *Freudianism and the Literary Mind*, New York, 1959, p. 329.
[87] *The Armed Vision: A Study in the Methods of Modern Literary Criticism*, New York, 1952, p. 33.
[88] p. 31.   [89] p. 32.   [90] *op.cit.*, pp. 32-34.

ous. The notion of parody implies a certain degree of distortion. Yet this distortion in turn could only be appreciated if the parodied material remained still discernible; this it cannot be in Kafka's novel or this particular article, which points to the Job image and does not attempt to discuss its possible aesthetic effect, would be more or less redundant. Like Schoolfield's suggestion that at a certain point in *Die Schlafwandler* the characters drop their mythological masks, the idea of parody is rather a critic's sleight of hand, a defense mechanism to conceal the impropriety of the analogy.

Although some of the above interpretations have subsequently been rejected, their opponents have themselves not given much methodological foundation to their criticisms. Grimsley's criticism of *The Metamorphosis of Don Juan* is correct but not supported. Dorrit Cohn calls Schoolfield's reading of *Die Schlafwandler* "fanciful," but does not really tell us why it "remains unconvincing."[91] Theodore Ziolkowski also calls it imaginative ("geistreich"),[92] but refutes the notion of a motif from the *Aeneid* on essentially genetic grounds. An article by Alfredo Dornheim, proclaiming Mignon, in Goethe's *Wilhelm Meister*, and Echo, in Thomas Mann's *Doktor Faustus*, as two versions of the Divine Child archetype—"Goethes 'Mignon' und Thomas Manns 'Echo': Zwei Formen des 'Göttlichen Kindes' im deutschen Roman" —has also been rejected (by Plöger in his *Das Hermesmotiv in der Dichtung Thomas Manns*),[93] but again the workings of Dornheim's argument are not exposed. Yet upon looking at the article, one can see that the distinction between myths and archetypes is blurred.

The title of the article reveals quite clearly Dornheim's

[91] *op.cit.*, p. 62.
[92] "Zur Entstehung und Struktur von Hermann Brochs *Schlafwandlern*," *op.cit.*, p. 46.
[93] p. 158.

correct observation that Echo and Mignon could be compared in the light of their common archetype: that of the
Divine Child, described by Karl Kerényi.[94] Dornheim sees
in both figures a "direct projection of the eternal phenomenon" ("unmittelbare Projektion des ewigen Phänomens")[95]
and the archetype of the child ("Archetypus des
Kindes").[96] The fatal distortion only occurs when Dornheim
proceeds to compare Echo with further examples of the
Divine Child archetype in mythology. Comparisons of a
dubious nature between Echo and both Hermes and Eros
are brought in.[97] But since the nebulous "divinity" of the
Divine Child in *Doktor Faustus* simply implies that he has
some message of love to offer, Echo could easily be likened
to all the myths of the Divine Child constellation, if one
were to admit the loose concept of ritual function upon
which Dornheim bases his reading. Nevertheless, only some
of these allusions are pertinent to *Doktor Faustus* and en-
rich our understanding of Echo's role; others are merely
critical importations devoid of justification.

Further Distinctions: the Number of Archetypes,
Myths and Legends, "Popular" and "Literary" Myths

For the purpose of isolating and focusing on mythological
motifs, a rough division has been made between archetypal
and mythological elements. But this is a very superficial
classification. To give it more depth, it will prove helpful to
outline some further ideas which these blanket terms cover,
but which I will seldom need to differentiate hereafter.

The number of archetypes, for example, varies from critic
to critic. For Joseph Campbell, "the standard path of the

[94] *Einführung in das Wesen der Mythologie*, pp. 41ff.
[95] *op.cit.*, p. 319.
[96] *op.cit.*, p. 320.
[97] "Das göttliche Kind [and now he means Echo] ist Hermes, der
Götterbote, der dem Musiker die Botschaft der Liebe bringt . . .
Hermes, der nun auch Eros ist," *op.cit.*, p. 323.

mythological adventure of the hero is a magnification of the formula represented in the rites of passage: *separation—initiation—return*."[98] Northrop Frye works with only one archetype, the quest, which in many ways corresponds to the "monomyth" of the hero. Harry Slochower argues that "the myth contains two basic categories: *creation* . . . and the *quest*."[99] And Karl Kerényi, Maud Bodkin, Theodore Ziolkowski (in his book on Hesse) and E.M.W. Tillyard all review a number of archetypes. For my purposes, however, "archetype" is largely used as a general contrast to specific myths and further distinctions need not arise. Likewise, various possible sub-divisions of myths (including astral, heroic, aetiological, soteriological and patriotic) will be dispensed with here for the same reason.

Another frequent distinction, one not usually maintained in the rest of this study, is that between myths and legends. It is a contrast which has nowadays become more difficult to uphold, since the word "legend" in turn seems as elusive as "myth."

Philip Edwards uses "legend" in the wide sense in his article on "*Ulysses* and the Legends." And when William Trevor mentions the "wise old legends of the Greeks" in his review of John Bowen's *A World Elsewhere*,[100] he is not employing the word to mean anything but myths. However, the general tendency in modern criticism is to prefer "myth" to signify myths *and* legends,[101] instead of extending

[98] *The Hero with a Thousand Faces*, p. 30.
[99] "The Uses of Myth in Kafka and Mann," p. 118.
[100] "New Novels," *The Listener*, 8 March 1965, p. 345.
[101] In *Hamlet oder Die lange Nacht nimmt ein Ende*, Alfred Döblin refers to "den Mythos von König Lear" (p. 238), where we might have expected "Legende," "Fabel" or "Märchen" to be used. Goldberg writes of the "myth of Shakespeare" (*The Classical Temper*, p. 67) discussed in the library episode of Joyce's *Ulysses*. Tillyard talks of the "Arthur myth" (*op.cit.*, p. 11) and Jethro Bithell underlines the uncertainty in terms by using both words: "The action of *Lotte in Weimar* returns ostensibly to modernity—the date of 1816—but the

the meaning of "legend" in the way that Edwards and Trevor do. Thomas Mann invariably uses the word "myth" in an even wider sense. In an explanation of this usage, André von Gronicka writes:

> Mann's formula ["Myth plus Psychology"] calls for a brief amplification. "Myth" as used in it stands for rather more than the term conventionally defines. It encompasses legend, history, and the literary traditions of the more recent past. . . .[102]

"Myth" here is the equivalent of "prefiguration."

Traditionally, legends were distinguished from myths because they described the lives of heroes, whereas the gods appeared in myths. The *Larousse Encyclopedia of Mythology* still maintains this distinction, for instance, in the following entry: "Another poem of ancient origin which describes the construction of the Temple of Ba'al is purely mythical in substance and contains no mortals."[103] The classicist Michael Grant also observes this distinction in *Myths of the Greeks and Romans*,[104] and Richard Chase has expressed it in some detail in *Quest for Myth*:

> The division of Greek mythological literature made by Heyne and Herder has become more or less standard in modern times. Sir James Frazer carries this division to its logical conclusion. *Myths proper*, he writes, are concerned with the origins of the world and man, the motions of the stars, the vicissitudes of vegetation, weather, eclipses, storms, the discovery of fire, the invention of the useful arts, the mystery of death. *Legends* are "traditions, whether oral or written, which relate the fortunes of real people in the past, or which describe events, not necessarily human, that are said to have occurred at real places."[105]

---

foundation matter is still myth, the myth or legend of *The Sorrows of Werther*" (*Modern German Literature 1880-1950*, London, 1959, p. 316).

[102] "Myth Plus Psychology: A Stylistic Analysis of *Death in Venice*," p. 46.

[103] p. 77.   [104] For example, on p. 34.   [105] p. 74.

Such taxonomy differentiates between euhemerisms (myths that have arisen from the stylization of actual historical events and characters), and cosmogonic and aetiological myths (fictive explanations of natural phenomena, origins and causes). Possibly valid in anthropology,[106] it seldom proves a very useful tool in literary criticism. In a world of mainly scientific explanations, there is a diminishing need for aetiological myths in most spheres of experience. The major exceptions, as Kermode's *The Sense of an Ending* suggests, are myths of creation and apocalypse; but these do not play a major role in mythological novels.[107] This again indicates that myths are not being used in literary contexts where one might think of them as myth.

The principal objection to any distinction between myths and legends is that the question of whether an event or a character belonged to a myth or a legend before being used in a literary work invariably becomes a red herring. Such a distinction between myths and legends distracts critical interest from the manner in which the material is transfigured in the novel. To understand the limitations of this contrast, one has only to consider the figure of Virgil in Broch's *Der Tod des Vergil*. Before entering Broch's work he was a historical figure, at most a legend, but in this novel his dying hours have an aura of myth about them. On the other hand, the fact that Hercules was a mythological figure when Agatha Christie came to him does not detract from our realization that the main character in *The Labours of Hercules*, one of her detective novels concerning Hercule Poirot, has less mythical stature than Broch's Virgil. Litera-

---

[106] Even this is in question. See G. S. Kirk, *Myth: Its Meaning and Functions in Ancient and Other Cultures*, pp. 9ff.

[107] For example, one aspect of the *Epic of Gilgamesh* which Guido Bachmann's *Gilgamesch* does not develop is the Great Flood. And novels which have used apocalyptic flood motifs (Stefan Andres's *Die Sintflut*, Werner Bergengruen's *Am Himmel wie auf Erden* and John Bowen's *After the Rains*) have not presented them within any pronounced mythological framework.

ture clearly has the ability to create a myth from history or take a myth and divest it of its mythical quality. And it can do both of these things within a single work. Broch's Virgil is historical, legendary and mythical at various points in the novel. In literature, as Frye has pointed out, "myths of gods merge into legends."[108] These in turn may often blend into fictionalized history, one might add. In such a domain, a simple distinction of the myth/legend kind is not very useful.

In establishing an analogy or a contrast, prefigurations taken from myths and legends act similarly. If they differ at all, it is in respect of something to which little consideration will be given here: they may well endow the modern novel with a different kind of status. A comparison between the friendship of two characters and that between two mythological figures, e.g. in the use of Chiron and Prometheus for George and Peter in John Updike's *The Centaur*, will transfer some of the myth's archaic grandeur to the modern protagonists. A college friendship presented in the light of the Faust-Devil configuration, in John Hersey's *Too Far to Walk*, has a less grandiose nimbus. One can perceive this range of status, given by different orders of motif, within the variety of Hans Erich Nossack's post-war novels. In *Spätestens im November*, a non-classical prefiguration from the legend of Paolo and Francesca appears eminently suitable for a treatment of love and disillusionment in West Germany's industrial belt, whereas Greek mythological motifs are evoked for Nossack's accounts of the Second World War in *Nekyia* and *Interview mit dem Tode*. Even so, any consideration of the mock-heroic tone, such as one frequently finds in Joyce, suggests that this distinction alone would not be enough to account for the status of the modern hero. Structurally at least—and the structures will be

---

[108] *Anatomy of Criticism*, p. 51.

my main concern—motifs from mythology and legend have a comparable role to play in modern fiction.

One can avoid the problem of distinguishing between myths and legends by subordinating one of the concepts to the other. I have done this by allowing "myth" and "mythology" a wide definition incorporating the idea of "legend." One can, of course, subordinate "myth" to "legend,"[109] although this goes more against the grain of generally accepted contemporary usage. Another solution is to subsume both of these terms under a third one. Margret Dietrich has adopted this approach in her discussion of "Antiker Mythos im modernen Drama," using the untranslatable term "Leitgestalten" (on the analogy of leitmotif). She argues that there are three kinds: mythical, biblical and historical. This neatly avoids having to distinguish between myths and legends and also suggests the idea of motif-structure by means of the prefix "Leit-."[110]

One further distinction that frequently arises in discussions of the mythological novel will be ignored here, and that is the one between "popular" and "literary" myths. Apart from incurring the criticism that such a contrast also leads away from the modern novel and back to the status which the prefiguration had before it became an ingredient, it again becomes difficult to put into practice.

The degree of inevitable subjectivity surrounding any question of esotericism must depend on the critic's own familiarity with mythology. One can see, for example, how the problem can arise in the case of the Don Juan figure. Eva Kushner finds him literary. "Les vrais mythes," she writes, "différents en celà des mythes créés par la littérature, comme celui de Faust et de Don Juan, appartiennent

---

[109] This E. W. Herd does in "Myth and Modern German Literature" (p. 55). In his scheme, myths = what I have called archetypes; legends = what I have called myths.

[110] As was pointed out in Chapter One, this is also the advantage of the term "prefiguration."

71

à la société, et non seulement au poète."[111] Leo Weinstein, however, holds the contrary view: "the figure of Don Juan is more popular than literary."[112] He argues, from the premiss that the other three among what he considers to be the four great myths of modern literature—Don Quixote, Don Juan, Faust and Hamlet—can all be traced back to one particular writer for their fame, if not always their origin, whereas Don Juan cannot be linked with one author in this way. In fact, one could counter that the situation is more complex than this: that Faust is both popular and literary, and that many of the Don Juan prefigurations that occur in modern novels[113] come specifically from Da Ponte's libretto (sometimes via Kierkegaard's *Either/Or*) and do not reside in any general, cultural inheritance of the folk kind.

Nevertheless, such a distinction may not always be pure sophistry. Just as it might help our understanding of some works to consider whether they choose myths or legends as prefigurations, there are also times when it would be enlightening to assess the degree of esotericism in a writer's choice of motif. The objection here is largely that one cannot operate all the time with such either/or categories as "popular" or "literary."

The problem underlying this distinction is a vexed one. The relationship of both novelist and reader to mythology is always tacitly assumed to be one of familiarity. But to what extent is it so nowadays? In George Steiner's opinion:

> the world of classical mythology, of historical reference, of scriptural allusion, on which a preponderant part of European and English poetry is built . . . is receding from our natural reach.[114]

[111] *Le Mythe d'Orphée*, p. 19.

[112] *The Metamorphosis of Don Juan*, p. 4.

[113] This includes Hermann Broch's *Die Schuldlosen*, Brigid Brophy's *The Snow Ball*, Peter Härtling's *Niembsch oder der Stillstand* and James Joyce's *Ulysses*.

[114] *Language and Silence: Essays 1958-1966*, Harmondsworth, 1968, p. 81.

Other writers agree. In his introduction to *The Greek Myths*, Robert Graves writes in a similar vein:

> the Classics have lately lost so much ground in schools and universities that an educated person is now no longer expected to know (for instance) who Deucalion, Pelops, Daedalus, Oenone, Laocoön or Antigone may have been.[115]

Or if they do, they may well be familiar with these figures indirectly through the medium of modern mythological literature. Various writers supply evidence that would seem to support this. Edmund Wilson admits that, without extraneous assistance, he could not have "divined . . . the complicated scheme of Homeric parallel in Joyce's *Ulysses*."[116] Stuart Gilbert, who largely did just that, admits having had to return to an intensive study of the *Odyssey* in order to appreciate the allusions to it in *Ulysses*. Philip Toynbee concedes the "ignominy" of being "driven to the *Odyssey* for the first time by Joyce."[117] In his book on Thomas Mann, Herbert Lehnert has shown that the source of most of the mythology in *Der Tod in Venedig* is not the classical works themselves, but certain quotations from them in Erwin Rohde's *Psyche*. Hermann Broch writes in a letter to Abraham Sonne of how he had to return to a study of the classics, for the first time since his schooldays, to write *Der Tod des Vergil*.[118] So the hero of Alberto Moravia's *Il disprezzo* runs true to form when he sets out to write a film version of the *Odyssey* with no knowledge of Greek and only an indirect familiarity with the theme through Petrarch.

[115] *The Greek Myths*, I, p. 11.
[116] "James Joyce," *Axel's Castle: A Study in the Imaginative Literature of 1870-1930*, London, 1947, p. 213.
[117] *James Joyce: Two Decades of Criticism*, ed. Seon Givens, New York, 1948, p. 245.
[118] ". . . es war eines der Schlafwandler-Gedichte, und Du hast es mit dem Vermerk 'lacrimae rerum' bestätigt, was vielleicht in mich den ersten Keim zum Vergil gelegt hat, denn ich habe daraufhin mir zum ersten Mal seit den Schultagen wieder die Aeneis vorgenommen" (*Briefe*, Zürich, 1957, pp. 385f).

Such a situation, where mythological allusions are likely to pass unnoticed, must be taken into account in any serious examination of mythology's role in the modern novel. The relationship of the reader to mythology has changed since Hölderlin's day and possibly even since Joyce's time. Nevertheless, one should not always assume that an allusion is meant to be immediately recognizable in all mythological novels. One need not agree with Gustav Hillard, who goes so far as to suggest that some benevolent editor should come to the aid of those reading *Joseph und seine Brüder* by supplying notes such as one finds to *The Waste Land*.[119] Such an attitude betrays a misunderstanding of what is at stake in many mythological novels: the element of a gradually revealed pattern to the events. What Herman Meyer says about quotations in literature could also be said about mythological allusions:

> If the quotation is blended into the new linguistic totality to the point of being unrecognizable, then it loses its specific character and its specific effect. In general it might be maintained that the charm of the quotation emanates from a unique tension between assimilation and dissimilation: it links itself closely with its new environment, but at the same time detaches itself from it, thus permitting another world to radiate into the self-contained world of the novel.[120]

Any critic who, in an attack on the esotericism of "literary" myths, urges that all mythological motifs, and by the same token presumably all allusions, be explained in footnotes, forgets the necessary tension between assimilation and dissimilation which Meyer describes. By ignoring what Meyer calls this "outright game of hide-and-seek,"[121] one fails to do justice to the gradual revelation of pattern which is the strength of such novels. The obscurity of myths is functional

---

[119] "Thomas Manns Mythenspiel," p. 121.
[120] *The Poetics of Quotation in the European Novel*, p. 6.
[121] *op.cit.*, p. 7.

in many novels; and in examining this side of the work's efficacy, it would be necessary to determine how well-known or obscure a prefiguration is, although it is doubtful whether any binary categorization of this type is adequate to the task.

The terminology and problems of taxonomy outlined in this chapter, the distinctions observed and those ignored, and the examples of misinterpretation discussed, have all centered upon the initial problem of distinguishing the mythological from the archetypal. However, any identification of what is and what is not a mythological novel, although it may have proved a stumbling block in numerous cases, can only be the first and least important step in the analysis of such works.

Approaches to the Mythological Novel

A Priori *Judgments*

Is the view of nature and of social relations which shaped the Greek imagination and Greek art possible in the age of automatic machinery, and railways, and locomotives, and electric telegraphs? Where does Vulcan come in against Roberts and Co.; Jupiter, as against the lightning rod; and Hermes, against the Crédit Mobilier. . . . What becomes of the Goddess Fame by the side of Printing House Square?[1]

These questions, posed over a hundred years ago by Karl Marx, touch upon some of the key problems concerning the introduction of mythology into modern fiction. They raise issues of accommodation; not only accommodation in the sense that the novelist has to find a way of adapting his archaic material to the modern world (Northrop Frye would call this a problem of "displacement"), but also because the reader may have to adjust his sensibility to this kind of fiction. In order to appreciate the nature of this operation and assess its success or failure in individual cases, it will help to explore some adverse reactions to mythological fiction, to examine the dominant approaches critically and, *en route,* to seek a viable method of doing justice to the subject.

The presence of mythology in modern literature, Horst Rüdiger has suggested, is a subject which lends itself admirably to an unbiased critical approach. His reason is that

---

[1] Introduction to *A Contribution to the Critique of Political Economy,* translated from the second German edition by N. I. Stone, Chicago, 1904, pp. 310-311.

Hellenism is a common European experience; thus a supra-national set of fixed symbols of this kind offers a counter-balance to the general hazy pluralism and chauvinism of much literary criticism.[2] Admittedly, chauvinism can hardly be a valid standpoint from which to judge literature. One can only agree with George Steiner that "chauvinism has cried havoc in politics; it has no place in literature."[3] And in this sense at least, Rüdiger's argument that mythological literature favors a more suitably unprejudiced approach than the national attitudes to the novel that one often finds, would seem sound enough in principle. In practice, how-ever, many other allegiances apart from national ones can influence judgments in this field; a great deal of criticism has been marred by dogmatism and partisanship of various other kinds. Sometimes chauvinism of another brand creeps in, in the guise of an attack on atavistic or simply anach-ronistic influences on twentieth-century literature. Occa-sionally one witnesses the classicist's indignation at finding "his" literature debased by the modern interpretation of some myth, or the modernist's view that the introduction of gods and heroes into a modern novel is *ipso facto* an unde-sirable avatar and a sign of intellectual regression to the simplicity of paradigms or ritual. Unfortunately, these monistic judgments are not founded on any aesthetic basis; they stem from preconceived attitudes to primarily non-aesthetic phenomena which are then transferred to the dis-cussion of mythology in the specific context of literature.

The first category of opinions I shall examine includes

[2] "Hier liegen Forschungsaufgaben bereit, die sich in besonderem Maße zur Untersuchung eignen: nicht nur weil der Mythos meist schon in der Antike in exemplarischer Weise dichterisch gestaltet worden ist, was unseren schwankenden kritischen Maßstäben Halt verleiht, sondern weil dem Forscher mit ihm ein gemeineuropäisches Bezugssystem gegeben ist, ein unverrückbarer, durch nationale Vorur-teile unbelasteter, in diesem Sinne also wertneutraler Fixpunkt" ("Na-tionalliteratur und europäische Literatur," *Definitionen: Essays zur Literatur*, ed. Adolf Frisé, Frankfurt a.M., 1963, p. 52).

[3] *Language and Silence*, Harmondsworth, 1968, p. 28.

those which either declare or imply that it is essentially good or bad to introduce mythological material into a modern novel.

Frank Kermode has frequently voiced the view that myth in modern literature is a sign of regressive tendencies. One finds this opinion set out in a review of C. G. Jung's *Man and his Symbols*:

> A yearning for ritualistic satisfactions can have a bad effect in literature as well as in politics, and it is a common enough complaint that the search in novels for mythical order reduces their existential complexity. It remains something of a mystery, this anachronistic myth-hunt.[4]

The criticism here is presumably directed more against the presence of myth, in the archetypal sense, in modern literature. It is a criticism which finds its counterpart in the recent attacks on the search for archetypal patterns behind all literature. In *Concepts of Criticism,* René Wellek concludes that "the dangers of this method are obvious: the boundary lines between art and myth and even art and religion are obliterated. . . . After decoding each work in these terms, one is left with a feeling of futility and monotony."[5]

A fuller version of this charge of over-simplification—and this time made with definite reference both to mythological and archetypal patterns—appears in Kermode's essay "The Myth-Kitty."[6] Here it is accompanied by the suggestion that mythological works betray the atavistic tendencies of their authors (and pander, presumably, also to those shared by their readers):

[4] "This Time, That Time," *Continuities*, London, 1968, p. 40.
[5] p. 361. As Kermode himself observes in the case of *Anatomy of Criticism*, very much a myth-orientated work: "Professor Frye forgets the fictiveness of *all* fictions" (*The Sense of an Ending*, p. 41).
[6] The compound "myth-kitty" comes from Philip Larkin. Kermode certainly seems to associate himself with this poet's declaration that

Mythology . . . raises the whole question of belief. This would scarcely be so if it was thought of only as a breeding-ground of images; in fact it is too often the anti-intellectualist substitute for science.[7]

Kermode's strictures may be more applicable to such phenomena as the Celtic revival or "Blut und Boden" literature: in *The Sense of an Ending*, the concentration camps are often evoked as a warning of what "the yearning for ritualistic satisfaction" can inspire. But he discounts the fact that more often than not mythology, far from being the sole or even the most important force at work in literature, forms part of a larger aesthetic context. While Kermode's earlier pronouncements often have the ambiguity that one soon grows to expect in discussions of myth, it becomes more apparent in *The Sense of an Ending* that his misgivings are largely directed against a predilection for myth in the archetypal sense. Here an important point is made about the relationship between myths and archetypes, or, as Kermode calls them, "fictions" and "myths": "Fictions can degenerate into myths whenever they are not consciously held to be fictive."[8] It is, in other words, largely dependent on how the reader thinks.

Many novelists themselves show an awareness of the danger to which Kermode here draws our attention. "Das

---

he has no "belief in 'tradition' or a common myth-kitty or casual allusions in poems to poems or poets" (quoted by Charles Tomlinson in *The Modern Age*, ed. B. Ford, Harmondsworth, 1964, p. 458).

[7] *Puzzles and Epiphanies*, p. 38.

[8] p. 39. The exception to this generalization, which Kermode then makes for *Ulysses*, applies to the non-mythical technique of using mythology common to most of the novels to be discussed later in this study. For, like *Ulysses*, the mythological novel, as I have defined it, generally "studies and develops the tension between paradigm and reality, asserts the resistance of fact to fiction." For this reason, Kermode concludes that Joyce's novel is not mythical (though it remains obviously mythological): "we might well ask whether one of the merits of this book is not its *lack* of mythologising: compare Joyce on coincidence with Jungians and their solemn concord-myth, the Principle of Synchronicity" (*The Sense of an Ending*, p. 113).

Schlimmste ist der Rückfall," Hans Erich Nossack, another mythological novel-writer, warns.[9] Also haunted by the false mythologies of the Third Reich, Thomas Mann takes great pains, both in the *Gespräch in Briefen* and in numerous speeches and essays, to clarify his position in relation to mythology and to counter any such charge of atavism. In "Die Stellung Freuds in der modernen Geistesgeschichte," Mann carefully distinguishes between two possible forms of interest in myth: cultural atavism and a healthier, inquisitive interest in the myths of the past:

> Es gibt keine Predigt und keinen Imperativ des großen Zurück, keine Inbrunst zur Vergangenheit um der Vergangenheit willen, die anders als zu dem offenkundigen Zweck der Verwirrung diesen Namen für sich in Anspruch nehmen könnte, womit nicht gesagt sein soll, daß etwa der revolutionäre Wille von der Vergangenheit und Tiefe nichts wüßte. Das Gegenteil soll besagt werden. Er muß und will sehr viel davon wissen, sehr gründlich darin zu Hause sein; nur daß diese dunkle Welt ihn nicht um ihrer selbst willen lockt, daß er sie nicht um scheinfrommer, scheinreligiöser Erhaltung willen, kurz aus reaktionärem Instinkt zu seiner Sache macht, sondern als ein Erkennender und ein Befreier in ihre mit Greueln und Schätzen gefüllten Verliese dringt.[10]

[9] "The worst thing is regression." Quoted from a tape-recording: "Aus der Dichterwerkstatt—Hans Erich Nossack" (prepared by Inter Nationes, Bonn, 1968).
[10] *Die Forderung des Tages*, Berlin, 1930, p. 207. H. T. Lowe-Porter's translation of this passage reads: "No teaching or incitement to the great 'back, back!', no zeal for the past for its own sake, can write the word upon its banner save for the open end of confusion. By this I do not mean that the revolutionary will knows nothing of the past or of the deeps. The contrary should be asserted. It must and will know much of them, be very thoroughly at home therein; if only these dark precincts do not allure it for their own sake, if only it does not make common cause with them to preserve the pseudo-religious and the sham-traditional, in short, out of reactionary instinct; but instead presses on as liberator and enlightener into those *oubliettes* so full of horrors and priceless treasures" ("Freud's Position in the History of Modern Thought," *Past Masters and other Papers*, London, 1933, pp. 178-179).

It was within the following decade and a half that this distinction—between the dark myths of Fascism, including *The Protocols of the Elders of Zion*, a misconstrued Zarathustra, and Rosenberg's nefarious *Mythos des 20. Jahrhunderts* on the one hand, and Mann's own enlightened, "humanized" myths on the other—was to become of crucial importance to this author.

Mythology is ambivalent, as Mann reminds us when talking of a world of myth, its caverns filled with both horrors and treasure-chests. Treasures are offered, not only in the sense that there are positive myths of humanism as well as evil, regressive ones, but also because even negative myths can be manipulated and exploited to moral advantages. The important factor must be what the novelist does with the myths he treats; it cannot simply be the fact that he uses them at all. Here opinion divides. Some maintain that the novelist is obliged to remain faithful to his sources, others that he should change myths radically in accordance with the realities of our age: "au rythme de notre époque," as Cocteau puts it in an important introduction to his *Oedipe-Roi*.[11]

In Alberto Moravia's *Il disprezzo* (entitled in English *A Ghost at Noon*), one finds a tongue-in-cheek example of just how doctrinaire the would-be liberal approach to prefigurations can become. Here we have a parody of what many might take to be the radical, modernist attitude to incorporating mythology into a novel; but its exaggerated mood soon becomes a restriction in itself. The following view, expressed by Rheingold, one of the two characters in the novel who are engaged in work on a film version of the *Odyssey*, gives a slightly distorted description of what Moravia himself is doing with Homer's epic in his own novel. To approach a myth in modern times, Rheingold argues, one has to be unencumbered by any scruples about the original:

[11] Paris, 1928, p. 2.

ma io non amo lo stesso *Il lutto si addice ad Elettra* . . .
e sa perché? . . . Perché O'Neill si è lasciato intimidire
da Eschilo . . . giustamente ha pensato che il mito di
Oreste poteva essere interpretato psicanaliticamente
. . . ma, intimidito dall'argomento, ha fatto una
trascrizione troppo letterale del mito . . . come un
buono scolaro che trascriva un tema sopra un quaderno
con la carta rigata [. . .] egli non doveva rispettare
troppo l'argomento, ma buttarlo all'aria, sventrarlo,
rinnovarlo . . .

Rheingold, a kind of mock-Wagnerian, as the name implies,
expounds his radical solution at this point: "aprirla, come
si apre un corpo sul tavolo anatomico, esaminarne il mec-
canismo interno, smontarlo e poi rimontarlo di nuovo
secondo le nostre esigenze moderne."¹² This advice represents a brash version of the standard opinion, voiced for
example in Gilbert Highet's observation that "every writer
who attempts to create anything on a basis of myth must
add, or subtract, or alter."¹³

Nevertheless, the radical *modus operandi* advocated by
zealous Rheingold is far less frequently encountered than
the idea of strict, even pious fidelity to the original. Prais-
ing Goethe's *Iphigenie*, Grillparzer's *Medea* and Wilder's
Alcestis, in a typical mood of reverence, Stefan Andres adds
the significant reservation that this applies only inasmuch

¹² p. 143 (author's punctuation, except where square brackets indicate ellipsis). In Angus Davidson's translation, these two passages
become: "I don't care for *Mourning becomes Electra*—d'you know
why? Because O'Neill allowed himself to be intimidated by Aeschylus
. . . He thought, quite rightly, that the Orestes myth could be interpreted psychoanalytically; but, intimidated by the subject, he made
too literal a transcription of the myth . . . Like a good schoolboy
writing out an exercise book with ruled paper [. . .] he ought not to
have respected his subject too much, but should have torn it to pieces,
turned it inside out, put new life into it." And: "open it up, as a
body is opened up on the dissecting table, examine its internal
mechanism, take it to pieces, and then put it together again according
to modern requirements" (*A Ghost at Noon*, Harmondsworth, 1964,
p. 116).
¹³ *The Classical Tradition*, p. 533.

as they retain a pious attitude towards their mythological material.[14] (The notion seems more appropriate to sacred scriptures than to another society's dead myths.) On analogous grounds Henri Peyre is content to admire Jean Giono's *Naissance de l'Odyssée* for the principal reason that "unlike many of his contemporaries" the author "refrains from belittling Hellenic themes with irony and facile anachronism when he goes to them for inspiration."[15]

E. M. Butler's interpretation, of *Doktor Faustus* displays the same purist inclination. She expresses her disappointment at finding the outlines of the Faust prefiguration obscured in Mann's novel by the introduction of much alien material. She feels that the Faust prefiguration in the novel "loses some of its fearful fascination . . . by the deliberate parallel drawn between Leverkühn and Nietzsche. . . ."[16] Mann, however, himself observes, albeit not without irony, that *Doktor Faustus* is "im Grunde ein Nietzsche-Roman und also auch wieder ein wenig mythisch angehaucht."[17] The myth of Faust, equated by E. M. Butler with the literary presentation of it in the Spies *Faustbuch*—in an approach reminiscent of Stanford's contention that the earliest literary version of a myth is the most important factor in the influence on any future adaptation—becomes the standard by which *Doktor Faustus* is judged. Hence it can be suggested that "dragging Nietzsche in *via* Deussen, considerably diminishes the total effect."[18]

In fact, there are two debatable assumptions here: that *Doktor Faustus* is primarily about Faust rather than about Leverkühn or Nietzsche, and that it is a bad version of the

---

[14] "schöne Dichtungen . . . nur in dem Maße, als sie den alten Stoff unverändert übernahmen, also in der Haltung des ehrerbietigen Verarbeitens verharrten" ("Mythos und Dichtung," p. 15).

[15] *The Contemporary French Novel*, New York, 1955, p. 130.

[16] *The Fortunes of Faust*, p. 322.

[17] *Gespräch in Briefen*, p. 123: "fundamentally a Nietzsche novel and therefore once again inspired mythically to some extent."

[18] *op.cit.*, p. 335.

Faust story because it does not concentrate enough on what the critic erroneously takes to be the main theme. If it can be said to be Mann's "theoretically satisfactory solution . . . to transpose the events of the Urfaustbook into the mental sphere,"[19] his aim was also to use the myth as a motif, and to counterpoint the theme—the life of Leverkühn—with a number of motifs from the lives and works of Beethoven, Kierkegaard, Nietzsche, Schönberg, Shakespeare, Wolf and others. One possible reason for the assumption that *Doktor Faustus* will be a modernized version of the Faust tale is the failure to realize that the titles of modern works often refer to a motif rather than the main theme. As will be argued in more detail later, the title cannot be taken as an indication that a novel is primarily about a particular myth because it names it; the title merely alerts us, in this case, to the fact that the book has *some*, as yet undefined, connection with the myth.

The novelist's choice lies, one of the standard arguments runs, between a rather epigonal handling of mythological materials and infidelity to the myth, or—if one sees this in a more favorable light—poetic license. For Henri Peyre, infidelity to mythology occurs at that point in a work where mythology is no longer mythical:

> Chez certains modernes hyperintelligents (un Gide, un Valéry), médiocrement primitifs, ou ne réussissant qu'à demi (tel un Cocteau) à se rendre bêtes, Oedipe ou Philoctète, Narcisse ou la Pythie ne servent guère que de thèmes commodes, et se vident de tout leur contenu réligieux de l'interprétation anthropomorphique de la nature qu'avaient pu retrouver un Ronsard, un Keats, un Shelley.[20]

This Romantic-sounding suggestion that myths have only been justifiably treated, if they retain a cosmogonic quality,

[19] *op.cit.*, p. 322.
[20] *L'Influence des Littératures antiques sur la Littérature française moderne*, p. 11.

is itself far more atavistic than most of the novels produced with such motifs in the twentieth century. However, the most frequent complaint leveled against mythological novels is simply that the traditional myths are not presented in an optimistic enough light. Reacting to Joyce's *Ulysses,* Hermann Pongs makes the characteristic charge of what might be called the "elegiac school" of critics: that the modern works are irresponsible parodies of the gods of a bygone age.[21] The viewpoint of the elegiac critics is well summed up by the title of J. Duvignaud's article: "La dégradation des mythes."[22]

"Most artists have used myths to ennoble contemporary life," Gilbert Highet suggests.[23] In fact, many critics have assumed that the presence of mythological motifs exercises an essentially ennobling effect upon modern fiction, just as it decorated rococo literature. This idea can in turn be interpreted in two ways: either as a sign of weakness in certain modern writers who feel the need to turn to such subjects, or merely as a fact and not necessarily an admission of imaginative sterility. In an example of the former approach, a reviewer of James Merrill's *The (Diblos) Notebook* summarily dismisses the Greek mythology incorporated as a "wayside halt for tired novelists."[24] Similarly, Michael Hamburger notes with obvious relief that "Musil does not need to resort to the far-fetched framework of a poetic myth" and contrasts this, Musil's strength in *Der Mann ohne Eigenschaften,* with the use of mythology in

[21] "Indem die Griechen durch die Gegenwartsgosse gezogen werden, wird zugleich diese glorreiche Gegenwart auf ihren nihilistischen Grundsatz gebracht. . . . eine einzige blutige Parodie ist diese Ulyssesfiktion . . . müssen alle Helden unseres Zeitalters erst einmal Parodien des Heldischen sein?" (*Im Umbruch der Zeit. Das Romanschaffen der Gegenwart,* Göttingen, 1956, pp. 47-48).

[22] *Les Lettres Nouvelles,* xxxiv, 1956, p. 138.

[23] *The Classical Tradition,* p. 512.

[24] *TLS,* 9 September 1965, p. 769.

Mann's *Doktor Faustus*.[25] Henri Peyre also attributes many modern novelists' desire to work with mythological material to an inherent weakness:

> le manque de fougue imaginative, la crainte de puiser à même la vie, souvent vulgaire et brutale, et la préférence pour la matière déjà épurée, sublimée et filtrée par maint prédécesseur.[26]

"Leaning on crutches" and "hitching a lift" are phrases which often occur when misgivings of this kind are being voiced. For the East European critic, such a device is escapism pure and simple. Writing of the Faust motif in Maxim Gorky's *Bystander*, Ralf Schröder expresses the essential, ideological objection to prefigurations when referring to:

> die Anknüpfung an klassische Vorbilder, die Parodie oder Adaption als formprägendes "Leitseil" oder als "symbolical framework," die bei den Modernisten letztlich eine Kapitulation vor der gesellschaftlichen Wirklichkeit und ihrer ästhetischen Bewältigung bewußt oder unbewußt verdecken . . .[27]

Such is the orthodox Marxist view of prefigurations,[28] but although this is a dogmatic viewpoint in the strict sense of the word, it does not differ greatly in quality from the

---

[25] *From Prophecy to Exorcism: The Premisses of Modern German Literature*, London, 1965, p. 97.

[26] *L'Influence des Littératures antiques sur la Littérature française moderne*, pp. 80-81.

[27] "Gorki, Mann und die spätbürgerliche Romankrise," *Weimarer Beiträge*, II, 1967, pp. 313-314: "the use of correspondences with classical models, parody or adaptation as a structural guide or as 'symbolical framework,' with which the modernists in the last analysis either consciously or unconsciously hide a capitulation in the face of social reality and the problem of depicting it. . . ."

[28] Despite such strictures, comparable "symbolical frameworks" have now appeared in recent East German fiction: in Franz Fühmann's "König Ödipus" and "Böhmen am Meer" in the cycle *König Ödipus*, and with the use of the *Iliad* in Klaus Beuchler's *Aufenthalt auf Bornholm*.

others looked at above. Its basic tenet, like theirs, is that the technique is indictable on non-aesthetic grounds.

A more considered criticism of the device, with which one can occasionally feel a degree of sympathy, is the view that the introduction of mythology into a modern novel sounds both pretentious and irrelevant to the theme. Margaret Dalziel remarks in her lecture on "Myth in Modern English Literature" that:

> the free use of myth, especially in novels, has now become part of a literary fashion of writing. . . . The age and associations, the suggestive and evocative power of myths have lured many people into using them as images for no very good reason, and the fashion has, I think, given rise to much pretentious and therefore bad writing.[29]

Still, myth "as a fashionable gimmick," as Dalziel puts it,[30] can only be, I suspect, a distorted view of the device. It may well be "inconceivable that Jane Austen or George Eliot should have written a novel based on the story of the Grail, or of Faust or Philoctetes, the centaur or the unicorn."[31] But then, Jane Austen and George Eliot did not live in a post-Freudian age, at a time when myth has formed such an integral part of modern politics, psychology and image-making and where we have been made so aware of its role.[32] Mythological motifs represent less often than is here suggested "an effort to create an object of senseless veneration, to claim for your book a depth of meaning it does not possess."[33] They are far more often a challenge to the read-

[29] p. 49. The works which Dalziel finds specifically objectionable in their use of prefigurations are John Bowen's *A World Elsewhere*, Carl Frederick Buechner's *A Long Day's Dying*, Bernard Malamud's *The Natural*, Iris Murdoch's *The Unicorn* and John Updike's *The Centaur*.

[30] *op.cit.*, p. 46.

[31] *op.cit.*, p. 45.

[32] On this subject, see Wolfgang Schmidbauer's "Mythos und Psychologie," especially pp. 896ff.

[33] *op.cit.*, p. 45.

er to think out for himself just where the modern tale stands in relation to the myth—perhaps to reject any great affinity —and are rarely intended as an identification of the two (and only an identification could inspire the kind of veneration implied here).

The view that mythology ennobles modern novels is undoubtedly an inheritance from earlier times: the supposition that even pagan deities are noble and also more interesting than contemporary man as a literary subject.[34] Such opinions share with their more negative counterpart (that we should not, as Langbaum puts it, "render modern facts more poetical by decorating them with outworn mythological allusions"[35]) a very questionable assumption: namely that the motif is guaranteed *by its source* to be noble and is bound to decorate the modern plot in some way. Yet many of the prefigurations chosen by writers in this century appear simply as a loose parallel or contrast, rather than an ennobling analogy to modernity. Furthermore, Daedalus, Hermes, Odysseus, Prometheus[36] and Sisyphus are far from being bestowers of a classical aura in many of the literary contexts in which they occur. There is little archaic grandeur transferred from mythology to the modern events, for instance, in Agatha Christie's *The Labours of Hercules* or John Updike's *The Centaur*. Indeed, it would be difficult to name a single novel for which such a motivation seemed appropriate.

A variant of this image of mythology as literary decora-

---

[34] For two examples of what is a very widespread assumption, see Franz K. Stanzel, *Typische Formen des Romans*, Göttingen, 1964, pp. 49-50, and Gertrud Mander, "John Updike: *Der Zentaur*," *Neue deutsche Hefte*, III, 1966, pp. 181-183.

[35] "Browning and the Question of Myth," p. 575.

[36] For modern writers it is not so much the Romantics' Prometheus the noble Fire-bringer, for example, who appeals to the imagination as Prometheus Bound. Louis Awad even writes of "the new cult of Prometheus Absurdus which we find in Kafka, Camus and the Temporal Existentialists . . ." (*The Theme of Prometheus in English and French Literature*, p. 447).

tion is found in the interpretation of mythological motifs as a deliberate exercise in the comedy, or at least whimsy, of anachronism. This was Peyre's charge, and one finds the notion well put in Borges's evocation of:

> one of those parasitic books which places Christ on a boulevard, Hamlet on the Cannebière and Don Quixote on Wall Street . . . useless carnivals, only suitable . . . for evoking plebeian delight in anachronism.[37]

For such delight in anachronism to be effectively awakened in the reader, the mythological matter would have to be readily noticeable and put in relief to contrast to modern events. This alone would discount a large number of mythological novels, for their motifs are often as submerged within the narratives as icebergs are in the sea. Yet one might still try to locate a few novels which do deal in anachronisms to see how they are handled.

Novels which have achieved this effect, such as Harry Brown's *The Stars in their Courses*, Agatha Christie's *The Labours of Hercules* and John Updike's *The Centaur*, largely derive their sense of anachronism from inappropriate correspondences. The petty feud between rival cowboy factions in *The Stars in their Courses* is compared with an event of the magnitude of the Trojan War; what was a lion in one of the original labors of Hercules becomes a pekinese in Agatha Christie's thriller; John Updike's centaur is in turn transformed into a small-town schoolteacher. In Paul Schallück's *Don Quichotte in Köln*, much of the action takes place on bicycles instead of on horseback. And in Alfred Döblin's *Berlin Alexanderplatz*, the sacrifice motif of Isaac and Abraham, and that of Orestes, is put into a grotesquely anachronistic context by being compared with the modern mechanized slaughter of the North Berlin *abattoirs*. Yet despite these incidental features, anachronism in the mytho-

---

[37] *Fictions*, London, 1965, p. 45.

logical novel is rare. When used, it leads to ironic rather than comic effect, and there appears to be nothing in fiction to compare with the more lighthearted use of anachronism in Giraudoux's plays.

The argument that it is detrimental to a modern work to include mythological material, or that prefigurative motifs are by their very nature certain to improve any novel in which they appear, rests upon false *a priori* assumptions: if—so we are given to understand—a writer chooses a given subject or a group of motifs, then there will be a certain inevitable result in the quality of his work. Clearly, no axioms apply so mechanically to all fiction. A novel can hardly be welcomed for the negative reason that it at least "refrains from belittling Hellenic themes with irony and facile anachronism when [it] goes to them for inspiration."[38] By the same token, all mythological novels cannot be criticized categorically for "charming us with the primary idea that all epochs are the same, or that they are different."[39] Of course, all of us will invariably find in the mythological novel those qualities which our predisposition towards mythology leads us to expect and conditions us to appreciate. Unfortunately, many of the above partisan views are then presented apodictically, as if certain hard-and-fast rules could be abstracted to relate literary quality to chosen mythological material. A novel, it is implied, is bad because it operates in a particular way, or good because it chooses a certain set of images and handles them with due respect. In fact, a work is good or bad, not because it works with a certain kind of infrastructure, or even because it is a good or bad example of a certain technique. I consider John Bowen's *A World Elsewhere* to be an admirable example of the technique of juxtaposing mythological and contemporary elements, but this does not constitute a judgment of the work as a whole. A mythological novel is largely successful when it manages to present the reader with an important

[38] Henri Peyre, *op.cit.*, p. 130.   [39] Borges, *op.cit.*, p. 45.

realistic theme and at the same time makes him feel the chosen analogy has enriched his understanding of the primary material. When the reader feels the contemporary subject-matter and the mythological motif are ill matched, when the prefiguration either appears to be gratuitously pretentious or unnecessarily obscure, then mythology is clearly not serving any aesthetically useful purpose. Viewed in these terms, Joyce's *Ulysses* and Michel Butor's *L'Emploi du Temps* are novels that make extensive and effective use of their mythological analogies; Anthony Burgess's *A Vision of Battlements* and Geno Hartlaub's *Nicht jeder ist Odysseus* involve a less happy handling of the same device—largely because one does not feel that the prefiguration has added much to the novel. Elisabeth Langgässer's *Märkische Argonautenfahrt* conveys a rather banal mythological scheme; yet in Macdonald Harris's *Trepleff* what might have been an equally facile system of analogies is exploited to some comic effect. In fact, the mood in which correspondences are presented is almost as important as their ramifications. Faced with this spectrum of works, why has criticism so frequently been dogmatic in its judgments? Partly, one suspects, because myth is a subject which draws out a certain partisan stance in many people. But also because of a lack of perspective. Seeing a bad example of a certain technique and knowing no better instance of it, one might be tempted to condemn the technique as well as the novel in question. Hence the solution to this detrimental narrowness of perspective (often the result of viewing literature within national confines) would seem to lie in wider comparative studies; but these have, to date, fallen into certain rigid categories.

Diachronic Accounts of Mythology in Literature

Most of the more general work on myths in modern literature has been carried out with a historical bias. A large number of diachronic studies offers an account of the metamorphoses and the vicissitudes of a particular myth over a certain period of time.[40] Because their sections on modern literature are constricted by their wide scope, they generally betray an oversimplified view of the treatment of mythological material in recent years. The pattern that Eva Kushner ascribes to the development of the Orpheus myth is representative of conclusions about others.[41] In her final chapter, she observes that during the Symbolist period there was:

> autour du mythe d'Orphée tout un mouvement de pensée idealiste et mystique. Puis, le mythe s'humanise, et Orphée ne représente plus qu'une sagesse toute humaine, reflétant ainsi l'idéal d'une époque qui se plaît à compter sur la raison pour assurer le progrès, donc le bonheur de tous. La guerre de 1914 met fin à l'ère des interprétations idéalistes. Tout au plus Orphée continue-t-il à représenter l'idéal dans le domaine esthétique, en poésie et en musique. A partir du moment où l'influence de Freud pénètre en France, l'attention des écrivains se détourne d'Orphée pour se tourner de plus en plus vers Eurydice. Le mythe assume une signification de plus en plus sombre, de plus en plus "infernale"; la descente aux enfers—enfers de la souffrance, du souvenir, de l'inconscient—devient le thème central. Orphée s'y enlise, sans trouver le bonheur dans ce monde ou dans l'autre. Enfin les poètes chrétiens reviennent à une interprétation plus optimiste; ce n'est pas là un optimisme facile, mais un optimisme qui ne perd jamais de vue la réalité de l'enfer sachant pourtant qu'au delà de l'enfer la

[40] Geneviève Bianquis's *Faust à travers quatres siècles*, Eva Kushner's *Le Mythe d'Orphée dans la Littérature française contemporaine*, Raymond Trousson's *Le Thème de Prométhée dans la Littérature européenne* and Leo Weinstein's *The Metamorphosis of Don Juan* are some recent noteworthy examples of such a metachronic approach.

[41] For similar opinions, see Jakob Rothschild, *Kain und Abel in der deutschen Dichtung* (pp. 144ff.); Awad, *The Theme of Prometheus in English and French Literature* (pp. 472ff.); and Weinstein, *The Metamorphosis of Don Juan* (pp. 168ff.).

résurrection est au moins une possibilité toujours ouverte. De toute manière, le mythe d'Orphée, une fois dépassé le mouvement d'études inspiré par le Symbolisme, n'est plus jamais redevenu un objet de vénération en soi. Bien plutôt, c'est un très riche réservoir de symboles, que les écrivains utilisent soit pour exprimer leur idéal esthétique et leur nostalgie de la beauté, soit dans un sens psychologique, pour y projeter leur propre situation.[42]

The two major historical landmarks stressed—the growing influence of Freud's ideas and the despair following the First World War—are both associated with a process of secularization that most myths have undergone since the Symbolist movement. But these are very general fluctuations, they would do little to account for the difference between, say, the image of Orpheus in Hans Erich Nossack's *Interview mit dem Tode* and Hermann Broch's *Der Tod des Vergil*, or that of Faust in James Blish's *Black Easter* and John Hersey's *Too Far to Walk*.

Chronologically ordered studies of mythological literature through the ages, with a chapter on each age and its reading of a myth, are inclined to concentrate on content rather than specific techniques, on similarities rather than dissimilarities in any age. Yet the differences between writers working in any single epoch, and especially in an age of pluralism such as our own, are as great as those between various ages. Apart from being prone to this leveling tendency, accounts of mythology's role in literature also run the risk of concentrating on major, explicit themes and ignoring disguised or implicit motifs. A novel that retells a myth *in toto* remains readily classifiable (and the concept of ready recognizability must be very important to someone engaged in such a mammoth undertaking). Hence historical accounts of the metamorphosis of myths have always re-

[42] Kushner, *op.cit.*, pp. 347-348.

vealed a willingness to include the work with a mythological theme, or even just an oblique mythological title; but the prefiguration has usually been ignored.[43]

Henri Peyre has argued that:
a consideration of the intercessors or heroes whom each age selects through its writers is, if prudently attempted, enlightening on the aspirations of that age. Cain and most biblical heroes or themes have almost disappeared from our recent fiction and essays. But Prometheus, the other great hero of the Romantics, is still with us. . . . Narcissus, whose presence pervaded the age of the Symbolists, and Ulysses (who tempted many moderns, from Joyce to Kazantzakis and Vorenca, and Giono, Fondane, and several French) have not yet been studied as the myths of the generation preceding that of 1930 to 1945. Orestes, Sisyphus, Antigone have become our patron saints, and the Centaur again haunts our contemporaries who are fascinated by the theme of metamorphosis.[44]

If executed with enough circumspection to include the mythological motif, such an approach would do much to supplement and redefine the findings of many historical studies; but until our knowledge of the structure and patterning of these images has substantially increased, this cannot avoid remaining too preoccupied at a superficial level with the subject-matter of mythological literature. For, as Peyre himself puts it elsewhere: "Ces recherches risquent en effet de s'égarer dans la thématologie, c'est-à-dire dans

[43] For example, Weinstein's list of omissions refers to "straight translations, continuations, and parodies of works by well-known authors, unless of special interest. . . . Works containing the name 'Don Juan' in their title but having no real connection with the legend" (*op.cit.*, p. 187). Clearly, this allows little opportunity for considering Don Juan's prefigurative role. In fact, most diachronic studies list works with a prefigurative title, even if the mythological element is introduced then simply as a motif.
[44] "The Study of Modern French Literature: Where do we stand? Where do we go from here?" *Modern Language Quarterly*, XXVI, 1965, pp. 36f.

la poursuite, à travers plusieurs siècles ou plusieurs littératures, d'un sujet extérieur et fuyant."[45] In other words, another kind of one-sidedness may predominate, if the technique's idiosyncrasies are not studied more closely. And perhaps the most vexed question is that of why novelists choose such a method of portrayal.

Motivations for a Motif

Occasionally a historical link is established between the myth and the modern tale. In *Proserpina: Eine Kindheitsmythe*, for example, Elisabeth Langgässer stresses the relevance of her classical prefiguration by referring to the time when Roman legions tramped across the Rhineland region where her tale is set. Similar attempts at historical motivation can be found in John Bowen's *A World Elsewhere*, Heinrich Mann's *Die Göttinnen*, Thomas Mann's *Doktor Faustus* and Alberto Moravia's *Il disprezzo*. The technique entails setting the modern story in a geographical location once inhabited by the appropriate myth-producing society. Abstruse essays at establishing the historical appropriateness of a mythological motif have also been made by some critics and even retrospectively by a few novelists: e.g. Stuart Gilbert's "brief outline of the legendary connection between ancient Ireland and the Mediterranean,"[46] composed possibly upon Joyce's own prompting. Nevertheless, these historical links are always peripheral. Erich Kahler rightly points out that for the modern age myths have a mainly symbolic import and lack the historical roots they once had in primitive societies:

> Nicht nur historische und öffentliche Figuren, auch erdichtete Figuren wachsen sich zu Mythen aus: Don Quixote, Dr. Faust, Ahasver, Don Juan, Tyl Ulenspiegl,

[45] *L'Influence des Littératures antiques sur la Littérature française moderne*, p. 12.
[46] *James Joyce's "Ulysses,"* pp. 65-68.

Münchhausen, Volpone, Tartarin de Tarascon, Rübe-
zahl und Schwejk—in ihnen allen ist ein spezifischer
Typus des Menschen oder eines Volkes oder einer
Landschaft lebendig geworden als irrationales Bild,
nur beschreibbar, nicht erklärbar und nicht weiter
zurückzuführen als bis zu der so und nicht anders
beschaffenen Gestalt mit ihrem Erlebnis. Die Menschen erkennen sich darin, sie finden darin ihre zeit-
losen Ahnen und Archetypen, ihre spirituellen Stamm-
väter. Aber während die antiken Mythologien in der
Vorstellung der Menschen eine unmittelbare, der hi-
storischen vergleichbare Wirklichkeit besaßen, ist die
Wirklichkeit dieser modernen Mythen die übertragene,
abstrakte Wirklichkeit des Symbols.[47]

To pursue the point one step further: in ancient mythologies, myths not only partook of a quasi-historical significance as fictions; as euhemerisms, they were frequently
historical in origin. Now the situation has changed. The
Gilgamesh myth in Hans Henny Jahnn's *Fluß ohne Ufer* and
Guido Bachmann's *Gilgamesch* is only relevant to the modern plot in archetypal or symbolic terms. The novelist presents no important historical links between the modern
Europe of these two novels and the Sumerian background
to the chosen prefiguration; nor does the reader expect him
to justify or present his motif in this way. On the other
hand, the classical story-teller could often add a great deal
of power to his tale by putting it into a familiar locale; the
famous crossroads on the way to Delphi is an instance of
this bringing the myth close to home.

[47] *Die Verantwortung des Geistes*, p. 207. "Not only historical and
public persons, but also fictive figures develop into myths . . . in all of
them a specific type of man or people or scenery comes to life as an
irrational image, only capable of being described, but not of being
explained and taken back beyond this figure, created thus and not
differently, with his particular experience. People recognize themselves in them, there they find their timeless forefathers and archetypes, their spiritual forebears. But whereas ancient mythologies possessed in the human mind an immediate reality comparable to that of
history, the reality of these modern myths is the figurative, abstract
reality of the symbol."

One may generalize by saying that in modern literature
there will be some sort of usually non-historical, archetypal
or symbolic relationship between the mythological and the
modern characters, a correspondence which seems difficult
to describe in preciser terms. It has usually been expressed
very loosely, often merely hinted at by means of a hyphen:
"Mutter Gisson-Demeter," "Faust-Leverkühn," "Zerlina-
Martha," "Don Giovanni-Boylan" and "Marco-Odysseus."[48]
Such combinations do little more than postulate indeterminate relationships existing between the characters whose
names are thus hyphenated. Usually the hyphen stands for
an equals-sign in such interpretations. For example, Vernon
Hall, a critic who uses hyphens in his essay on *Ulysses*, concludes soon enough that "Don Giovanni is Hugh E.
(Blazes) Boylan, Zerlina is Molly Bloom, Zerlina's bridegroom, Masetto, is Leopold Bloom."[49] Few critics who use
the hyphen to imply some link between mythological prefiguration and modern hero proceed to elaborate what kind
of connection it really represents. Where hyphens are
avoided, metaphor takes over. In his thesis on Thomas
Mann's use of the Hermes motif, Jürgen Plöger gives a long
résumé of the various theories advanced by critics to describe the relationship between Joseph and Hermes in
Joseph und seine Brüder.[50] Nearly all these approaches in-

---

[48] The respective sources for these usages are: Franz Schonauer,
"Hermann Broch und sein Werk," *Hochland*, XLVIII, June, 1956, p.
476; Jürgen Kreft, *Hamlet—Don Juan—Faustus*, p. 231; Vernon Hall,
"Joyce's Use of Da Ponte and Mozart's *Don Giovanni*," p. 82; Hall,
op.cit., p. 81; Joseph Brennan, *Three Philosophical Novelists*, p. 180.
[49] *op.cit.*, p. 79.
[50] "Für Käte Hamburger schimmern Hermes' Umrisse 'hier und da'
hinter Joseph auf . . . und seine Ministerschaft ist 'die vollendete
Inkarnation des vermittelnden, witzig-zweideutigen Hermesgeistes'.
. . . Nach Ferdinand Lion gehört Joseph 'auf irgendeine Weise'
Hermes an. . . . Jonas Lesser stellt fest: 'Joseph takes the roguish god
Hermes as a model' . . . und 'Echnaton erzählt die Streiche des
jugendlichen Gottes auf eine Weise, daß Josephs mythische Hoch-
stapeleien sich aufs erheiterndste in ihnen spiegeln'. . . . Für Hans
Mayer 'spielt Joseph die Rolle des Hermes,' 'Seine Laufbahn lenkt

volve familiar metaphors: the idea that Joseph and Hermes are brothers, that one perceives Hermes' silhouette beyond the Joseph figure, that the god's actions are mirrored in Joseph's own or that Hermes is Joseph's divine counterpart. There is even an astrological version of this type of vague statement of affinity: the notion that Joseph stands under the sign of Hermes.[51] Such metaphors are elusive counsels of despair, for they say very little.

The one single relationship that can be rejected as a totally unacceptable explanation of myths in novels is that of identity. A character in a novel cannot *be* a mythological god in the literal sense. Perhaps because earlier critics were prone to view novels in these terms, current literary heroes state quite explicitly at times that they are not identical with their prefigurations. As the hero of Geno Hartlaub's *Nicht jeder ist Odysseus* realizes, upon hearing the remark "Ich frage mich, ob du Odysseus bist, der sein Ithaka sucht. Dann wäre Franca Penelope, Victor Telemach,"[52] such equations can be nonsensical:

---

hinüber zum Hermes der Griechen, dem Merkurius der Römer' . . . Max Rychner: 'Joseph, der Günstling des Schicksals und Herr mannigfaltigster Lebenslagen, so als erfolgreicher Wirtschaftsminister Ägyptenlands . . .' und: in Joseph habe Thomas Mann 'einen Vertreter der Hermeswelt erkannt, ja er hat ihm Züge und Gaben des Griechengottes verliehen'. . . . Gustav Hillard: 'es kommt bis zu einer Art Identifizierung von Joseph und Hermes'. . . . Nach Beda Allemanns Formulierung ist Hermes 'ein wichtiges mythologisches Schema für die Josephs-Gestalt'. . . . Walter Jens erblickt in Joseph einen echten 'Bruder des Hermes, Abbild und Kopie des Gottes,' 'der sich die Züge seines Gottes so sehr zu eigen macht, daß am Ende die Grenzen seiner Individualität nicht mehr genau bestimmbar sind und es unklar bleibt, wo Göttliches endet, Menschliches beginnt'. . . . Heide Heimann: 'Dieses Epos, unausschöpfbar wie das Meer, hat in Joseph seine Zentralfigur und in Hermes' schillernder Gestalt dessen göttlichen Gegenpart'. . . . Nach Erich Hellers Urteil unterhält Joseph Beziehungen zu Hermes" (*Das Hermesmotiv in der Dichtung Thomas Manns*, pp. 22f.).

[51] "Hermes . . . eine Gottheit, in deren Zeichen sowohl Joseph als auch Felix Krull stehen" (Ignace Feuerlicht, *Thomas Mann und die Grenzen des Ich*, Heidelberg, 1966, pp. 4-5).

[52] p. 79. "I wonder whether you are Odysseus, looking for his Ithaca. Then Franca would be Penelope and Victor Telemachus."

Er soll aufhören, der elende Alleswisser, der jedes
Ereignis zwischen Himmel und Erde in die Schablonen
seiner Begriffe und Bilder preßt. Er plündert die Bibel
und die Antike aus, dies Kabinett mit den Gipsab-
güssen der Vater-, Mutter-, Sohn- und Tochterfiguren,
die wir noch aus der Schulzeit kennen: Orest, Odysseus, Ödipus. Das stimmt ungefähr und niemals genau.
Unser Mörder heißt Wiesenthal [the man who uses
these constricting metaphors]: er nimmt uns unsere
Namen, er zwingt uns, die Masken fremder Tragödien-
figuren zu tragen. Paul Verhoeren ist weder Orest noch
Odysseus noch Ödipus und schon garnicht der ver-
lorene Sohn, der ins Vaterhaus zurückkehrt. . . . Ich bin
ich, das ist die einzige Gleichung, die stimmt.[53]

One of the main figures of John Bowen's *A World Elsewhere* distances himself from the prefigurations in a like
manner: "However I may use myself, however cast myself,
these people are fictions. I am outside them, and so I intend
to stay."[54]

Sometimes the idea of "identity" is used when "identification"—a psychological process of transference—is really
meant. I shall consider this later in a discussion of "mythical
imitation" (which is really only another name for the same
idea). Otherwise, identity is not a helpful term.

Three types of description—sometimes used as metaphors by the critic, sometimes really part of the novel's contents—do merit further consideration as serious attempts
at accounting for the function of prefigurative motifs:

[53] *ibid.* "He ought to stop it, this miserable know-all, who forces
everything that happens between heaven and earth into the molds of
his concepts and images. He plunders the Bible and antiquity, this
cabinet of plaster-casts of father-, mother-, son- and daughter-figures
which we still know from our schooldays: Orestes, Odysseus, Oedipus.
It's roughly right, but never precisely so. Our murderer is called
Wiesenthal: he deprives us of our names, he forces us to wear the
masks of strange tragic figures. Paul Verhoeren is neither Orestes nor
Odysseus nor Oedipus, and certainly not the Prodigal Son returning to
his father's house. . . . I am myself, that is the only equation which is
true."
[54] p. 158.

1. Jung's idea of the "collective unconscious" as a source of mythological models;
2. reincarnation or some ghost-like return from the dead;
3. the idea of imitation or identification on a character's part.

These theories, very frequently advanced as explanations of any kind of motif, as I suggested in Chapter One, apply in the case of some novels, but not many. Even then, one must make a careful distinction between the motivation actually given in the novel and the motif's unstated, but nevertheless equally important aesthetic function. Theories of imitation, reincarnation, the racial memory (or collective unconscious) can all be offered as unverifiable rationalizations for the myths chosen by any novelists. To clarify where and when they hold water as genuine reasons for the use of a prefiguration, one must look at some illustrations of where they are supported by the nature of the work and where they can be rejected as critical metaphors.

Myth, the Collective Unconscious and the Idea of Reincarnation

Not many novelists could preface their mythological works with the kind of creed that David Stacton expresses at the beginning of *Kaliyuga*: that "we have our racial memory. The Jungian consciousness does exist."[55] Most prefer even the Jungian overtones of their use of mythology to remain rather discreet.

At one point in Hermann Hesse's *Demian*, Pistorius does admittedly offer the hero a view of the psyche which sounds very Jungian:

> Wir ziehen die Grenzen unserer Persönlichkeit immer viel zu eng! Wir rechnen zu unserer Person immer bloß das, was wir als individuell unterschieden, als abweichend erkennen. Wir bestehen aber aus dem

[55] p. 12.

ganzen Bestand der Welt, jeder von uns, und ebenso wie unser Körper die Stammtafeln der Entwicklung bis zum Fisch und noch viel weiter zurück in sich trägt, so haben wir in der Seele alles, was je in Menschenseelen gelebt hat. Alle Götter und Teufel, die je gewesen sind, sei es bei Griechen und Chinesen oder bei Zulukaffern, alle sind mit in uns, sind da, als Möglichkeiten, als Wünsche, als Auswege. Wenn die Menschheit ausstürbe bis auf ein einziges halbwegs begabtes Kind, das keinerlei Unterricht genossen hat, so würde dieses Kind den ganzen Gang der Dinge wiedererfinden, es würde Götter, Dämonen, Paradiese, Gebote und Verbote, Alte und Neue Testamente, alles würde es wieder produzieren können.[56]

The prefigurations of Hesse's novel—Eve and Abraxas—with their air of primeval age could be explained in this light, although their further aesthetic function as milestones along the hero's path of development is also relevant to *Demian*.

One can have mythological archetypes divorced from the more mystical aspects of Jung's thought, of course. The observation in the preface to John Bowen's *A World Elsewhere*—that "a myth is by its nature universal. Each of us is Oedipus, each Ajax, each Orestes"—implies a straightforwardly symbolic type of classification. No racial memory is evoked. Yet something akin to a belief in the deep springs

---

[56] *op.cit.*, p. 138. "We always set too narrow limits on our personalities. We count as ours merely what we experience differently as individuals, or recognize as being divergent. Yet we consist of the whole existence of the world, each one of us, and just as our body bears in it the various stages of our evolution back to the fish and further back still, we have in our soul everything that has ever existed in the human mind. All the gods and devils whether among the Greeks, Chinese or Zulus are all within us, existing as possibilities, wishes, outlets. If the human race dwindled to one single, half-developed child that had received no education, this child would rediscover the entire course of evolution, would be able to produce gods, devils, paradise, commandments and interdictions, the whole of the Old and New Testament, everything" (*Demian*, trans. W. J. Strachan, London, 1958, p. 117).

of the collective unconscious is uttered at one point in Alfred Döblin's *Hamlet oder Die lange Nacht nimmt ein Ende*:

> Man beherbergt vieles in sich, eine ganze Menagerie, und von Zeit zu Zeit klebt man auf dieses Tier, und von Zeit zu Zeit auf ein anderes Tier oder eine Gestalt das Etikett "Ich" und läßt ihm den Vortritt, die Repräsentanz des Ganzen. Wir haben in uns, nein, wir sind ein ganzes Volk, mit Bürgern, Proletariern, mit Adel und mit Kammern, mit einem Repräsentantenhaus, mit einem König. . . .[57]

It is not actually made clear here, as it is in Hesse's novel, whether this rich storehouse of *personae* remains part of a lifetime's memories, our stock of private intellectual acquisitions or whether it was there already when we were born, as part of our alleged racial memory. In any case, the collective unconscious can always be advanced as a quick hypothesis to explain why we attach ourselves persistently to certain myths in our lives. We have consciously recognized, so it could be argued, something already impressed upon our collective unconscious.

The crux of the issue does not come when certain novelists legitimately use this explanation of events in their works (for they are entitled to their mysticism), but when it is advanced in subsequent interpretations. What, for example, does it mean when Anthony Burgess talks of "Adam, Humpty Dumpty, Napoleon, Parnell [and] HEC himself, who is all their reincarnations?"[58] The metaphor hangs

---

[57] *op.cit.*, pp. 423-424. "We house much inside ourselves, a whole menagerie, and from time to time we attach the label 'I' to this animal, from time to time to another animal or character, and we allow it precedence, the representation of the whole. We have within us, no, we *are* a complete people, with bourgeoisie, proletariat, with nobility and governing chambers, with a house of representatives, with a king. . . ."

[58] Introduction to *A Shorter "Finnegans Wake,"* London, 1966, p. 10.

ambiguously between the author and the critic and makes us wonder to whom it should be assigned.

In an interpretation of Michel Butor's *L'Emploi du Temps*, Gerda Zeltner-Neukomm attributes the Minotaur motif in it to "a generally collective store of memories" ("ein allgemein kollektives Erinnerungsgut").[59] This notion of collective experiences shifts, in John Sturrock's interpretation of the same novel, from sociology to depth-psychology. At first mythology seems to mean no more than the kind of character-typology that John Bowen uses:

> There are two aspects . . . to Butor's use of myth; not only does a myth represent a means of making sense of reality, it also points to the collective nature of the problem facing each of us as individuals. His busy narrators are not freaks but exemplary men.

But from the notion of collective problems, Sturrock then proceeds to quote a passage from Lévi-Strauss's *Tristes Tropiques* which hints at the collective unconscious:

> Car les grandes manifestations de la vie sociale ont ceci de commun avec l'œuvre d'art qu'elles naissent au niveau de la vie inconsciente, parce qu'elles sont collectives dans le premier cas et bien qu'elles soient individuelles dans le second. . . .[60]

Whereas Zeltner-Neukomm throws herself into Jung's arms, Sturrock contents himself with an ambiguous nod in his direction. But what light could Jung bring to bear on such a novel? Jacques Revel, the hero of Butor's novel, has to have the full significance of the Theseus myth, seen on the tapestries at the fictitious English city of Bleston, spelled out to him by someone else. One could therefore presumably argue that his collective unconscious has rendered him

---

[59] *Das Wagnis des französischen Gegenwartromans*, Hamburg, 1962, p. 113.
[60] *The French New Novel*, London, 1963, pp. 156-157.

highly susceptible to the lure of a myth which lay dormant[61] in his "racial memory" and that in the novel the reader shares in a process whereby the contents of the collective unconscious of the principal character are gradually exposed to the conscious mind. But the unconscious of literary characters is always a treacherous region. As a working hypothesis this argument can often appear to explain any hero's sympathies with the myth used to comment on him. As an account of mythological motifs, the Jungian theory, now widely in disrepute[62] even if it does appeal to the creative imagination, has an obvious drawback: while it cannot be disproved, it also remains impossible to corroborate. Apart from being overtly hypothetical to all but a few devotees, it is also counter-productive, for it does nothing to account for the narrative function of prefigurations. Only in a work where an omniscient narrator steps in, or some observant mentor holds forth, to tell us that this is the justification for the inclusion of a myth, can one feel happy with this explanation.

Ingmar Bergman uses the device of a return from an

[61] Sturrock points to the significance of his name: Revel/Reveil, "the agent who can bring what is dark in Bleston partially but not wholly into the light of the waking state" (*op.cit.*, p. 117).

[62] In the context of literary criticism, René Wellek has spoken of "the dangerously occult idea of the collective unconscious, or racial memory" (*Concepts of Criticism*, p. 336). Richard Chase writes disparagingly of "the fantastic Jungian hypothesis of a 'collective unconscious' into which primitive thought is eternally plunged and into which we regress in our dreams, art and neuroses. . . . Jung's theory involves a belief in 'the racial memory,' according to which the general experience of mankind is recorded in the 'collective unconscious.' This idea certainly overestimates the conservatism of the psyche and of culture" (*Quest for Myth*, p. 145). In "Mythos und Psychologie," Schmidbauer expresses his criticism of "die dem Ovid moralisé in vielen Zügen ähnliche Mythendeutung C. G. Jungs . . . die durch eine psychologische Um-Mythisierung dem entgötterten Menschen Zugang zu den 'Archetypen' schafft" (p. 896). Kirk similarly writes of "the unproductive idea, bandied from Reik, Abraham and Rank to Freud and Jung, that myths are in some sense the collective dreams of the tribe" (*Myth*, p. 270).

afterlife to motivate the Don Juan motif in his film *The Devil's Eye*. And in fiction, both Mikhail Bulgakov and Anthony Burgess introduce mythological figures in the same way. The devil comes back to this world in *The Master and Margarita*, and a statue of Venus actually comes to life in *The Eve of Saint Venus*. But one does not find many examples of a return from the dead or of reincarnation in modern novels. One exception comes at the end of Hermann Broch's *Der Versucher*. Here, the mystical Demeter-like powers previously possessed by Mutter Gisson, an old woman of the village where the novel is set, are transferred, after her death, to another figure: Agathe. In this case, one could talk of Agathe being a reincarnation of the Demeter *persona*. But the general dearth of such events as reincarnations or returns from the dead underlines once more the lack of belief, in most modern uses of myth. For rebirth and a return from the dead imply identity between modern and classical figures.

In practice, it often becomes just as difficult to diagnose a true case of reincarnation in fiction as it is to perceive the difference between an implied racial memory and a store of memories built up by someone during a lifetime. Certainly, in Thomas Mann's Joseph tetralogy, Elezier, whose identity is described as "gleichsam nach hinten offen,"[63] turns out to be not so much a reincarnation of divine office from one generation to the next (such as one finds with the Dalai Lama), but a conscious stylization in the light of his forefathers.[64] And while Molly Bloom may mention metem-

---

[63] In the passage from "Freud und die Zukunft," quoted in Chapter One (*Adel des Geistes*, Stockholm, 1948, p. 581). Elezier is "as it were, open behind" because he can make no distinction between himself and his ancestors of the same name. Feuerlicht (*op.cit.*, p. 85) has compared Elezier's self-stylization with Lévy-Bruhl's "participation mystique," but this interpretation tends to underestimate the old man's ingenuity.

[64] Robert Graves cites similar instances in *The Greek Myths*: "The lives of such characters as Heracles, Daedalus, Teiresias, and Phineus

psychosis to her husband in Joyce's *Ulysses*,[65] any critic supposing that this doctrine offers a rationale for the novel's use of mythology would deserve the same reply that Molly gives to her husband's pronouncements on the subject that Bloomsday morning. Indeed, such ideas are given short shrift later in the novel. "The hypothesis of a plasmic memory, advanced by the Caledonian envoy," in the "Oxen of the Sun" chapter, is ironically summed up as "worthy of the metaphysical traditions of the land he stood for."[66] Furthermore, like the theory of the collective unconscious, the proposition that reincarnation is relevant tells us little about mythology's aesthetic role in modern fiction.

Mythical Imitation

Imitation is the most frequently suggested motivation for mythology in the modern novel. Occasionally it does help to account for certain motifs. Many of Thomas Mann's characters, including Joseph, Leverkühn and Krull, seem consciously to imitate models. At the other end of the literary scale, Agatha Christie's Hercule Poirot selects twelve appropriate cases to solve so that he can imitate the twelve labors of Hercules. In Brigid Brophy's *The Snow Ball*, the characters assembled at a masquerade soon begin to surrender to the spell of their fancy dress and reenact the roles suggested by them. The scriptwriter in Alberto Moravia's *Il disprezzo* also tends to be haunted by the role he should play as Ulysses to his wife's Penelope and his director's Antinous. Yet in all cases, the imitation theory only accounts for part of the device's effect.

I shall be looking more fully at John Bowen's *A World Elsewhere* later, but it will serve to illustrate here the essen-

---

span several generations, because these are titles rather than names of particular heroes" (i, p. 20). In fact, like Elezier (cf. *Exodus* xviii, 4) they are all allegorical names.

[65] *op.cit.*, p. 64.
[66] *op.cit.*, p. 411.

tial drawback of the imitation theory. Reduced to its arche-typal pattern, the plot grows from the following situation. A politician on an island, with a symbolic bow (his reputation as a statesman) and a symbolic wound (his antisocial behavior), is to be lured back to the world of public affairs. Like the M.P. sent out from London to perform this task, Neoptolemus was commissioned to bring back the lame Philoctetes with his magic bow from imposed exile. An imitation of the Philoctetes myth would seem to be one way of describing *A World Elsewhere*. There is more than a suggestion of conscious self-stylization in the novel:

> Turner as Neoptolemus, himself as Philoctetes—whatever part Turner might choose to play, there was no doubt how the Old Man had cast himself. He could no longer say he had done so unconsciously, because, once one recognized what had been unconscious, it became *voulu*.[67]

But this only partly indicates the range and nature of the prefiguration, because the Philoctetes figure refuses to pursue his role at a later point in the novel. He does not want to be inveigled into leaving his island for the modern counterpart of Troy. Indeed, for the majority of the time, the Old Man not only refuses to imitate the figure from the classical myth as we know it from Sophocles; he is even working towards a reinterpretation of the myth in the light of his own wishes and experiences:

> It occurred to the Old Man that, in his own version of the myth, Philoctetes did not wish to leave the island either. No other version—certainly not that of Sophocles—made such a suggestion. Odd. Of course, one did not expect a myth to be probable, yet it was strange that nobody had realized that, when one animated Philoctetes, when one placed oneself inside him, saw with his eyes, felt his pain and his humiliation, then he

[67] *op.cit.*, p. 157.

could only refuse: he must stay. The Old Man had done this, and knew this, and could not write against his knowledge.[68]

A confrontation of reality with the myth, the reality of a modern society which does not offer the community of a Greek army to return to, leads to a rejection of the myth, not to a manipulation of reality in any wilful way to conform to the classical myth's ending. I say "apparently" because the Old Man probably does leave the island in the end, as we shall see later. Yet this fact would not be enough to reinstate the idea of imitation (except in the loose sense, mentioned in my opening chapter: whereby one considers the novelist to be imitating his source-material). One can only talk of imitation, if one adds the rider that it applies only to some parts of the novel—i.e. the middle third or so. And the conclusion drawn here, that imitation applies only to a part of the work, holds for any mythological novel. A piece of fiction that did slavishly imitate its prefiguration, if it is a feasible thing at all, would be a work devoid of surprise and lacking in life.

Again, the idea of imitation is only partly viable as an explanation of the relationship of Thomas Mann's *Doktor Faustus* to the legend. In an interpretation of the novel, Birgit Nielsen writes of "Adrian Leverkühns Leben als bewußte mythische imitatio des Dr Faustus" (the title of her article). By calling the imitation a conscious act ("bewußt") she shifts the emphasis to the work's hero and avoids the more careless notion of authorial imitation. In one sense, Nielsen's study represents a milestone in work on *Doktor Faustus*. Unlike earlier critics, primarily concerned with examining the prefiguration in simple terms of identifiable allusions,[69] she introduces the more fundamental con-

[68] *op.cit.* p. 158.
[69] The most informative of these approaches are Geneviève Bianquis's "Thomas Mann et le 'Faustbuch' de 1587" and Gunilla Bergsten's *Thomas Manns "Doktor Faustus,"* pp. 55-60.

siderations of perspective and aesthetic function into her discussion. Leverkühn, she contends, consciously models his life on Faust's, rather in the way that Napoleon modeled himself on Charlemagne.[70] Nielsen proposes the imitation of a myth as something capable of accounting for the whole of the novel's plot. Echoing Mann's words in "Freud und die Zukunft," she argues that mythical imitation involves a complete identification with the model: "eine völlige Identifikation mit dem Vorbild."[71] Ignoring how this would vitiate a complete identification, she interprets the novel as an example of a single mythical imitation, although this is a novel absolutely bursting with prefigurations. And not only does the imitation theory distort by ignoring other prefigurations, it also offers too much hindsight knowledge about Leverkühn's early life to be helpful. Does Leverkühn really learn Hebrew and choose to study theology simply in order to follow his model, as is argued here?[72] I would suggest that the prefiguration is only helpful for the later parts of the novel, if one wants to see it as a mythical imitation. I find myself in agreement with Leslie Miller over this question. He asks when Leverkühn is likely to have recognized the pattern of his life and arrives at a point much later than the one suggested by Nielsen. The fulcrum of his argument is a remark of Zeitblom's:

Ich weiß nicht, wieweit Adrian damals etwas "merkte," ob er sofort oder erst allmählich, nachträglich und in erinnerndem Abstand, gewisse Verhältnisse, in eine andere, aber nicht ferne Tonart transponiert, wieder-

[70] It should be remembered that Napoleon, one of Mann's own illustrations of "mythical imitation," only stylized himself as Charlemagne for part of his political career.

[71] op.cit., p. 131.

[72] "Schon während seines letzten Schuljahrs lernt Adrian hebräisch, um sich auf ein theologisches Studium vorzubereiten. Hier müssen wir annehmen, daß er seine bewußte Faustnachfolge anfängt: Er fühlt den Gegensatz zwischen Musik-Magie und Theologie und wählt wie Doktor Faustus zunächst die Theologie" (op.cit., p. 139).

erkannte. Ich neige zu dem Glauben, daß ihm die Entdeckung zunächst unbewußt blieb, und daß sie ihm später erst, vielleicht im Traum, überraschend aufging.[73]

From this key passage, Miller deduces that it is "only later, alas, too late, when it is no longer possible to change the course of his life, he recognises the nature of his mythical identity."[74] Yet one important dimension is still missing from our appreciation of the correspondences between Faust's life and Leverkühn's. By failing to note that *two* perspectives are pertinent to a discussion of the parallels— first the reader's, and in this instance, only later Leverkühn's—one misses much of the dramatic irony in such a use of prefiguration. One cannot but paint a somewhat misleading picture of the novel, if one underrates the tension between the role of prefigurations within the plot and the aesthetic function of the device. It is really only for the later parts of *Doktor Faustus* that evidence can be produced showing that Leverkühn must be aware of the parallels between his life and Faust's and is even modeling his personality on the myth. From the point where Leverkühn's language corresponds in style to the Spies *Faustbuch*, and even includes quotations from it, the reader can no longer assume merely coincidental similarities. Both Nielsen and Bergsten give a great deal of documentation to these parallels in language and direct quotation,[75] without seeing them as the fundamental turning-point where the reader's

---

[73] *Doktor Faustus*, p. 273. "I do not know how far Adrian took notice at that time; or whether it was only afterwards, gradually and from memory, that he recognized certain correspondences, transposed, as it were, into another but not far removed key. I incline to the belief that the discovery at first remained unconscious and only later, perhaps as in a dream, came to him as a surprise" (*Doctor Faustus: The Life of the German Composer Adrian Leverkühn, as told by A Friend*, trans. H. T. Lowe-Porter, London, 1959, pp. 204-205).

[74] "Myth and Morality: Reflections on Mann's *Doktor Faustus*," p. 210.

[75] Nielsen, pp. 142ff.; Bergsten, pp. 55-60.

awareness of the Faust analogy must be shared by the hero.

A more revealing approach than the interpretation of mythological parallels with exclusive reference to the hero's perspective and within the context of the plot, is to ask how the two perspectives, the reader's and the fictive character's, relate to one another. There are far more complicated issues than simply deciding when imitation begins or if it does. As Bruce Morrissette has shown, the question of perspective becomes quite involved in the case of Alain Robbe-Grillet's *Les Gommes*:

> One question of theoretical difficulty arising in *Les Gommes* is the following: if, in the novel, everything is seen or described from some particular character's viewpoint, how can such hidden allusions as those to the Oedipus myth . . . be communicated to the reader, if all the characters remain ignorant thereof? More importantly, how can such "metafictional" elements be tolerated at all? The answer must lie close to the basic paradox of all fiction. Reflection will show that the universe "observed" by the characters cannot be their own creation, in any real sense, but must emanate from the novelist . . . he can therefore hide or reveal, at will, features recognizable by the reader but not by the characters.[76]

To show just how this can be done takes one a long way beyond quantitative allusion-spotting, of course. The leading questions are matters of perspective: at what point (if at all) does the character notice parallels to the prefiguration? At what juncture, through the title or later, does the reader become aware of the motif, how ambiguous is the model, even when it has been transmitted to the reader, does the reader spot the prefiguration before the fictive character or do they share the experience? The common denominator of all these questions is their relevance to the

[76] "The Evolution of Narrative Viewpoint in Robbe-Grillet," *Novel*, I, 1967, p. 26.

aesthetic function of the prefiguration—how it affects our reading of the novel. It is primarily, although not always solely, from the reader's perspective that the device is to be understood. Plot motivations may be of partial relevance, but this is only the case with some novels. In fact, only five or six of the works mentioned in this study can be explained by such theories as imitation.

The novel's "main structural feature," as Malcolm Bradbury has reminded us, "lies in a developing action."[77] Mythological works develop their motifs, and a failure to account for this process is one of the shortcomings of many interpretations. (It is, however, this quality of development, above all, which clears many mythological novels of the charge of paradigmatic simplification so often leveled at them.) Development means change of attitude, shift of emphasis and a focus on a different part of the prefiguration. Hence, prefiguration becomes a kind of unraveling commentary. It is this function of the pattern which Joseph Warren Beach forgets in his analysis of *Ulysses*: "The point of this juxtaposition of contemporary Irish futilities with heroic Greek adventure is obviously the ironic exposure of contemporary Irish futilities. But never does Joyce interpose to make his point."[78] Joyce does not need to, the pattern does this for him; instead of interposing, he juxtaposes. The motif remains essentially one of the means at the author's disposal of commenting on his characters, of introducing important questions in the reader's mind about the direction the plot is taking and giving further levels of significance and complexity to the modern theme. "Though the author can to some extent choose his disguises," Wayne Booth observes, "he can never choose to disappear."[79] Nevertheless, these

---

[77] "Towards a Poetics of Fiction," *Novel*, I, Fall 1967, p. 52.
[78] *The Twentieth-Century Novel*, New York, 1932, p. 420.
[79] *The Rhetoric of Fiction*, Chicago and London, 1963, p. 20.

motifs, and most other prefigurations, offer him one kind of mask. Some readers may feel that it is a very false, histrionic mask to don in a modern novel, but this would not be an unmitigated condemnation. As Wayne Booth points out, we live in an era of circumlocution: "many of the symbols employed in modern fiction as a substitute for commentary are fully as obtrusive as the most direct commentary might be."[80] And one only has to look at Moravia's Molteni, in *Il disprezzo*, and Mann's Joseph to realize that the histrionics of the technique may in fact be a mirror of the characters involved.

Mythology as a Structural Principle

The charge that a sense of development in the novel is neglected applies not only to many analyses of the relationship between modern character and prefiguration, but also to the prevalent idea that mythological motifs are really used as a system for organizing the material of fiction. Theories of mythopoeic structure have tended to treat the novel as if it were a static entity and thereby failed to note the very real structuring properties of the myths employed.

The feeling that a mythological pattern offers a rigid structural aid, somewhat like the preparatory network of lines used by some painters, is encouraged particularly frequently by novels with an extended sequence of correspondences, such as one finds in *The Centaur, Doktor Faustus* or *Ulysses*. It was in fact *Ulysses* that gave rise to some of the most influential remarks on this subject in T. S. Eliot's essay on "Ulysses, Order and Myth":

> In using myth, in manipulating a continuous parallel between contemporaneity and antiquity, Mr. Joyce is pursuing a method which others must pursue after him. They will not be imitators, any more than the scientist who uses the discoveries of an Einstein in pursu-

[80] *op.cit.*, p. 197.

ing his own, independent, further investigations. It is simply a way of controlling, of ordering, of giving shape and significance to the immense panorama of futility and anarchy which is contemporary history. . . .[81]

It is, I seriously believe, a step toward making the modern world possible for art . . . toward order and form.[82]

Ezra Pound talks in like manner of Joyce's Homeric correspondences as "a scaffold, a means of construction"[83] and critics have made the same point about other works. Malcolm Bradbury has suggested that "the myth of Mars, Venus and Vulcan is used as a kind of scaffolding" in Iris Murdoch's *Under the Net*.[84] For Northrop Frye "the use of myth in Joyce and Cocteau, like the use of folk tale in Mann, is parallel to the use of abstraction and other means of emphasizing design in contemporary painting."[85] In their discussions of Thomas Mann's *Der Tod in Venedig*, both Isadore Traschen[86] and Hans-Bernard Moeller[87] quote Eliot's remarks about the use of myths as a structural device in *Ulysses* and proceed to argue that Joyce was not the first to do this, that Mann had used the same structural aid eleven years earlier.[88]

Such statements often leave unclear whether the structural aid is more important to the novelist during the act of creation or subsequently to the reader. In the following two statements—the first about his own work, the second about

---

[81] *op.cit.*, p. 201.   [82] *op.cit.*, p. 202.
[83] *Literary Essays*, ed. T. S. Eliot, London, 1954, p. 406.
[84] "Iris Murdoch's *Under the Net*," p. 49.
[85] *Fables of Identity*, p. 31.
[86] "The Use of Myth in *Death in Venice*," pp. 166ff.
[87] "Thomas Manns venezianische Götterkunde," pp. 184ff.
[88] Both Traschen and Moeller miss the point that, although *Ulysses* and *Der Tod in Venedig* are mythological works, their motif-structures differ considerably. While Mann's *Novelle* incorporates a fragmentary series of mythological references, none of these spans the action in the way that the Homeric correspondences do in *Ulysses*.

Joyce's—Anthony Burgess is more concerned with genesis than with final aesthetic ends. He talks of the Homeric parallels in his novel *A Vision of Battlements* as "a tyro's method of giving the story a backbone . . . a device for taming the Rock [Gibraltar, where his novel is set] by enclosing it in myth."[89] And in his introduction to *A Shorter "Finnegans Wake,"* Burgess writes: "What Joyce found in Vico was what every novelist needs when planning a long book—a scaffolding, a backbone."[90] Harry Levin even pronounces quite categorically his belief that the Homeric framework of *Ulysses* is "more important to Joyce than it could possibly be to any reader."[91] Yet if the mythological motif's structuring powers are to be of valid concern to literary criticism, our main interest must lie with the function of the device from the reader's perspective. It is doubtful whether any device which was of great assistance to the novelist will be of no interest at all to the reader. The matter is a question of degree, as Harry Levin suggests. In the case of *Ulysses,* for instance, David Wykes has argued that one can "draw a careful distinction between the correspondences which are critically useful to the reader and those which were chiefly of use to Joyce."[92] Certainly, what might be called the "scaffold theory" is in need of modification. S. L. Goldberg has some useful remarks on this subject in *The Classical Temper,* where he rejects:

> the belief that the structure of the book is modelled on that of the *Odyssey* or of some other myth. The truth is, of course, that the structure of *Ulysses,* like that of most great books, grows by an inner necessity, and is no more a re-enactment of the *Odyssey* . . . than it is a fictionalized guide to Dublin. A serious artist would waste his time as little on the one project as on the other.[93]

[89] *A Vision of Battlements*, p. 8. [90] *op.cit.*, p. 9.
[91] *James Joyce: A Critical Introduction*, Norfolk, Conn., 1941, p. 53.
[92] "The *Odyssey* in *Ulysses*," p. 305. [93] *op.cit.*, p. 201.

And if this observation is true of such a highly organized work as *Ulysses*, it is even truer of most other mythological novels.

Without doubt, Goldberg is right to object that the Homeric motif is not *the* structural principle of the novel. In this overgeneralized sense, none of the above statements about *Der Tod in Venedig, A Vision of Battlements, Finnegans Wake* or *Ulysses* can be acceptable. Yet Goldberg manages to throw out his baby with the bath water. Although not the sole structural principle informing the novels in question—it is doubtful whether there is ever just one structural pattern governing any work of fiction—the motifs still exercize a structuring influence in a more liberal sense. The idea of structuring, usually expressed in too simple a form, needs to be modified rather than rejected out of hand. When Eliot advocates "making the modern world possible for art" and Burgess talks of "taming" his wartime experiences, it would be too easy to dismiss this as part of an all too familiar rhetoric of crisis or as irrelevant self-indulgence in justifying the choice of a motif. On the other hand, most of the novelists in question have successfully managed without myths in other works,[94] so there is no cause to be overgenerous in assessing these comments. Rather, one should try to find a way between these two positions.

Instead of static metaphors, evoking "scaffolds," "molds" or "frameworks," one must allow for more protean notions of structure, adequate to the constantly changing shapes and patterns these novels generate. The models offered in the next two chapters are put forward with three aims in mind: to consider with what means a modern novel can

[94] Mann in *Buddenbrooks* and *Königliche Hoheit*, Burgess with his novels about Mr. Enderby, and Joyce in *Dubliners*. Indeed, Burgess is the only one of the three for whom this appears to be a "tyro's method."

effectively introduce classical material in order to pattern our reading of the work; to highlight the function of prefigurative motifs as part of a constantly developing continuum; and to examine what relationship can be found between the kind of pattern chosen and the effect this has upon the narrative. In pursuing these lines of investigation, I shall be considering a narrative situation which was nicely characterized in a piece of dialogue from Samuel Delaney's *The Einstein Intersection*:

> "You may be Orpheus; you may be someone else, who dares death and succeeds. . . . The stories give you a law to follow."
> "—that you can either break or obey."
> "They set you a goal—"
> "and you can either fail that goal, succeed, or surpass it."[95]

While such a set of open possibilities includes the option of imitation, this is only as one thread in a much more complex pattern.

[95] *op.cit.*, pp. 135-136.

Chapter Four

The Unilinear Pattern of Development

Establishing a Prefiguration

"The novel had to be fairly long, since a pattern had to be established; and for that you need a considerable number of variations. . . . As soon as the pattern emerges, the novel, as written, ceases to exist."[1] The novel in question is Max Frisch's *Mein Name sei Gantenbein*,[2] a work which includes a Hermes motif and also uses Philemon and Baucis as prefigurations. What Frisch says here about variations and a final pattern is of more general import; to see how, the relationship between myths and patterns has to be looked at in some detail.

A pattern is something which both genuine myths and mythological motifs share. "To become a myth a man must complete a pattern," according to the hero of Michael Ayrton's *The Testament of Daedalus*.[3] The kind of simple pattern, a configuration of events or characteristics, which motifs and myths have in common is archetypal. However, the patterns to be considered in this and the next chapter, although they are the products of such designs, are both more complex and more related to the intrinsic study of literature than the archetypes which Maud Bodkin and others have traced. Motif-patterns are more complex be-

[1] The statement comes from a radio interview for the Deutschlandfunk broadcast on 8 November 1964, quoted by U. Weisstein, *Max Frisch*, New York, 1967, p. 84.
[2] The novel came out in 1964 and appeared in translation as *A Wilderness of Mirrors* in 1965.
[3] London, 1962, p. 56.

118

cause they refer the reader not only to the archetypal patterns in the novel's plot when it is actualized, but because they are presented in such a way as to generate in the reader patterns of hypothesis, conjectures and illusions concerning what is going to happen to the fictive characters.

Since the novel is a serial form of art in which the order of events is of crucial concern, a unilinear model would seem to be the best one with which to approach the subject of establishing a motif. Substantial references to the myth used are invariably presented to us before the main part of the work. The usual development of motifs in this type of fiction consists of the initial establishment of a highly ambiguous prefiguration, activating in its turn an extensive set of expectations about the course the plot is likely to take, and thereafter the gradual offering of additional pieces of less ambiguous information until, as Frisch puts it, "the pattern emerges." As a result of this technique, the reader's expectations about what can possibly happen later in the work, if the prefiguration is further adhered to,[4] gradually diminish in number as the work progresses. In this sense, the novel "ceases to exist" in the end, because the range of permutations has been exhausted. Although most motifs begin at an early point in the narrative, thereby raising certain questions about how closely the novel will adhere to the familiar myth's archetypal pattern, some works have what might be called a "delayed action" prefiguration. The retroactive kind emerges late on in the narrative and invites the reader to reexamine the plot in the light of the analogy which then obtains for it. This occurs, for instance, in Rainer Maria Rilke's *Die Aufzeichnungen des Malte Laurids Brigge*[5] where the tale of the Prodigal Son is intro-

[4] Viewed in terms of information theory, this is the path between "repertoire" and "realization."

[5] See Theodore Ziolkowski's reading of Rilke's novel in the first chapter of his *Dimensions of the Modern Novel: German Texts and European Contexts*, Princeton, 1969, pp. 3-36.

duced right at the end of the novel, and we can then reconsider the whole of the work in the light of this analogy. In other works—for example, Michel Butor's *L'Emploi du Temps*, or Heinrich Mann's *Die Göttinnen*—the motif is introduced about halfway through, with comparable effects. But generally, motifs appear to be established early on in the narrative.

This chapter will be mainly concerned with the way in which mythological motifs can be introduced, particularly with the functional order in which information of such a symbolic kind can be conveyed to the reader. Admittedly, a typology of techniques in terms of sequence of appearance can only be an approximate approach, since a number of devices (mythological similes, metaphors and quotations) could appear at almost any point in a novel. But in general, despite such anomalies, the model adopted seeks to emphasize the importance of placing an allusion at the right spot; a prefiguration achieves most effect if put in an ambiguous position and then gradually clarified. Therefore one needs to place less stress on the traditional method of asking what devices are used to signal a motif, and to enquire how the degree of engendered ambiguity, or (at times) clarity, relates to the position of a cue in the context of the plot's development. Location is as important as type of allusion, when it comes to establishing a mythological motif.

The title is the first point in his work at which a novelist can introduce a mythological motif. Almost all mythological novels with such titles refer again to the title-figure, following up the first allusion with an extended motif. Principally, the role of the title is to create an awareness that the motif is to come, it is not there to establish a prefiguration once and for all. To take a familiar illustration: the title *Doktor Faustus* alerts the reader to certain similarities between Adrian Leverkühn's life and the story of Faustus, but gives away little of the plot. The reader still cannot guess whether this Faust-like figure will be eventually redeemed or eternally damned, whether he will prove to be Faustian as an alchemist (in some trendy version of occultism) or Faustian in his demands as a lover, whether he will emerge as an updated Romantic hero or as a modern anti-hero. Nevertheless, sets of expectations stemming from such simple possibilities are put into play, and these can only be exploited for ambiguous potential, provided that too much information is not given away early on in the narrative.

In the first chapter of Mann's novel, the impetuous narrator Zeitblom alludes to the Faust prefiguration given in the title with a reference to "die Ausübung eines gräßlichen Kaufvertrages."[6] Like the title, his comment hides as much as it reveals; for the least one can expect of a Faust-like figure is that he contract a pact of some kind. At this point, one cannot be too sure whether the pact will be tacit, as it is in a novel like Mikhail Bulgakov's *The Master and Margarita*,[7] or a ritual one as it is in James Blish's *Black Easter*. Eventually, it turns out to be quite a solemn affair bordering on ritual, even if Ronald Gray rightly misses the ceremonious handshake.[8] Similarly, one does not know whether "horrible" ("gräßlich") is a transferred epithet pointing to the outcome of the whole novel or referring strictly to the pact itself. When one later discovers the nature of the blood pact—deliberately contracted venereal disease—the question is left open once more. Had the vehicle of the pact itself not been so ugly, the adjective would certainly have alluded to the outcome of the work and a number of permutations could have been quickly excluded. Now it can still

[6] *Doktor Faustus*, p. 11; "the issue of a horrible bargain" (Lowe-Porter translation, London, 1959, p. 4).
[7] For details, see Elisabeth Stenbock-Fermor's "Bulgakov's *The Master and Margarita* and Goethe's *Faust*."
[8] *The German Tradition in Literature 1871-1945*, Cambridge, 1965, p. 212.

refer to both, or just to the pact, for all we know at this juncture in the narrative; such is the strength of a motif handled in this way. Subsequently, a large number of references to the Faust legend occur, all to some extent playing with the reader's expectations until the final parallels between Mann's plot and the Faust story emerge and the novel "ceases to exist" (in Frisch's sense).

Mann talks of his novel as being almost mathematically composed ("durchkomponiert"), with the prefigurations occurring in the well-worked-out manner that we associate with the leitmotif. Although *Doktor Faustus* is an extreme instance, it does illustrate, nevertheless, a feature common to most mythological works: a persistent interweaving of theme and motif.[9] Prefigurative titles have in fact occurred in fiction before the twentieth century, but without being elaborated into a motif-pattern.

In giving the title *Hyperion* to a novel, Friedrich Hölderlin suggests a prefiguration for the hero, but little is made in this work of the tales and legends specifically connected with the god, associating him with Theia and their offspring. The fact that Jean Paul should choose to entitle a novel *Titan*, rather than employ a particular Titanic deity as symbol, again indicates the vaguely evocative quality of such images in Romantic fiction. Later in the nineteenth century, in a period devoted to the less mythopoeic aims of Realism and Naturalism, we find a number of works with symbolic titles: including Keller's *Romeo und Julia auf dem Dorfe*, Leskov's *Lady Macbeth of Mtsensk*, Turgenev's *A King Lear of the Steppe* and the *Novelle, Papa Hamlet*, published by Johannes Schlaf and Arno Holz under the

---

[9] These are in themselves ambiguous terms; see Eugene H. Falk, *Types of Thematic Structure: The Nature and Function of Motifs in Gide, Camus and Sartre*, Chicago and London, 1967. For my purposes a narrower definition will suffice: the theme will be understood to mean the contemporary events of the plot; the motif will designate the system of references to the prefiguration.

pseudonym Barne P. Holmsen. The use of Shakespearean allusions can be seen as something of a compromise in prefigurative symbolism. The Realists and Naturalists would hardly have wished to use myths and legends in their works; but Shakespeare's dramas offer a different kind of mythology, which can be used in much the same way. With the exception of *Papa Hamlet*, these works make further concessions to realism in restricting the Shakespearean allusions to their first and last few pages. The prefiguration remains a loose kind of framework which comments on the plot without intruding into it. Keller, for example, begins his tale thus:

> Diese Geschichte zu erzählen, würde eine müßige Nachahmung sein, wenn sie nicht auf einem wirklichen Vorfall beruhte, zum Beweise, wie tief im Menschenleben jede jener Fabeln wurzelt, auf welche die großen alten Werke gebaut sind. Die Zahl solcher Fabeln ist mäßig; aber stets treten sie im neuen Gewande wieder in die Erscheinung und zwingen alsdann die Hand, sie festzuhalten.[10]

Henceforth, it is left entirely to the reader to note the parallels between Keller's tale and *Romeo and Juliet*. There are no further allusions to establish a concentrated motif-pattern.

In this century, a large number of novels have used a title to draw attention to the motif-pattern that is to come. And in these cases, the motif has generally been pursued more rigorously. Many merely cite the name of a prefiguration: *Trepleff*, *Ulysses*, *The Centaur*. Others name the prefiguration, but include a further qualification: *Le Vol d'Icare*,

---

[10] *Sämtliche Werke*, vi. *Die Leute von Seldwyla: Erzählungen*, Berlin, 1958, p. 69. "To tell this story would be a useless imitation, if it did not stem from a real occurrence, which shows how deeply rooted in people's lives is each of those stories upon which the great works of old are built. The number of such stories is limited; but again and again they reappear in a new guise and force the writer's hand to record them."

Forget not Ariadne, Proserpina: *Eine Kindheitsmythe,* or *Cassandra at the Wedding.* Others have a double title reminiscent of those in Baroque dramas and novels: *Hamlet oder Die lange Nacht nimmt ein Ende* or *Triptychon des Teufels—Ein Buch von dem Haß, dem Börsenspiel und der Unzucht: Mars, Merkur, Venus.* This extended, symbiotic type of title emphasizes the author's intention of combining, but not identifying, myth and modernity. But the function of the title has seldom been considered. Indeed, as Eberhard Lämmert has pointed out, theories of fiction have tended to consider those devices which comment retrospectively on the action rather than those which point forward to what has yet to happen in the work.[11]

In an account of the effect Aeschylus' *Agamemnon* would have on its audience, Michael Grant notes that, due to a pre-knowledge of the pattern of events, the Greek audience is "by . . . dramatic irony linked with the myth that is working itself out"[12]—linked with the myth, that is, but not so much with the individual characters. A certain distance is also set between character and reader in prefigurative fiction, since the latter is often continuously aware of the mythological precedent for what is happening. Such vital information is seldom possessed by the hero from the outset, if at all. Aesthetic distance is achieved by means of prefigurative signals to the reader, but it is not the kind of distance that Brecht once ascribed to the use of captions on the stage of the modern epic theatre.[13] For one reason, myths, like oracles, seldom speak unequivocally. An initial indication that the Faust myth is relevant to a novel only raises the kind of questions outlined above. Furthermore,

[11] *Bauformen des Erzählens*, Stuttgart, 1955, p. 272.
[12] *Myths of the Greeks and Romans*, p. 182.
[13] In the section "Titeln und Tafeln" (*Schriften zum Theater*, Frankfurt a.M., 1957, pp. 30f.), Brecht describes a situation where the audience knows in advance *what* is going to happen in a scene and can therefore concentrate on *how* it comes about.

the relationship between the theme and motif can be very loose indeed in some works. The reader may make many conjectures about the feasible course and outcome of the plot, therefore. The difference between four modern Faust novels, such as *Bystander*, *Doktor Faustus*, *The Master and Margarita* and *Black Easter*, bears ample witness to the potential of the motif.

The central figure in Michel Butor's *L'Emploi du Temps* is also put in an ambiguous light. He would have to desert his Ariadne deliberately at the end of the tale, if the Theseus myth were as closely followed as some readers might be expecting it to be earlier on. Instead, we find him admitting eventually: "Toute une figure s'est achevée dans cette exclusion de moi-même."[14]

If the mythological model is not an unequivocal anticipation of the novel's plot and if such titles do not achieve a degree of distance by alienation in the way Brechtian captions do, how do they affect our attitude to the characters? They do this, I would suggest, by turning the plot of the novel into a kind of game. The reader is invited to speculate whether or not the rules of the game (the patterns set by the prefiguration) are going to be respected.[15] Being concerned with these supra-personal questions, the reader will be distanced to a large extent from the individuals in the work.

There are, in contrast, some novels with prefigurations

[14] *L'Emploi du Temps*, p. 258.
[15] When games themselves are used as prefigurations, they have a disturbingly dehumanizing effect: characters are reduced to the role of mechanical components, figures on a chessboard (Nabokov's *The Defence*), acting in the sequence of a card game (the same author's *King, Queen, Knave*) or automata according to some other set of rules (Cortázar's *Hop-scotch* or Hesse's *Das Glasperlenspiel*). The mythological motif, though it shares certain qualities with these devices, does not dehumanize so radically. On this subject, see Strothar B. Purdy's "*Solus Rex*: Nabokov and the Chess Novel," *MFS*, XIV, 1968, pp. 379-395, and the second half of my "Myths and Patterns in the Modern Novel."

where we share the hero's perspective and where it would destroy the dramatic effect of this parity of vision, if the title revealed something that the protagonist has not yet realized. In Alberto Moravia's *Il disprezzo*, it is not until the eighth chapter (about a third of the way through the novel) that the hero, Molteni, realizes that there is an appropriate prefiguration for his wife's contempt ("disprezzo") for him. It is only when he starts working on a film version of the *Odyssey* with a co-scriptwriter, Rheingold, that the analogy appears: "il pensiero di Emilia mi disturbava e ancor di più la strana rassomiglianza dell'interpretazione omerica di Rheingold ai miei fatti personali."[16] The ironic quality to certain earlier passages in the novel is only realized after the Homeric parallel has been introduced. For example, this adds a dimension to Molteni's awareness that he is "ricalcando le orme di tutti i mariti non amati dalla propria moglie."[17] Even an earlier description of the role of the scriptwriter takes on a note of irony when it is realized how close this is to the prefigurative role of Ulysses: "Lo sceneggiatore, dunque, è l'uomo che rimane sempre nell'ombra; che si svena del suo miglior sangue per il successo di altri. . . ."[18] By not mentioning his prefiguration in the title of the novel and by maintaining a first-person perspective through this character who lacks insight, Moravia allows the irony of these comments to be revealed

[16] *op.cit.*, p. 96. In Angus Davidson's translation of the novel (*A Ghost at Noon*, Harmondsworth, 1964, p. 79), the passage reads: "the thought of Emilia upset me and, even more, the strange resemblance between Rheingold's interpretation of Homer and my own personal affairs."

[17] *op.cit.*, p. 60; "following in the footsteps of all husbands who are not loved by their wives" (*A Ghost at Noon*, p. 48).

[18] *op.cit.*, p. 41. "The script-writer, in short, is the man who remains always in the background, who expends the best of his blood for the success of others . . ." (*A Ghost at Noon*, p. 34). For a discussion of dramatic irony and the relationship between love and artistic creation in *Il disprezzo*—both important aspects of this passage—see Donald Heiney, *Three Italian Novelists: Moravia, Pavese, Vittorini*, Ann Arbor, 1968, pp. 51-58.

retrospectively to the reader only. The same retrospective prefigurative pattern is to be found in Michel Butor's *L'Emploi du Temps*, Alain Robbe-Grillet's *Les Gommes* and Hans Erich Nossack's *Spätestens im November*. However, the fact that the majority of mythological novels favor revelatory titles or other early signals results in a certain degree of either comic or foreboding distance between reader and hero. An appropriate emblem for most novels of this kind would be the sword of Damocles. Indeed, some literary characters are very much aware of the note of fatalism which the classical analogy also introduces. In Alfred Döblin's *Berlin Alexanderplatz*, one of the minor figures refers to the Greek world from which the novel's Orestes motif is drawn and rhetorically rejects its fatalistic *Weltanschauung*: "Man soll sich nicht dicketun mit seinem Schicksal. Ich bin Gegner des Fatums. Ich bin kein Grieche, ich bin Berliner."[19] Yet producing this contrast so early in the novel, Döblin invites the reader to see the rest of the action in such polarized terms: Athenians/"Spreeathener" (a nickname for Berliners), Orestes/Biberkopf, fatalism/free will. Just as traditional tragedy was often in a sense prefigured by some oracular pronouncement delivered early in the proceedings, many mythological novels have a title which evokes a similar inexorability.

Even the title is not without its peculiarities and problems as a prefigurative technique. Wayne Booth observes in *The Rhetoric of Fiction* that "it is interesting to note how much more importance titles and epigraphs take on in modern works, where they are often the only explicit commentary the reader is given."[20] They in fact remain the most direct narrative device the modern author can choose to

[19] *op.cit.*, p. 40. In Eugene Jolas's translation (*Alexanderplatz: The Story of Franz Biberkopf*, London, 1931, p. 47), the passage runs: "We shouldn't brag about our fate. I'm an enemy of Destiny, I'm not a Greek. I'm a Berliner."

[20] *op.cit.*, p. 198.

127

trigger off a prefigurative pattern. The problem is that we are accustomed to associate titles with main themes and may be unable to see the modern use of prefigurative (i.e. motif-oriented) titles in the right perspective.

Hermann Broch's last novel *Der Versucher* illustrates a problem which can arise in the case of titles: the kind of misinterpretation found earlier in E. M. Butler's reading of *Doktor Faustus*. The novel was edited by Felix Stössinger in 1953, two years after the author's death, and given the controversial title it now bears. There is nevertheless some reason for believing that Broch might have entitled the novel "Demeter oder die Verzauberung,"[21] although a new critical edition has now appeared under another tentative title: *Bergroman*.[22]

Since 1953 much effort has been expended by scholars trying to argue either for or against various titles on internal evidence alone. Nearly all have employed the concept of an "appropriate" title, reasoning that this would ideally concentrate attention on the main theme of the work. In fact, titles may contain direct statements of subject-matter or be apparently inappropriate. As Booth observes, they can operate at an unexpected level of sig-

[21] Broch referred to the novel at various times by a number of different titles and descriptions: "Bergroman," "religiöser Roman," "Bauernroman," "Demeter," "Demeter oder die Verzauberung," "Ein Jahr Gebirgseinsamkeit" and "Der Wanderer." Any of these descriptions could have become a title; after all, Broch originally intended to call *Die Schlafwandler* by the generic title "Historischer Roman" (*Briefe*, Zürich, 1957, p. 13). Critical opinion is very much divided on the merits of various titles. Schoolfield, Kahler, Koebner and Durzak support the Demeter title. On the other hand, Binde, one of the editors of Broch's collected works, has informed me (letter, 8 May 1966) that he hopes to demonstrate from unpublished evidence that the proposed title "Demeter oder die Verzauberung" was not intended for the final work. With Stössinger, he favors the present title. Hannah Arendt, in turn, advocates the title "Der Wanderer," which was proposed for the projected trilogy, of which the present novel represents only an unfinished first draft.

[22] *Bergroman: Drei Originalfassungen*, ed. F. Kress and H. A. Maier, Frankfurt a.M., 1969.

nificance or reveal the novel's subject-matter from a fresh (possibly mythological) perspective. To take a pair of illustrations from secondary literature, for a change: Wladimir Weidlé once wrote a book on modern literature entitled *Les Abeilles d'Aristée*, and Edmund Wilson set the mythological archetype for one of his critical works with the title *The Wound and the Bow*. It would be foolish to suggest that Wilson's title is more valid than Weidlé's, simply because the Philoctetes image is expounded at length in *The Wound and the Bow*[23] whereas the Aristaeus myth is never considered in Weidlé's book. To correlate the measure of appropriateness with the degree of explicitness makes little sense here, or in the case of the modern novel. With the title *Der Versucher*, Broch's novel is one kind of work; it would be a different, more explicitly mythological novel with the title "Demeter oder die Verzauberung." To argue, as Stössinger does in his epilogue to the novel, that the Demeter title was mythologically untenable, or to suggest conversely that the title is more relevant to Broch's plans than the one chosen by Stössinger,[24] is to miss an essential point about the way in which titles frequently operate in modern fiction. One cannot presume the mythological title is necessarily an indication of theme rather than motif. In Jean Giono's *Naissance de l'Odyssée* and Georg Britting's *Lebenslauf eines dicken Mannes, der Hamlet hieß*, it is; in Alfred Döblin's *Hamlet oder Die lange Nacht nimmt ein Ende* and James Joyce's *Ulysses*, it is not. If titles should refer to themes rather than motifs, one might well concede that the sub-title of *Doktor Faustus—Das Leben des*

[23] "Philoctetes: The Wound and the Bow," *op.cit.*, London, 1961, pp. 241-264.

[24] "mythologisch nicht haltbar," Stössinger, "Nachwort" to *Der Versucher*, p. 666; "treffender im Broch'schen Sinn . . . als der von Stössinger gewählte," Liselotte von Borcke, *Das Romanwerk Hermann Brochs: Eine systematische Untersuchung seiner Aussage*, diss., Bonn, 1957, p. 47.

deutschen Tonsetzers Adrian Leverkühn, erzählt von einem Freunde—is more "appropriate" to the novel than its main title. To do this would not only be perverse; it would also obviate serious consideration of why titles often tend to be tangential. With mythological works, the obliquity becomes quite important: the actual relationship between the character mentioned in the title and the hero of the novel is revealed gradually, if at all. Questions are left open, to maximum effect.

To perform this function, the title generally remains direct and unmistakable as the alert-signal of what is to come. It names the myth involved and only seldom alludes to it less openly. Janice Elliot's *The Singing Head* and Hans Erich Nossack's *Nekyia* are two exceptions to this generalization. With these, the reader may not discover immediately that in both titles veiled references are being made to Greek mythology, but he will at least be aware that something beyond any immediate, realistic milieu is being implied. And so curiosity and expectations must even here be aroused to some extent.

Malcolm Bradbury's interpretation of Iris Murdoch's *Under the Net* as a modern version of the myth about Hephaestos ensnaring his wife Aphrodite and her lover Ares in a net[25] assumes that the net referred to in the novel's title is the one used in the ruse. This reading of the title has been denied by Iris Murdoch because it was not intended,[26] yet what proves of interest to us here, apart from the academic question of whether or not a particular myth was presaged by the title *Under the Net*, is the general observation that an obscure mythological title of this kind would defeat its purpose as signal.

[25] "Iris Murdoch's *Under the Net*," *Critical Quarterly*, IV, 1962, pp. 47-54.

[26] Iris Murdoch has since claimed that the net image is borrowed from Wittgenstein's *Tractatus logico-philosophicus*; see A. S. Byatt's *Degrees of Freedom: The Novels of Iris Murdoch*, London, 1965, p. 14.

The other method by which a novelist can introduce his chosen prefiguration before the novel proper begins is to preface his work with a literary quotation. The passage that precedes Thomas Mann's *Doktor Faustus* forms an integral part of the work by hinting at the implications of the pact to come:

> Lo giorno se n'andava, e l'aer bruno
> toglieva gli animai che sono in terra
> dalle fatiche loro, ed io sol uno
> m'apparecchiava a sostener la guerra
> sì del cammino e sì della pietate,
> che ritrarrà la mente che non erra.
> O Muse, o alto ingegno, or m'aiutate,
> o mente che scrivesti ciò ch'io vidi,
> qui si parrà la tua nobilitate.[27]

The average German reader cannot necessarily be expected to understand these lines. However, the reference that Mann then assigns to them—DANTE, INFERNO, II. GESANG—it self acts as prefiguration enough. The reader needs little more than a mention of the inferno in conjunction with the title *Doktor Faustus* to activate his imagination. Then, the uncomprehended passage acquires for him the same daemonic quality that Leverkühn's other-worldliness has for Zeitblom.

"'Le temps, qui veille à tout, a donné la solution malgré toi' (Sophocle)." This quotation prefacing Alain Robbe-Grillet's *Les Gommes*, although in French and hence at least immediately comprehensible to his reader, has a similarly dark allusiveness that only becomes fully realized when one has read the whole novel. This proves to be more than an apposite quotation from Sophocles embroidering a work,

---

[27] "The sun sank; the night darkened and brought to all the creatures of the earth, after their day's burden, peace; only I alone armed myself for the difficult battle, that of the journey as well as that of pity, which my memory shall reproduce faithfully. O Muses, help me; help me, lofty spirit, memory, who writes what I have seen, here you will reveal your nobility."

for the novel in fact operates with the Oedipus prefiguration. And this indirect kind of reference is a common occurrence in quotations setting a motif-pattern.[28] Whereas the mythological title tends to offer a more direct kind of symbolism, usually recognizable at first glance, and clearly signaling a precedent for what is happening, the prefatory quotation can often remain vague and only be fully appreciated later. This is hardly surprising, for quotations preceding many works are little more than arabesques and we do not read them with the same seriousness as a title, so the author adapts his approach accordingly.

The novelist may also use mythological chapter headings for comparable effects. When James Joyce removed such captions from the final version of *Ulysses*, he deprived English fiction of one of its few examples of this technique.[29] In German literature, on the other hand, there are numerous instances of the technique, perhaps a reflection of an urge to systematize and label. Headings such as "Kain," "Jakobs Kampf," "Frau Eva" (all in Hesse's *Demian*) and "Steinerner Gast" (in Broch's *Die Schuldlosen*) function in much the same way as book titles do. However, a greater amount of variation can be achieved with this device, as can be seen

---

[28] Other examples include: the quotation preceding Anthony Burgess's *The Eve of Saint Venus* ("'Cras amet qui nunquam amavit/quique amavit cras amet . . .' Pervigilium Veneris"); the quotation from *Faust* prefacing Mikhail Bulgakov's *The Master and Margarita* ("Say at last—who art thou?"/"That power I serve/Which wills forever evil/Yet does forever good"); and the passage from Shakespeare's *The Winter's Tale* (III, 3, 1-4) affixed to Franz Fühmann's "Böhmen am Meer": "Bist du gewiß, daß unser Schiff gelandet/An Böhmens Wüstenei'n?"/"Ja, Herr, doch fürcht'ich,/Zur schlimmen Stunde: düster wird die Luft/Und droht mit bald'gem Sturm" (*König Ödipus: Gesammelte Erzählungen*, Berlin and Weimar, 1968, p. 366).

[29] Originally the chapters were to have been headed: Telemachus, Nestor, Proteus, Calypso, The Lotus-Eaters, Hades, Aeolus, Lestrygonians, Scylla and Charybdis, Wandering Rocks, Sirens, Cyclops, Nausicaa, Oxen of the Sun, Circe, Eumaeus, Ithaca, and Penelope. See Stuart Gilbert, *op.cit.*, p. 30.

from Alfred Döblin's *Hamlet oder Die lange Nacht nimmt ein Ende.* Because there are so many different kinds of chapter title in Döblin's novel, we cannot rely on any pattern of precedent. "Szenen aus der Unterwelt," "Pluto und Proserpina" and "Wie Pluto Proserpina raubte" are, despite their apparent similarity, three entirely different types of heading.[30] The first gives a title to the story of Pluto and Proserpina told at an evening gathering. It therefore reflects the central theme of the chapter in which it appears. The other two titles refer in contrast to subordinate motifs. The second alludes to a painting discussed at one point in the chapter, a picture which itself becomes symbolic of events at this stage, and the third refers to mythological figures introduced as metaphors and similes in the narrative. Since the variety of chapter headings in Döblin's novel is so wide, the reader is kept alert to the device's ambiguities by having to guess what the relationship between the title and the contents of each chapter is likely to be.

One final method of prefiguration which also appears in the framework surrounding the narrative and not in the novel proper, is the use of a foreword or an appendix to tell the reader of certain parallels. Anthony Burgess's *A Vision of Battlements* has an introduction informing us that "Ennis is close to Aeneas, Agate to Achates, Turner to Turnus, Lavinia is Lavinia, Barasi is Iarbus, his name anagrammatised . . . Concepciòn is Dido."[31] And John Updike has added a "Mythological Index" to *The Centaur,* telling his readers on which page his mythological "referents" occur.[32] But these seem to be counsels of despair, if not handled with irony (and these two are not). For the novelist appears to be undecided about whether he wants the reader

[30] These headings occur on pp. 276, 288 and 384 respectively.
[31] *op.cit.,* p. 8.   [32] *op.cit.,* pp. 271-272.

to have assimilated or unassimilated mythological material. Perhaps a better, though still obvious way to integrate prefigurative figures is through allegorical names. "The simplest form of characterization is naming. Each 'appellation' is a kind of vivifying, animizing, individuating."[33] Or, in the case of mythological names, it can be a typifying process. Mythological names for characters can often present the motif to the reader alone, as the devices discussed so far do, for many mythological figures seem decidedly uninquisitive about their own names. Or the name can give the hero something to live up to.

Stephen Dedalus is probably the best-known bearer of such a symbolic name,[34] but there are many others: Diane, the modern huntress who seduces Felix Krull in a Paris hotel, for instance; or Proserpina, the eponymous heroine of a novel by Elisabeth Langgässer, Elvira and Zerlina in Broch's *Die Schuldlosen* or Hercule Poirot in Agatha Christie's *The Labours of Hercules*. Some names, such as Demetria, that of the Mother Superior in Langgässer's *Märkische Argonautenfahrt*, sound so anachronistic that readers have found them objectionable.[35] So in general, to combat such stridently archaic names, writers have tended to modify them in some way. The range of possibilities stretches from anagram (Herr von Juna for Don Juan in Broch's *Die Schuldlosen*) to looser affinities such as shared sounds or even just a shared initial letter. In James Merrill's *The (Diblos) Notebook*, which portends to be the published rough draft of a mythological novel—hence the hesitant parenthesis in the title—the author is undecided

---

[33] Wellek and Warren, *Theory of Literature*, p. 208.

[34] Gilbert Highet suggests there is a process of assimilation here, whereby Daedalus is changed to Dedalus to look more like such Irish names as Delaney and Devlin (*The Classical Tradition*, p. 697).

[35] See Eva Augsburger, *Elisabeth Langgässer: Assoziative Reihung, Leitmotiv und Symbol in ihren Prosawerken* (Nuremberg, 1962), p. 13.

whether his hero should be called Orson or Orestes, but generally prefers Orson as a form of assimilation. The Faust-like hero of John Hersey's *Too Far to Walk* is called John Fist: a literal translation of one meaning of the German word "Faust." In Harry Brown's *The Stars in their Courses*, prefigured by the *Iliad*, one meets in a cowboy setting such gunslingers as Pax Randal (Paris), Mark Lacy (Menelaus), Nelse Macleod (Nestor), Arch Eastmere (Achilles), Soap Damson (Polydamas) and Phil Tate (Philoctetes); and the woman who starts the feud is called Ellen. The character prefigured by Trigorin, from Chekhov's *The Seagull*, is called Egon in Macdonald Harris's *Trepleff*. And Michel Butor's Ariadne in *L'Emploi du Temps* has the English name Ann—a nice twist, because the French for Ariadne ("Ariane") drops the "d" and sounds much closer to the English name. Perhaps if we did not have his "Mythological Index," we might not even notice the tenuous links that exist in John Updike's *The Centaur* between some of his characters and their prefigurations: Vera for Venus, Appleton for Apollo, March for Mars, *but* Hummel for Hephaestos, Zimmerman for Zeus, Caldwell for Chiron and Peter for Prometheus. Usually the names have to be closer to each other than this for any sense of prefiguration to occur to the reader.

While still on the subject of how the author can signal a motif directly to the reader without giving it any plot-motivation, we can consider two other devices: the use of quotations from earlier works of literature and mythology, and the inclusion of a scheme of prefigurative figures of speech. In fact, neither of these approaches is very common, for good reasons.

It would be superfluous to consider to any great extent the technical aspects of prefiguration through quotation, for Herman Meyer has pursued this subject in detail in *The Poetics of Quotation in the European Novel*. Yet I do not think it is by chance that his illustrations end with Thomas Mann. The reason why few novelists employ this device nowadays was considered towards the end of my second chapter. It lies in our age's decreasing familiarity with myths in literary forms. There remain few mythological sources with which a literary public, even if well-read, can be guaranteed to be conversant enough to recognize quotations taken from them when presented in pastiche. How many readers of *Ulysses* nowadays would be able to say whether the phrase *"Pater, ait"* uttered by Dedalus in the "Scylla and Charybdis" chapter is specifically from Ovid's account of the flight of Icarus, as Stuart Gilbert claims it is, or whether Joyce has in fact modified the phrase to make it more recognizable to the less classically minded audience (which is really the case)?[36] Plot-prefigurations from the plays of Shakespeare or other well-known dramatists have a better chance of being spotted, as Holz and Schlaf's *Papa Hamlet*, Huxley's *Brave New World* and Macdonald Harris's *Trepleff* show.

The narrator can of course step in and make his chosen prefiguration apparent by explicitly drawing attention to it, but he does this at the risk of sounding avuncular. When the narrator of Peter Härtling's *Niembsch oder der Stillstand* explores the relevance of Kierkegaard's *Either/Or* to the choice of a Don Juan motif in the novel, the general reader senses an air of possible condescension. What the author is more likely to do, to avoid the impression of academic parentheses, is to restrict allusions to figures of speech: to similes and metaphors.

After the Philomela myth has been introduced into Carl Frederick Buechner's *A Long Day's Dying*, we find the heroine thinking: "Somehow, immediately, she must silence

[36] Random House ed. (New York, 1961), p. 210. Cf. Gilbert, *op.cit.*, p. 338.

Steitler, like a tyrant in a myth must cut out his tongue and thus prevent him from confirming any part of what Motley had suspected. . . ."[37] The preciosity of the image interrupts the flow of the narrative in a way that a larger complex of expected mythological allusions would not. For this reason, some novelists favor a whole chain of similes and metaphors introducing aspects of mythology. These at least soon form a consistent part of the author's technique and appear more acceptable, as we come to expect more of them.

In *Proserpina: Eine Kindheitsmythe*, a work typical of the escapist "magic realism" in early post-war German literature, Elisabeth Langgässer first establishes her mythological motif with the title and then employs various tropes based on Greek mythology. Even then, the simile tends to predominate in a rather precocious manner. The reader can hardly fail to wilt at the following comparison: "wie einst die blumenpflückende Kore durch das offene Blütenauge hinabgezogen wurde in die Arme des Todes, sank . . . die fühlende Seele hinein."[38] One senses a certain incongruity here, a cross between *Kitsch* and rococo mythology, between the young heroine of the novel and the myths used to describe this "fühlende Seele." At another point, her head becomes "wie einer Venus Haupt"[39]—also a pretentious image to apply to a young child. "Wie Daphne einst floh vor der schöneren Gottheit, so wehten die kindlichen Züge gleich Blättern ins Leere hinüber."[40] At the death of the gardener, the young girl's aged mentor, another heavy analogy is presented: "ein Anruf wie einst rudernden Schiffern, die Botschaft zuzutragen: *der große*

---

[37] *op.cit.*, p. 162.
[38] *op.cit.*, p. 36; "as once flower-picking Kore was drawn down through the open eye of the bloom into the arms of death, so the sensitive creature sank into it."
[39] *op.cit.*, p. 55; "like the head of Venus."
[40] *op.cit.*, p. 111. "Just as Daphne once fled from the more beautiful deity, her childish features were swept like leaves into the void."

CHAPTER FOUR

Pan sei gestorben, tot sei der gewaltige Pan."[41] From time
to time, the pedantry is relieved by the pretense of coyly
searching for the missing mythological partner for an allusion—"weil es Proserpina war, wurde er Pan"[42]—but on the
whole the device betrays a rather labored self-conscious-
ness which contrasts sharply with the idyllic suggestion of
a childhood myth ("Kindheitsmythe"). Everything, the narrator assures us, is as in bygone days ("wie einst"), although the reader notices that this is not the case. And there
is seldom any irony to relieve the resultant disparity of
moods.

In a discussion of another such work—Emil Barth's
Enkel des Odysseus—Theodore Ziolkowski notes that the
author has "the annoying habit of pointing out all classical
references, as if he questioned the reader's intelligence."[43]
But in most of these cases, what results is an assault on literary sensitivities as well as on intelligence. Obviously, the
clumsiness of the mythological motifs in *Enkel des Odysseus* and *Proserpina*—or in *Märkische Argonautenfahrt* for
that matter, since most of the allusions mentioned earlier
come from similes—cannot be ascribed only to the use of
this figure of speech. But it is a significant factor in creating
the impression of an analogy too anachronistically handled
for the modern reader.

In general, few mythological similes or metaphors are to
be found in the modern novel (unless, that is, one sees the
whole mythological motif as an extended metaphor, which
it is possible, though not very helpful, to do). Apart from
the novels already cited, Michel Butor's *L'Emploi du
Temps* and Alfred Döblin's *Hamlet oder Die lange Nacht
nimmt ein Ende* are the only two works I have come across

[41] *op.cit.*, p. 130; "a call to carry the message, as it had once gone
to rowing sailors: *that mighty Pan had died, dead was mighty Pan.*"
[42] *op.cit.*, p. 36, "because she was Proserpina, he became Pan."
[43] "The Odysseus Theme in Recent German Fiction," p. 233.

which use such figures of speech to any great degree. This avoidance of similes in particular is partly in keeping with the widespread antipathy to the simile as a rhetorical device in modern literature. It is a reaction that found much support among Futurists, Expressionists and Imagists alike and is still echoed in various programmatic declarations on the subject.[44] The simile, if not used with the irony that can rescue any hackneyed device, often represents more of an intrusion on the narrator's part than the reader is willing to tolerate. Not only is the mythological simile, and sometimes the metaphor, too labored and direct a comment for the modern reader, it may also possibly be too specific for the novelist's purposes. The figure of speech has to occur at a definite point in the narrative, usually thereby signaling that *at that time and place* the hero resembles his prefiguration. Such a specific task contrasts with the ambiguity sought in most motif-patterns. The information given would become too distinct and limited in scope; patterns of conjecture could hardly be triggered off.

James Joyce once pointed out the attraction for the reader of working out for himself the motif-pattern:

> When Max Eastman asked why he did not supply help to the reader, Joyce replied, "You know people never value anything unless they have to steal it. Even an alley cat would rather snake an old bone out of the garbage than come up and eat a nicely prepared chop from your saucer."[45]

Like Joyce's alley cat, the modern reader does not like things handed to him on a plate, and mythological similes and metaphors may deprive him of the experience of hunt-

[44] For example, in Gottfried Benn, *Probleme der Lyrik* (Wiesbaden, 1951), p. 16, and Jean Gebser, *Der grammatische Spiegel* (Zürich, 1944), pp. 26f.

[45] Quoted by Richard Ellmann in *James Joyce*, pp. 509f.

ing for them. Yet if a novel is called *Le Vol d'Icare* or has a character in it called Diane, or provides a pattern of elusive motifs running through it, the reader still has the chance to work out for himself the extent of the analogy's relevance. Indeterminate prefigurations are invariably more engaging for these reasons. And indeterminacy can be both achieved and made plausible in many ways.

Motivating a Prefiguration through the Plot

In a large number of cases, motifs receive some degree of motivation within a novel's plot and do not remain simply part of an Olympian exchange between narrator and reader, as the devices so far mentioned frequently do. The problem of plausible motivation may be a difficult one for the novelist to solve, especially if the myth chosen is uncommon. *Gilgamesch* (1966), the first novel of the young Swiss writer Guido Bachmann, illustrates the technical hazards well enough. Except in the title, one finds no reference to the Gilgamesh myth for a third of this novel of delinquent adolescence, but then it intrudes suddenly into a rather stilted conversation between the central character Roland and his priest. The latter admonishes Roland for his criminal ways and morbid preoccupations and suggests that he has an unnatural concern for his dead friend Christian:

> "Du darfst keinen Kontakt aufnehmen mit Christian—
> oder du wirst wahnsinnig! Ich sage dir Roland: Du bist
> nicht Gilgamesch!"
> "Gilgamesch? Gilgamesch? Doch—ich bin Gilgamesch.
> Und Christian ist Engidu!"
> "Du bist ein Heide geworden, Roland! Das Babylo-
> nische euerer Sitten wird sich rächen."
> "Ich pfeife auf die christliche Moral."[46]

[46] *op.cit.*, pp. 88f. " 'You must not enter into any contact with Christian—or you will go mad! I'm telling you, Roland: you are not Gilgamesh!' 'Gilgamesh? Gilgamesh? Yes—I'm Gilgamesh. And Christian is Enkidu!' 'You've become a heathen, Roland! You'll pay the

If not surprising that a priest can borrow an analogy from *The Epic of Gilgamesh*, it sounds a little out of character for Roland, with his criminal background and hitherto unliterary disposition, to recognize and assimilate this myth so readily into his speech. For someone to be plausibly conversant with a mythological image of his own situation, he has to have some more special reason than being a god's kindred spirit. Like Gustav Anias Horn, the hero of Jahnn's *Fluß ohne Ufer*,[47] Roland later sets parts of the epic to music,[48] but at the earlier point in the narrative which I have quoted the author is trying to give a plot-motivation to a motif which as yet has only aesthetic merit as authorial prefigurative comment.

If introduced from the hero's perspective, the motif is usually embodied in some significant object or symbolic work of art. There are few instances where characters become aware of the mythological parallels to their situation without some external impetus. Indeed, for this passion for mythology or prefigurations of another kind to occur unsolicited in the modern hero would hardly be in keeping with our age. A detailed acquaintance with mythology would be outside his probable intellectual range (though there is admittedly more to the device than this).

For one thing, the use of symbolic objects lends the chosen motif a certain plasticity. I shall be looking at Michel Butor's *L'Emploi du Temps* in more detail later, but it will serve to illustrate this property here. My illustration con-

---

penalty for your Babylonian ways.' 'I don't give a damn for Christian morality.' "

[47] The dust-jacket commentary to *Gilgamesch* tells us, in an over-benevolent statement of the case, that "die geistige Begegnung mit dem Werk Hans Henny Jahnns wurde Bachmann zum Sporn." The author's manipulation of the Gilgamesh material, however, remains too derivative, and the novel's strength lies elsewhere: in the description of Roland's tortured visions.

[48] References are made to this composition on p. 198 and p. 202.

cerns the hero's reaction to a symbolic tapestry noticed in
the local museum of the town where he is staying:

> Certes, je pense que j'avais reconnu dès l'abord le
> thème du onzième panneau, dans la cinquième salle,
> en face quand on entre, à gauche de la porte qui donne
> dans la sixième, éclairé de côté par les fenêtres qui
> donnent sur Museum Street et les miniscules baraques
> qui la séparent des voies de chemins de fer allant vers
> Hamilton Station:
> Un homme à tête de taureau égorgé par un prince
> en cuirasse, dans une sorte de caveau entouré de murs
> compliqués, à gauche duquel, en haut, sur le pas d'une
> porte ouvrant sur le rivage de la mer, une jeune fille
> en robe bleue brodée d'argent, haute, noble, attentive,
> tire de sa main droite un fil se déroulant d'un fuseau
> qu'elle tient entre le pouce et le médius de l'autre, un
> fil qui serpente dans les méandres et les corridors de
> la forteresse, un fil épais comme une artère gorgée de
> sang, qui va s'attacher au poignard que le prince
> enfonce entre le cou du monstre et son poitrail humain,
> une jeune fille que l'on revoit à droite, au loin, sur la
> proue d'un bateau qui file, sa voile noire gonflée de
> vent, en compagnie du même prince et une autre jeune
> fille très semblable mais plus petite et drapée de violet.
> Mais il m'est difficile de retrouver ma première im-
> pression devant cet ensemble prestigieux que j'ai telle-
> ment mieux regardé depuis, dont le style me déroutait
> sans doute quelque peu, bien que, dès le début, j'en
> suis sûr, j'eusse été ému par les paysages, par les arbres
> notamment, des panneaux 2, 3, 4 et 5, qui décrivent
> l'approche d'Athènes par Thésée, ses victoires sur les
> quatre criminels qui infestaient sa campagne, Sinnis,
> Sciron, Cercyon, Procruste, ces arbres représentés aux
> quatre saisons de l'année, si manifestement inspirés de
> ceux de l'Ile de France, peupliers, trembles, ou chênes,
> en bourgeons, en pleines feuilles de tous les verts, en
> pleine fantasmagorie de douces flammes, ou les
> branches nues.[49]

[49] *op.cit.*, pp. 70f.

142

It would be unrealistic to expect most works to achieve that sense of precision we associate with the *nouveau roman*, but I think this extreme example does illustrate the potential underlying such a symbolic device.

Often, like Revel, the hero of *L'Emploi du Temps*, a figure is allowed to chance upon a mythological painting, some classical sculpture or mythological tapestry which acts as a *mise en abyme* and often as a catalyst for the ensuing prefiguration. The mythological statues in Leopold von Sacher-Masoch's *Venus im Pelz*, Pamela Hill's *Forget not Ariadne*, David Stacton's *Kaliyuga* and Anthony Burgess's *The Eve of Saint Venus* perform a similar role. As a variant, the hero may travel on a boat with a mythological name; there is, for example, a ship named *Hermes* in Bachmann's *Gilgamesch*, which functions rather in the same prefigurative way as the ship *Phaedra* in Jules Dassin's film of the same name. He may perceive a mythologically named constellation of stars, as we shall find the hero of Nossack's *Nekyia* doing later on, or he may see a film which reminds him of mythology (*L'Emploi du Temps*). He may, on the other hand, encounter one of the many dogs with mythological names that seem to trot through modern novels: Pluto in *Der Versucher* and *Hundejahre*, Mr. Mars in *Under the Net*; and another Hermes in *Nicht jeder ist Odysseus*. In a world where we name our ballistic missiles, our space probes and our weaponry after classical figures from mythology, various other permutations of this device are readily available.

Novels that offer a plot-motivation for their images generally fall into two groups: those where the hero comes face to face with some objective correlative from mythology, and those where the main character himself draws our attention to a prefiguration by creating an image of it himself in a work of art. Examples of the former not already cited include the use of mythological motifs in the unicorn tapestry of Carl Frederick Buechner's *A Long Day's Dying*, the painting of Pluto and Proserpina in Döblin's Hamlet novel, the stage production of *The Seagull* in Macdonald Harris's *Trepleff* and the décor of a villa in Heinrich Mann's *Die Göttinnen*. Heinrich Mann's novel is a more complex novel than the others, since it uses the device to relate to a triple prefiguration.

Die Göttinnen oder Die drei Romane der Herzogin von Assy, as the trilogy is called in its entirety, produces its mythological images at a pivotal point in the long narrative in order to emphasize the prefigurations hitherto only mentioned in the sub-titles of the first two volumes: *Diana* and *Minerva*. In the first book of her biography, Duchess Violante is compared with Diana the huntress. The justification for this comparison lies in her political intriguing and machinations. Violante is playing as manly a role in the modern world as Diana the huntress did in the ancient. With Diana she also shares the classical attribute of chastity, a legendary source of various masculine virtues in women. Little, however, is made of the motif in the first book. Further associations with the goddess Diana, such as the idea that she was "the deity of sudden death,"[50] could admittedly account for the series of disasters that dog her progress in the novel. And the recurrent moon image may not be fortuitous as a further symbol from antiquity. Yet on the whole, this remains a very subdued prefiguration in the first volume. Since Diana is a goddess of action rather than contemplation, any lack of self-awareness *vis-à-vis* mythology on this modern Diana's part appears in keeping with the underplayed analogy.

The second volume introduces the Minerva-motif with something of a flourish. In a villa near Rome, Violante and some friends are admiring the mythological frescoes adorn-

[50] *Larousse Encyclopedia of Mythology*, p. 130.

ing three rooms: one is devoted to Diana and one to Minerva, the third being decorated with pictures of Venus. The group conveniently walks from the Diana Room to the Minerva Room and then on to the Venus Room, thus presaging the direction our heroine's life is to take in the third volume of the novel. In case any of the readers may have missed the point, the following conversation takes place. In the first room comes the exchange: " 'Die Diana dort oben, Herzogin, sind Sie.' 'Vielleicht war ich es. Jetzt bin ich es gewiß nicht.' " In the second room further hints are to be gathered: " 'Die Minerva dort oben, Herzogin, sind Sie.' Die übrigen sahen hin; keiner widersprach." Then later, when all the rooms have been described and the reader sees the mythological décor as a symbolic comment on the outlines of Violante's life, the point is pressed home once more. " 'Sie, Frau Herzogin . . . sind Diana gewesen, jetzt sind Sie Pallas. Der dritte Saal liegt noch in wüsten Träumen und wartet noch auf Sie. Venus ist noch abwesend.' "[51]

Although it is fitting that this manner of presenting the motif should occur in the part of the trilogy consecrated to Minerva, the goddess of the arts, the device is handled over-explicitly. The reader has long since grasped the point being made and the only possible defense for this ponderousness might be the dilettantish society in which the conversation takes place. But if overt references of this kind have something of the pedantry also to be found in prefigurative similes, there is an alternative way of motivating the motif.

The other main approach is to introduce the motif as part of the creation of an artist-hero. At some point in his de-

---

[51] *op.cit.*, pp. 9f: " 'You, your Grace, are the Diana up there.' 'Perhaps I was. But now I am certainly not.' " *op.cit.*, pp. 12f.: " 'You, your Grace, are the Minerva up there.' The others looked in that direction; no one contradicted." *op.cit.*, pp. 42f.: " 'You, your Grace, . . . have been Diana, now you are Pallas. The third room still lies in your wildest dreams and awaits you. Venus is still missing.' "

velopment, he produces a work which itself derives from mythology and hence prefigures his own predicament. Half the German novels cited in my bibliography use this technique, whereas only about one in ten of the others chooses it. Outside German literature, which has a strong addiction to artist-novels, we find Alberto Moravia favoring the work-within-a-work to motivate the *Odyssey* motif in *Il disprezzo*, James Merrill employs it in *The (Diblos) Notebook* and John Bowen has also chosen it to rationalize his use of the Philoctetes motif in *A World Elsewhere*. In Mikhail Bulgakov's *The Master and Margarita* the Faustian parallel is evoked by a variant of this technique: Berlioz, one of the main figures does not—it is continually stressed —have anything to do with the musician who wrote *La Damnation de Faust* and who enjoyed such a high reputation in Imperial Russia. Hence a motif is signalled dialectically by a denial of affinities.

When the hero is allowed to create the prefigurative object for himself, the enthusiasm and understanding he shows for mythology generally acquires a plausible motivation. Obviously this does not mean that the artist's aesthetic empathy is always more credible than any beholder's but merely suggests that we need adequate preparation in a work to accept the artistic and perhaps arcane inclinations of non-creative characters. Artist-novels like *Doktor Faustus* and *A World Elsewhere* give us such insight into the central figure's preoccupations with his work, so that any enthusiasm shown for his mythological creation has already been justified by our general sympathy with his intellectual character.[52]

---

[52] This is the implication of a remark made by Thomas Mann in *Die Entstehung des "Doktor Faustus"* (Frankfurt a.M., 1949, p. 40): "Nichts Läppischer, in einem Künstler-Roman, als Kunst, Genie, Werk nur zu behaupten, nur anzupreisen, von ihren seelischen Wirkungen nur zu schwärmen. Hier galt es Realisierung, galt *Exaktheit*—nichts war mir klarer."

It may seem more natural for the creator to identify in spirit with his mythological creation and to show a passionate interest in his source-material than for the average non-artistic hero or heroine to display these same emotions. One exception to this generalization is the classical scholar or connoisseur of mythology who appears in one or two novels. In Carl Frederick Buechner's *A Long Day's Dying*, the Philomela myth is introduced as part of a lecture delivered in some detail to an academic audience.[53] And Max Frisch's *Mein Name sei Gantenbein* has as one of its protagonists a figure who is an expert on Hermes and who bears many similarities to him.[54]

Another kind of creativity, not really included in the idea of the artist-hero, but encompassed by a wider, more psychological (even Nietzschean) concept of creativity, is relevant here: the stylization of one's life into a myth, or "mythical imitation." I shall look at this later in the case of Macdonald Harris's *Trepleff*. But there are few examples of this outside Thomas Mann's works. For although Mann saw it as a positive kind of artistry,[55] this kind of mythical imitation has been seen by critics as a kind of lived-out parody of the prefiguration.[56] But usually the motif is no more a vehicle of parody than it is of comic anachronism. It has a more serious function.

The creator-heroes are seldom novelists. They may be musicians, as Bachmann's Roland, Jahnn's Horn and Mann's Leverkühn are. Or, like Nossack's Berthold (in *Spätestens im November*), they may be dramatists, or film-writers like

[53] *op.cit.*, pp. 72-75.

[54] "Hermes ist das Thema einer Arbeit, die ihm den Ruf nach Harvard eingetragen hat," *op.cit.*, p. 60.

[55] "Der Joseph des Romans ist ein Künstler, insofern er spielt, nämlich mit seiner imitatio Gottes auf den Unbewußten spielt" ("Freud und die Zukunft," *Adel des Geistes*, Stockholm, 1948, p. 520).

[56] According to Ignace Feuerlicht: "Was Mann gelebten Mythus nennt, könnte man ebensogut gelebte Parodie nennen" ("Thomas Manns mythische Identifikation," p. 144).

Moravia's Molteni, producers of psycho-dramas like
Zelazny's Render (in *The Dream Master*), or poets like
Broch's Virgil and Härtling's Niembsch. For all that, it is
difficult to accept Maurice Beebe's conclusion that in these
roles they are no more than mirrors of their creators' art:
that "though the hero of an artist-novel may be a sculptor
or composer, as a self-portrait of his creator he is always a
writer."[57] Novelist and creator-hero resemble each other in
a way which only a biographical approach of impractical
depth would be able to determine. For the reader, the real
importance of the myth is as symbolic comment, not as a
defense mechanism for some writer choosing to appear in
the guise of a different kind of artist.

The similarity between what one might call the inner and
outer works is not one of such closeness as to imply the one
simply mirrors the other, but constitutes a loose enough
parallel to avoid this suggestion and yet remain striking
enough to draw our attention to the mythological *tertium
comparationis*. Usually the motif occurs explicitly in the
inner work and is transferred largely by implication to the
outer, i.e. the real, novel. Expecting close parallels rather
than a loose analogy, Maurice Blanchot cannot conceal his
disappointment at Mann's handling of the relationship between Leverkühn and Faustus:

> Mais plus frappant encore, ce fait que la représentation
> du mythe le plus vivant que la culture occidentale ait
> su garder, ne puisse plus être, aujourd'hui, qu'une
> représentation au second degré. Adrian Leverkühn
> n'est pas Faust, il ne peut pas être Faust, il n'en porte
> pas le nom, il n'en renouvelle pas l'histoire, mais il écrit
> une cantate de Faust: voilà tout ce qu'il a de commun
> avec l'image légendaire.[58]

[57] *Ivory Towers and Sacred Founts: The Artist as Hero in Fiction
from Goethe to Joyce*, New York, 1964, p. v.
[58] "Thomas Mann et le mythe de Faust," p. 21.

In fact, this is not the whole truth of the matter. They do have the work in common, to be sure, but this is only one of the numerous pointers to many other shared attributes. Admittedly, they are not identical, and the fact that they do not bear the same name draws attention to the differences. But Blanchot swings to the other extreme in denying much of what they do have in common. (This reading is at least a departure from the approach usually adopted. Whereas the clues for a mythological motif tend to be over-interpreted in so many cases, making a symbolic name or title into evidence of assumed identity, here they are practically ignored.) As was argued earlier, the mythological novel demands that its reader draw a number of inferences on the strength of certain veiled information. As a result, the form is open to certain misrepresentations at times.

Criticism has largely concentrated on prefigurative works where the motifs have only symbolic connections with the main themes. Therefore, to redress the balance, the novels to be looked at in detail now are those with prefigurations motivated within the plot. In each case, my aim is not to offer a comprehensive account of the motifs involved, but rather to limit the scope to certain aspects of this most frequent device.

Historical Symbolism: Thomas Mann's Doktor Faustus

The symbolic parallels in Thomas Mann's Faust-novel between the hero, Adrian Leverkühn, and Germany are largely of a chronological order. Events in Leverkühn's life can be related to certain episodes in German history. There are, for instance, historical counterparts to his association with the theological student-circle, and the general patriotic, mystical mood of the conversations at these meetings. Political symbolism can be read into the rejection of the Jewish impresario Saul Fitelberg and the central pact with the devil; for Leverkühn's climb to fame and his ensuing luetic decline there are also appropriate analogies. These and other symbolic aspects have already been studied in some detail by Gunilla Bergsten and Jonas Lesser.[59] Another dimension to the Faust-motif has, however, received little attention: namely, the implications of such prefigurative patterning for the novel's image of recent history.

It is generally agreed that the Faust myth, as portrayed in *Doktor Faustus*, is chosen for its "Germanness." Mann's image of Faust owes much to Spengler and to the Nazi myth of *Deutschtum*. It is this nationalistic quality which is stressed in the revised version of the novel's sub-title: *Das Leben des deutschen Tonsetzers Adrian Leverkühn, erzählt von einem Freunde.* (The adjective "deutsch" was only added to the description in a late emendation to emphasize the specifically German mood which pervades the novel.) The main prefiguration is clearly intended to imply that Germany produced Faust for much the same reason—a proclivity for the daemonic—as the German composer produces his Faust cantata. One exceptional aspect of this prefiguration is that it is not only used to describe a single character, but—because of the novel's complex time-structure—becomes the symbol of a whole nation. It would have made little sense to prefigure this deeply German novel with a myth of striving such as the quest for the Golden Fleece or the Tree of Life. Once these numerous parallels leave their mark on our reading of the novel, the plot suggests a certain historical inevitability and an uncommon note of determinism enters the work.

The presence of mythological motifs adds a touch of fatalism to the plot of many a modern novel; we sense the sword of Damocles hanging above the protagonist. All

---

[59] Bergsten, *op.cit.*, especially pp. 173ff.; and Jonas Lesser, *Thomas Mann in der Epoche seiner Vollendung*, Zürich, 1952, pp. 329ff.

kinds of prefiguration, if followed closely, will have such an effect. The reader expects a modern Theseus-like hero to enter and master the labyrinth, as the hero of Butor's *L'Emploi du Temps* does. Similarly, one assumes that modern characters prefigured by Persephone or Demeter are destined to return to the underworld, as Mutter Gisson does literally in Broch's *Der Versucher*, or to the kind of symbolic underworld of marital torments experienced in Döblin's Hamlet-novel. Furthermore, this sense of inevitability can be heightened by the kind of motif-pattern chosen. A complete pattern of mythological correspondences covering the whole of a novel is bound to generate a far greater mood of inexorability. Events then appear to be following some preordained course for which a familiar analogy assumes the role almost of an influence, and the prefiguration seems to retain its former religious aura. This may be seen as something positive, as the predestined homecoming is in Joyce's *Ulysses* and in the many other works which derive their symbolism from the *Odyssey*. Or a pattern of tragedy may be broken at the last moment and the reader may feel a sense of release.[60] Or, perhaps the most obvious alternative open to the novelist: the pattern of an inevitable tragedy may be fulfilled and the sword of Damocles may fall, as it does in Moravia's *Il disprezzo* and Schneider's *Der Tod des Nibelungen*.

Doktor Faustus emphasizes this relationship between the technique of oppressive prefiguration and determinism. "Das 'Schicksal' (wie 'deutsch' dies Wort, ein vor-christlicher Urlaut, ein tragisch-mythologisch-musikdramatisches Motiv!)"[61] Zeitblom's comment is an apt description of the novel's mood. Yet this very tragic vision remains the one

[60] Cf. the discussion of Harris's *Trepleff* (below, pp. 228-240).
[61] *op.cit.*, p. 463. In Lowe-Porter's translation, this passage reads: "our 'sending' (the very word we use is Germanic, the idea pre-Christian, the whole concept a tragically mythological, music-dramatic motif). . ." (*Doctor Faustus*, p. 301).

Mann thereby transfers to his image of recent German history in the novel.[62] In its account of the predetermined path of events, the novel seems to become fatalistic itself. Recent German history is seen as the result of a long process reaching back to the Middle Ages, rather than as the machinations of a single diabolical genius. By playing with a specifically German myth[63] and applying it to so much of the novel, Mann succeeds in insinuating that such an assignation with evil may well be an inherent part of modern Germany's historical role: that the country was as fated to make a pact with National Socialism as Faustus or Leverkühn were to sign one with the devil. In this light, one is tempted to see Faustus, Leverkühn and Hitler all as inevitable products of some conception of *Deutschtum*. The last sentence in the novel is a reminder of this parallel: "Gott sei euerer armen Seele gnädig, mein Freund, mein Vaterland."[64] With such a national dimension to its symbolism, the novel is unique in its handling of prefigurations.

Such a view of history appears dangerously reminiscent of the notion, so often attacked by Brecht, that historical disasters are the handiwork of some impersonal destiny. This Brecht recognized as a very German thought and he took great pains to combat it both in his plays and his theoretical writings. In *Schriften zum Theater*, for instance, he outlines the problem and how it can be tackled:

Nichtaristotelische Dramatik würde die Ereignisse, die sie vorführt, keineswegs zu einem unentrinnbaren Schicksal zusammenfassen, und diesem den Menschen

[62] Leslie Miller was one of the first to draw attention to this aspect of the novel. In "Myth and Morality: Reflections on Mann's *Doktor Faustus*," he points out that "more than once earlier commentators . . . have hinted at a degree of determinism in Leverkühn's life, although they have not discussed the problem as one of mythical imitation" (p. 208).
[63] André Dabezies gives an excellent account of the nationalistic overtones to the myth in his *Visages de Faust*, pp. 89-156.
[64] "God be merciful to thy poor soul, my friend, my fatherland."

hilflos, wenn auch schön und bedeutsam reagierend, ausliefern, sie würde im Gegenteil gerade dieses "Schicksal" unter die Lupe nehmen und es als menschliche Machenschaften enthüllen.[65]

The aim of an enlightened, modern writer, Brecht feels, should be to demonstrate that man is the master of his own fate. Brecht himself, notably in *Arturo Ui* and *Mutter Courage*, and Max Frisch, in *Biedermann* and *Andorra*, have both tried to combat this recurrent fatalistic image of the Second World War. The doctor's words in *Andorra* parodistically echo such a viewpoint:

Ich bestreite keineswegs, daß wir sozusagen einer gewissen Aktualität erlegen sind. Es war, vergessen wir nicht, eine aufgeregte Zeit. . . . Eine tragische Geschichte, kein Zweifel. . . . Ich bin nicht Schuld, daß es dazu gekommen ist.[66]

It is a viewpoint strongly attacked also in Sartre's *L'Etre et le Néant*.

There is a certain depersonalization of guilt in viewing the event as some great tragedy sent from above, or in Leverkühn's case sent from below. The adaptation of the Faust prefiguration in Mann's novel to refer symbolically to Germany's part in the war has something of the stylization—the *Dämonisierung*—of the war that National Socialist propaganda itself favored, especially when defeat seemed imminent. Goebbels's words to the German people on 20 April 1945 transmit the very image of the war which Brecht and Frisch so strongly deplored:

[65] *op.cit.*, pp. 243f. "Non-Aristotelian drama would in no way lump together the events it portrays as inexorable fate and abandon Man to it, leaving him helpless, albeit behaving admirably and in a meaningful way; on the contrary, it would put this very 'fate' under the magnifying glass and reveal it to be human machinations."

[66] London, 1964, p. 102. "I in no way deny that we are, as it were, the victims of a certain actuality. It was, let us not forget, a turbulent time . . . . A tragic story, without doubt . . . . I am not to be blamed that it happened."

Was wir heute erleben, das ist der letzte Akt eines gewaltigen tragischen Dramas, das mit dem 1. August 1914 begann, und das wir Deutschen am 9.November 1918 gerade in dem Augenblick unterbrachen, als es kurz vor der Entscheidung stand.[67]

If one were to ask how the symbolic depiction of the war in *Doktor Faustus* relates to these two standpoints, one would find oneself obliged to admit that it comes closer to Nazi propaganda than either Brecht's or Frisch's positions. For does not Mann's novel also make the end of the Third Reich seem like the last act of a powerful, tragic drama, a débâcle with strongly Wagnerian overtones?[68] An observation in *Betrachtungen eines Unpolitischen* gives some clue why Mann uses the political over-simplifications one finds in the symbolism of *Doktor Faustus* and which were already to be seen in the allegory of *Der Zauberberg*. Analyzing the way people will revert in war to a nationally typical way of behaving, such as they normally shrink from displaying as individuals, Mann writes of:

> die plötzliche groteske Personifizierung der Nationen . . . , die der Krieg mit sich brachte. . . . Ereignisse wie diese heben auf einmal die Individualität der einzelnen Völker, ihre ewigen Physiognomien mächtig hervor. . . . England, Frankreich, Deutschland, Italien, sie benahmen sich so richtig, so ganz wie es im Buche, im Märchenbuche steht.[69]

[67] "What we are experiencing today is the last act of a powerful tragic drama, that began with 1 August 1914, and that we Germans interrupted on 9 November 1918 at the very moment when we were about to reach a decision."

[68] Certainly, one must bear in mind that the whole novel is narrated not by Mann, but by the more dubious figure of Serenus Zeitblom. Mann's own behavior during the war hardly brands him as a fatalist in his attitude to history; he was much less a flower of his age than his narrator, in this sense. Rather, Mann exercizes here his favorite critical role as ironic seismograph of contemporary views.

[69] Frankfurt a.M., 1956, p. 142; ". . . the sudden, grotesque personification of nations . . . which the war produced. . . . Events such as these suddenly strongly emphasize the individuality of single peoples, their eternal features. . . . England, France, Germany, Italy, all behaved correctly, just as one finds in the book—the fairy-tale book."

Hence even Mann's image of the Faustian German, which some of his critics have charged with excessive banality,[70] can always be interpreted as one of the grotesque distortions brought about by the war itself. The fatalism of using a German prefiguration in *Doktor Faustus* is not so much a sign, therefore, of Mann's own deterministic interpretation of the rise of Fascism, or even just of Zeitblom's, but a symbol of the custom amongst belligerent societies to regress to atavistic national stereotypes: "wie es im Buche, im Märchenbuche steht." In this sense, Leslie Miller is quite justified in observing that:

> the very choice of Faust as the mythical model for Leverkühn is, despite the apparent condemnation of Germany this implies, a more ambiguous interpretation of the German problem, a more objective and penetrating approach to the question of guilt, than Mann's comments on the Faust myth [in *Deutschland und die Deutschen*] would suggest.[71]

Doktor Faustus undoubtedly emphasizes the historical roots of its motif to a greater extent than most prefigurative novels do. It is also one of the few novels where the use of mythological motifs has a directly political, and even teleological, implication, in contrast to the usual, more limited, psychological and aesthetic roles of the device. In the case of this novel, one can talk of identification—if not identity— with the original Faust-figure on the hero's part, but the irony lies in our awareness of the dubious nature of this relationship. The connection with madness gives the whole prefiguration a pejorative quality. It may be "a basic trait of mythical thinking" that, to quote Ernst Cassirer,[72] "analogy shifts everywhere into real identity" but this proves a rarity

---

[70] For an account of the novel's reception, including this issue, see Bernhard Blume's "Aspects of Contradiction: On Recent Criticisms of Thomas Mann," in *Thomas Mann: A Collection of Critical Essays*, pp. 155-169.

[71] "Myth and Morality," p. 199.

[72] *The Philosophy of Symbolic Forms*, II, p. 226.

in most fiction. Leverkühn, like the Fascist ideologues,[73] tends to think mythically, but it is an idiosyncrasy that the reader would do well not to share with him.

The Use of a Real Artist: Hermann Broch's Der Tod des Vergil

At about the same time as Mann was writing *Doktor Faustus* at Pacific Palisades, Hermann Broch, also in exile in the United States, was putting the finishing touches to his artist-novel *Der Tod des Vergil*, an equally monumental response to the Second World War. His Virgil-novel appeared simultaneously in English and German in 1945.

In its handling of mythological motifs, *Der Tod des Vergil* differs from most other novels of the kind I am looking at, since it is not set in modern times, but in the age of Virgil and Caesar Augustus. The mythological element does not provide the same direct commentary on the modern world, even though it still functions as description by analogy.[74] This divergence is in fact not as fundamental as it might at first seem to be, however, for the mythological motifs really operate in a similar way to most other prefigurations elsewhere. In this particular case, one sees what can happen if a real artist is chosen, one whose works the reader may well be expected to know before reading Broch's novel.[75]

The principal characters in *Der Tod des Vergil* are in

---

[73] On the subject of myth and Nazi propaganda, see E. H. Gombrich's *Myth and Reality in German War-Time Broadcasts*, London, 1970.

[74] Other novels, such as Huxley's *Brave New World*, Spencer's *Asylum* and Zelazny's *The Dream Master*, use prefigurations to comment on a world of the future. But within fiction, according to the conventions, this time then becomes the reader's present, just as Virgil's age does in Broch's novel.

[75] Peter Härtling's *Niembsch oder der Stillstand*, the only other novel with a historical hero that I have come across—Niembsch is the real name of the German poet Lenau—does not exploit our possible knowledge of Lenau's work in the same way.

most respects very familiar to the reader as archetypes: the poet, the soldier, the doctor and the wife. Their main preoccupations are timeless ones concerning life and death, art and commitment, love and infidelity; and one is not distanced essentially from them by any marked anachronistic interpolations from a narrator. There is no impression of descending into the mythical well of the past as there is in Mann's *Joseph und seine Brüder.*

Der Tod des Vergil takes the reader into the mind of the poet Virgil, during the last eighteen hours of his life. His mind is in turn something of a museum of the past, and a kind of arena for wider conflicts concerning his society. "Es ist der paradigmatische Fall der 'Krise' sowohl im persönlichen wie kulturellen Leben wie überall sonstwo, und wie sie immer wieder zu beobachten ist," as Broch was to observe after he had written the novel.[76]

Three poets figure in the novel, each existing on a different plane: the central character Virgil, the mythological Orpheus, and Virgil's own creation, the legendary Aeneas. (As we shall see, a case can be made here for reintroducing the distinction between myth and legend waived in Chapter Two.) Aeneas and Orpheus are used as prefigurations to comment on Virgil; similarly, their counterparts, Dido and Eurydice, prefigure Virgil's wife Plotia.

Quite early in the novel, Virgil recognizes that he is about to die and soon too he notes certain parallels between himself and Aeneas:

> . . . es war zum Abschied geworden. Und ebenderselbe Abschied war es gewesen, der dann nochmals und später und größer von dem Äneas erlebt werden sollte, da er, bemüßigt vom rätselhaft unergründlichen Schicksalsablauf der Dichtung, mit flüchtenden Schiffen ins Unwiderrufliche ziehend, die Dido verlassen

[76] *Briefe*, p. 267. "It is the paradigmatic instance of 'crisis,' both in personal and public affairs and everywhere else, just as can be observed over and over again."

hatte, für immer verzichtend bei ihr zu liegen, mit ihr zu jagen, für immer geschieden von ihr, die ihm süßer Schatten der Wirklichkeit gewesen, der süße Schatten der Lust, für ewig geschieden von der Nachthöhle der Liebe unter den Gewittern. Ja, Äneas und er, er und Äneas, sie waren geflohen in einem wirklichen Aufbruch, nicht nur im verharrenden Abschiednehmen der Dichtung . . .[77]

Aeneas is Virgil's own personal creation (there is an Aeneas in the *Iliad*, but Aeneas, as we know him, is Virgil's property because he was the one who for the Romans created a legend out of a minor Greek figure). Perhaps for this reason, the poet is inclined to see so much of himself in Aeneas. The novel is narrated from Virgil's perspective, hence the Aeneas prefiguration becomes a point of analogy at so many junctures. Orpheus, on the other hand, is a major traditional figure from Greek mythology and not Virgil's literary property in the same way, even though the poet also depicts him in the *Georgics*. Hence he emerges more often in the novel as a contrast-figure than in comparisons. Quite understandably, Virgil cannot feel the same closeness to a figure from a classical culture which he merely feels he is aping.

In Broch's novel, one discerns a marked progression through the various stages of prefiguration on the way to Virgil's death. Orpheus is only introduced after the earlier comparisons have been made between Virgil and Aeneas, as father-figures in Rome's glorious history, but then he be-

---

[77] *op.cit.*, p. 71. Jean Starr Untermeyer's translation of the passage reads: ". . . it became their farewell. And it had been the selfsame farewell that once again and on a grander scale had to be experienced later on by Aeneas when, forced by the enigmatic, unfathomably fateful course of poetry, bound for the irrevocable with his departing ships, he had forsaken Dido, forever forsworn from lying with her, from hunting with her, eternally divorced from her who had been his sweet shadow of reality, his sweet shadow of desire, divorced eternally from the night-cave of love beneath the thunders. Yes, Aeneas and he, he and Aeneas, they had fled in a real departure, not only in the lingering farewells of poetry . . ." (*The Death of Vergil*, London, 1946, pp. 65f.).

comes the major symbolic figure for the rest of the novel. Orpheus is not mentioned, in fact, until about a quarter of the way through the novel:

> . . . ihn, den Dichter, zum Erkenntnisbringer in der wiederhergestellten Menschengemeinschaft erhöhen, enthoben der Pöbelhaftigkeit und ebenhiedurch auch die Pöbelhaftigkeit selber aufhebend, Orpheus erkoren zum Führer der Menschen. Ach, nicht einmal Orpheus hatte solches je erreicht, nicht einmal er in seiner Unsterblichkeitsgröße rechtfertigte solch überheblich eitle Ehrgeizträume und solch sträfliche Überschätzung des Dichtertums![78]

This image of Orpheus as a kindred spirit—an image which is only erected to be destroyed very soon afterwards—returns to the poet a few minutes later. "Und nicht anders mußte es um Orpheus und um sein Gedicht bestellt gewesen sein, da er ein Künstler, da er ein Dichter gewesen war . . . doch nicht ein Heilsbringer der Menschen."[79]

References to Orpheus begin to proliferate as Virgil penetrates deeper into the realms of fever and subsequently death. Simultaneously, he descends further into the sphere of myths. In his earlier, more lucid moments, Virgil invoked the legend of Aeneas, a more concrete, quasi-historical analogy than the myth of Orpheus—and one more securely anchored in his own world, thanks to the *Aeneid*. As death approaches and he becomes aware of the relativity and vanity of his life as a writer, the more the tragic tale of

---

[78] *op.cit.*, p. 148; ". . . would exalt him, the poet, to the rank of perception-bringer in the restored community of men; lifted out of the mob pattern and therefore able to abolish that pattern, Orpheus chose to be the leader of mankind. Ah, not even Orpheus had attained such a goal, not even his immortal greatness had justified such vain and presumptuous dreams of grandeur, such flagrant overestimation of poetry!" (*The Death of Vergil*, pp. 134f.)

[79] *op.cit.*, p. 150. "And it could not have been otherwise with Orpheus and his poem, for he was an artist, a poet . . . but not the savior of man" (*The Death of Vergil*, p. 136).

Orpheus' failure captures Virgil's attention. Whereas Aeneas deserted Dido to go and found Rome, Orpheus lost Eurydice without any positive result of this kind, but merely as a result of his own imprudence.

Two main points of comparison are offered between Virgil and Orpheus: first, the obvious parallel in the descent into the underworld and the analogy in the death of Virgil;[80] second, a more unexpected parallel, based on the relationship between the poet and the masses.

The Latin poet at one time quotes from his *Georgics* the passage describing how the Ciconian women tear Orpheus to pieces.[81] Virgil interprets this passage as symbolic of the introspective poet's failure to communicate with the masses and his subsequent unpopularity. The sin of esotericism (which we in a sense see here in Virgil's own perverted allegorization of the myth) becomes the poet's main concern now, just as it had haunted Broch for much of his life. Virgil's other worry is that this esotericism cannot even be justified, for in his eyes his poetry lacks any great redeeming epistemological value. A parallel to the Ciconian women's attack on Orpheus is to be found in Virgil's recent experiences. Borne through the streets of Brundisium to the emperor's palace on a litter, he was mocked by the women of the city who saw in him a parasite whom they would also have liked to tear to pieces. Ironically, both Orpheus and Virgil love and wish to save their fellow men, but the isolation in which they find themselves is the result of their vain attempts at becoming spiritual leaders:

[80] In a letter to Albert Einstein, Broch once remarked: "Mir ist nämlich auf- und eingefallen, daß Vergil den Abstieg zum Hades nicht weniger als dreimal geschildert hat, daß also dies bei einem Menschen, der sich, wie er, immerzu viel Gedanken über sein Dichtergewerbe machte, etwas zu bedeuten hatte" (*Briefe*, p. 228). This is one of the few comments that Broch makes linking Virgil's own mythology with the motifs of *Der Tod des Vergil*.

[81] *Georgics*, iv, 520-527; *op.cit.*, p. 172, or in the English translation, p. 156.

Schlummerte der Erlöserwunsch nicht im Dichter mit noch weit größerer Traumesgröße als in allen anderen Menschen? Wollte nicht auch Orpheus sich dazu erkühnen, da er sogar die Tiere an sich heran und in seinen Bann zog, um sie ins Menschliche zu erlösen?[82]

Both poets fail—not only mankind in general, but also their loved ones. By disobediently turning around during his ascent from Hades, Orpheus betrays Eurydice. Likewise, Virgil is convinced that his commitment to a failed poetry instead of to life has made him betray his wife: "untaugliches Mittel bleibt die Kunst, und selbst Orpheus hatte daran scheitern müssen."[83] Orpheus' unsuccessful journey to the underworld is at least an act of love for Eurydice and hence a direct contrast to the way in which Aeneas treats Dido and Virgil neglects his wife. This ritual journey to the realm of death is presented not only as an act of a poet trying to transcend the barriers of finiteness, but also as a personal act of love—something which Virgil again cannot yet match:

> Der Liebe Erinnerungsstärke hatte Orpheus den Eintritt in die Hadestiefe erzwungen. . . . Er hingegen, liebelos von Anbeginn, unfähig das liebende Gedächtnis voranzuschicken und von keiner Erinnerung geführt, er war nicht einmal in die ersten Tiefen des erzbeherrschenden Vulcanus gelangt. . . .[84]

This passage, italicized in the novel, marks the point where Virgil begins to compare himself with Orpheus, not so

[82] op.cit., pp. 421f. "Was not the wish to be the redeemer a more compelling dream of grandeur in the poet than in other men? Did not Orpheus also wish to rise to that dream even as he tried to draw the animals into his spell in order to redeem them to humanity?" (The Death of Vergil, p. 382).

[83] op.cit., p. 422; "art remained an unsuitable vehicle, and even Orpheus had to fail because of this."

[84] op.cit., p. 174. "Love's power of remembrance had forced Orpheus to enter the depths of Hades. . . . He, unlike Orpheus, loveless from the beginning, unable to send forth the loving recollection and guided by no memory, had not even reached the first level of the iron rule of Vulcan. . ." (The Death of Vergil, p. 157).

161

much as a poet, but simply as a human being with deep personal commitments. Henceforth, love rather than art becomes the main touchstone of Virgil's process of self-realization. His jaded marriage to Plotia is sadly contrasted with Orpheus' heroic love for Eurydice and his search for her in the dangerous depths of Hades. However, Virgil's failure also resembles Orpheus' inability to bring Eurydice back. "Oh, Eurydike, oh, Plotia!"[85] he calls out in his fever, realizing that he too has failed his wife. But Virgil thinks that he can perhaps atone for this past lack of love by giving up an earlier deathbed resolution to burn all his works and by donating them to Caesar Augustus as a token of friendship. Thus, he feels, he will resemble the Orpheus who descended into the underworld as an act of love. The novel concludes by depicting Virgil's death after this ritual act of atonement.

To sum up, the steps in the development of these mythological-cum-legendary motifs are marked by: 1. similarities between Virgil and Aeneas, their ultimate rejection of love for what they take to be a higher cause; 2. the similarities between Virgil and Orpheus, both in the desire to save mankind through a knowledge of death and their failure to do so (Ciconian women motif); 3. a contrast between Orpheus' act of love for Eurydice and Virgil's offhand treatment of Plotia; and 4. Virgil's final gesture of giving the books of the *Aeneid* to Caesar Augustus as an attempt at once more narrowing the gap between himself and Orpheus. (After which, he does quite literally descend into Hades.)

Despite many dead mythological tropes, there are three main figures of symbolic quality in the novel, and two of these are from prefigurative sources. Beyond these levels of reality comes a fourth dimension, the unnamed sphere of the archetype in the final book of the novel. This section

[85] *op.cit.*, p. 273.

is a creation myth in reverse, the beginning of Virgil's death and the point where the hero moves beyond the realm of individuation, leaving behind his self and the two *personae*. Now all the earlier images of identity have lost their relevance. Virgil, Aeneas and Orpheus are hardly ever mentioned in the final book of the novel.

One feature of these prefigurations is the order in which they are presented; a corollary is the impression they give of being understated.

Because Virgil's works are likely to be known quantities for the kind of person attracted to a novel entitled *Der Tod des Vergil*, one does not find the same elaborate refraction between the fictional prefigurative work and the reader that usually occurs in mythological artist-novels. In *Doktor Faustus*, for example, Adrian Leverkühn's musical composition "Dr Fausti Weheklag" is only known indirectly to the reader through what is given in Serenus Zeitblom's account of it in chapter 46 of the novel. This acquaintance at one remove is limited in comparison with the detailed information about Virgil's work available to any reader. (The operative factor here is, of course, that one can transfer such information from the real to the fictional Virgil.) This essential difference has a noticeable effect upon the construction of Broch's novel. Whereas the elaboration of motifs in other novels generally tends to be more discursive, in *Der Tod des Vergil* the assumption that the reader will be familiar with the outlines of the Roman poet's work forms an integral part of the novel's more allusive technique.[86]

[86] Two concepts which frequently appear in Broch's theoretical writings are "Symbolketten," which Broch sees as the only way towards his ideal goal of a "Totalitätskunstwerk" (cf. *Dichten und Erkennen*, p. 161 and p. 193) and "Symbolabkürzung" (*Die Schuldlosen*, p. 363), a short cut enabling the novelist to master his encyclopaedic material within the space available to him. The motifs in *Der Tod des Vergil* satisfy these two programmatic demands. Since

One of the grounds frequently advanced to account for Broch's choice of hero is the religious significance of his work. Although in a pagan sense soteriology is already a salient aspect of Virgil's poems, in the Middle Ages they were allegorized and imbued with further, specifically Christian overtones, by Dante in particular. For this reason, Hermann Weigand argues that:

> it was certainly not the temper of Vergil's published work which gave Broch the cue for this book. Vergil's work does not manifest or even suggest that passion for the absolute with which Broch endows him. There are a great many quotations from Vergil's work and allusions to it interwoven with the narrative but none of these many passages would have supplied the spark for conceiving of Vergil's personality in the terms of this book.[87]

This is in a sense true, for Broch's whole novel sets out to depict the disparity between *the true* (i.e. *his*) Virgil and the pale imitation of this man we find in the works. The spark, Weigand maintains, comes from Dante. Stressing the "passion for the absolute" in Broch's hero, Weigand forgets that this itself links Broch's Virgil with the mythological figures in the novel (as Broch's letter to Einstein confirms). Weigand, however, believes that Dante's Christian image of the poet, a kind of *Virgile moralisé*, furnishes the key to our understanding of this metaphysical urge, a key which Virgil's own work would not offer. This, as the imagery of the prefigurations would suggest, is a matter open to some debate.

Virgil's works themselves abound with mythological motifs, these can be transferred in "Symbolketten" to Broch's novel. This partly explains the choice of Virgil, the only non-fictive hero in Broch's *œuvre*.

[87] Hermann J. Weigand, "Broch's *Death of Vergil:* Program Notes," *PMLA*, LXII, 1947, pp. 529f. In the light of what was said earlier about the paucity of prefigurative quotations and the problems involved in using them, I should point out that Broch tells his readers, in a postscript to the novel (*op.cit.*, pp. 539f.), just where the quotations occur and what work they are taken from.

Broch's decision not to emphasize unduly the fourth Eclogue—the very cornerstone of the medieval altar erected to the Latin poet—but to concentrate instead upon the mythological aspects of his hero's major works is an essential feature of the novel. Although Weigand writes that Broch "makes relatively little use . . . of the fourth Eclogue," he still proposes that "Dante, rather than the *Eclogues, Georgics* and *Aeneid,* was responsible for the formation of Broch's creative Vergil complex."[88] All of Broch's novels, with the exception of *Die unbekannte Größe,* are redolent with soteriological myths, without necessarily suggesting the Christian concept of the Savior in particular. Too much concentration on the fourth Eclogue would surely have invited a specifically Christian interpretation of the Virgil figure, one too limited in scope for Broch's purposes. It is for this reason that Broch denies the importance of Dante for his novel,[89] a novel which works with more general, *mythological* prefigurations.[90]

Patterns of expectation, surprise twists to the prefiguration or playing with the reader's assumptions about the course of the plot, resulting from indeterminate or even misleading analogies, do not inform the novel's rhetoric as they do that of most prefigurative novels. The ideal reader, a constant concern in Broch's correspondence, already knows far more about the hero's life than he could possibly do in the case of a fictive artist. So, to exploit this difference,

[88] Weigand, *op.cit.,* p. 530.
[89] *Briefe,* p. 243; "Hingegen hat Dante beim Entwurf des Plans überhaupt keine Rolle gespielt."
[90] Käte Hamburger has made the same point about interpreting the figure of Joseph in Mann's biblical tetralogy specifically in Christian terms. She asks "ob Thomas Mann die Joseph-Gestalt als eine christliche Heilsbringererscheinung auffassen wollte" and concludes: Mann "verwandelt . . . den ursprünglichen Erlösungssinn dieser Überlieferung in einen *humanistischen.* Und entsprechend stellt sich in Josephs Geschichte der Mythus des Christentums, seines transzendenten Sinnes entkleidet, in seinem *symbolischen,* menschlichen Gehalt dar," *Thomas Manns "Joseph und seine Brüder,"* p. 148.

Broch schematizes the pattern. He stylizes the material into a pattern of ordered progression: from history to legend, from legend to myth and from myth to the archetypal sphere of the dissolution of the individual in death. This is appropriate in a novel where even the title reveals a fore-knowledge of the course events will take, and where the four books mirror the ordered, elemental structure of the cosmos. That the choice of a real artist in a way interferes with the patterns of conjecture normally triggered off in the reader's mind by the device is one of the principal reasons why novelists in general prefer to invent their artist-heroes. Few of them want the highly organized pattern of prefigurations that Broch puts to good use here. As with the mythological simile, too much specific information presented too soon[91] may well be aesthetically undesirable. What Broch achieves with *Der Tod des Vergil* is a signal contrast to the way the motifs are handled by Alberto Moravia in my following illustration.

Myth plus Amateur Psychology: Alberto Moravia's Il disprezzo

> ormai il dopoguerra è finito e si sente il bisogno di una formula nuova . . . il neorealismo, tanto per fare un esempio, ha stancato un po' tutti . . . ora, analizzando i motivi per cui il cinema neorealistico ci ha stancati, potremo forse arrivare a capire quale potrebbe essere la formula nuova.[92]

[91] This "too soon" should be emphasized. My formulation is not intended to subscribe to the currently popular contention that ambiguity is always a virtue in literature. It is simply drawing attention to Frisch's point that most works of this kind involve a process of development whereby we move from ambiguity to explication, and that premature clarity would make much of the subsequent patterning redundant.

[92] *op. cit.*, p. 85. (In passages quoted from Moravia and his translator, the use of dots follows the original punctuation and does not indicate ellipsis.) Angus Davidson's translation of this passage (*A Ghost at Noon*, Harmondsworth, 1964) runs: "The after-the-war period is now over, and people are feeling the need of a new formula

What the film-producer Battista has to say about the neo-realist film in this passage from *Il disprezzo* is of importance for an understanding of the novel's style. For Moravia, a novelist generally associated with the neo-realist school of post-war Italian fiction has here (in 1955) turned to a mythologically prefigurative type of novel.[93] Battista, a kind of Italian Cecil B. de Mille, appears to be quite convinced why the neo-realist mode is dying out: the public wants something more spectacular. This, of course, is not an adequate reason for Moravia's change of style, for *Il disprezzo* hardly offers a mythological circus instead of the stale bread of early post-war fiction. But it does draw our attention to the fact that Moravia has deliberately written a different kind of novel for very specific reasons.

Like most mythological novelists, Moravia turns to mythology for certain aesthetic effects. Unlike them, however, he lays a trap by setting up two bogus theories of mythology's importance in the novel: the one represented by Battista, whose ideal version of the *Odyssey* "sarebbe stato un film ricalcato sopra i grossi film biblici e in costume di Hollywood, con mostri, donne nude, scene di seduzione, erotismo e grandiloquenza,"[94] and on the other side, the scriptwriter Rheingold, for whom "Freud ci servirà da guida in questo paesaggio interno di Ulisse, e non Bérard con le sue carte geografiche e la sua filologia che non spiega

. . . Everyone—just to give an example—is a little tired of neo-realism . . . Now, by analysing the reasons for which we have grown tired of the neo-realist film, we may perhaps arrive at an understanding of what the new formula might be" (pp. 69f.).

[93] Cf. Frank Baldanza, "The Classicism of Alberto Moravia," *MFS*, III, 1957, pp. 309-320. Although Baldanza begins with a consideration of the classical allusions in *Il disprezzo*, he is more concerned with the relevance of classical tragedy to Moravia's works in general. *Il disprezzo* is not seen to mark so much a change as to express "the essence of his aims as an artist" (p. 309).

[94] *op.cit.*, p. 89; "would be a film based upon the big Biblical and costume films of Hollywood, with monsters, naked women, seduction scenes, eroticism and grandiloquence" (*A Ghost at Noon*, p. 73).

nulla . . . e invece del Mediterraneo noi esploreremo l'animo di Ulisse . . . o meglio, il suo subcosciente."[95] It is between the Scylla of Battista and the Charybdis of Rheingold that both Moravia and his hero steer their way. As a result, a highly differentiated attitude to mythology emerges during the course of *Il disprezzo*.

Il disprezzo is the most introspective mythological novel that I shall be looking at. Its hero, the writer Riccardo Molteni, possesses the passion for self-analysis which so many of Moravia's heroes and heroines display. Being an artist-novel, this work includes many discussions of the very technique which Moravia himself adopts. Chapters 8 and 12, in particular, contain some generally perceptive comments about the problems involved in accommodating mythology to a modern audience; and although the issue in question is a projected film with a mythological theme, much of what is said is equally applicable to literary mythological motifs. Nevertheless, there is more to the quality of differentiation in this novel than the simple fact that the hero is continually analyzing his situation or its artistic reflection in the film to be made of the *Odyssey*. Molteni is brought face to face with two people who have long since made up their minds about mythology, whereas he has not and cannot. They represent two extreme positions, as we have seen, and it is clear that, contrary to their expectations, Molteni is not likely to side with either of them, although he is constantly being drawn into taking a stand. Presumably because of the producer's death, the film is not made in the end. Instead, since he is never forced to reach a final decision about mythology's contemporary significance, or about the relevance of the *Odyssey* in particu-

[95] *op.cit.*, p. 146. "Freud will serve us as a guide through this interior landscape of Ulysses, not Bérard with his maps and his philology which explains nothing . . . and, instead of the Mediterranean, we shall explore the mind of Ulysses—or, rather, his subconscious" (*A Ghost at Noon*, p. 119).

lar to his marital problems, Molteni finds himself continually measuring his experiences cautiously against the myth, speculating about his future on the basis of the model provided, and recapitulating how far the past has fulfilled a pattern. In short, his attitude is that of the reader of a mythological novel, and the choice of a first-person narrative emphasizes this closeness.

The plot of *Il disprezzo* runs parallel to the final part of the *Odyssey*: the homecoming. (It is characteristic of many modern works prefigured by the *Odyssey* that their concern is more with the psychological aspects of the husband's love and his homecoming than with the more epic elements.) Moravia's is a very simple story involving a husband whose marriage is bankrupt for no observable reason except that his wife has ceased to love him. The husband is invited to participate in writing a film-version of the *Odyssey*, but a triangular situation emerges when the wife begins to surrender to the director of the film. The novel closes rather abruptly when the wife, Emilia, and the director, Battista, are killed in a car crash while eloping together. The Odysseus-figure, Emilia's husband Riccardo, certainly has his revenge against his wife's suitor,[96] though at the cost of his own wife. But this tragic process is depersonalized: instead of having a modern Odysseus kill his usurper(s)—too "heroic" a task for the kind of character Moravia describes —an accident is used to dispose of the couple. The change in plot may be interpreted in the light of the way the two wives differ. The Penelope of the myth remains faithful to her husband and is suitably rewarded, whereas Emilia is untrue and the car crash becomes her punishment.

In many ways, *Il disprezzo* is Moravia's answer to the

[96] In both the novel and the projected film-script, the wife simply has one suitor, not many: ". . . I Proci, a noi converrà forse ridurre i Proci ad un solo personaggio, per esempio Antinoo. . ." (*op.cit.*, p. 192).

Odyssey: Molteni is something of an anti-Odysseus. Battista, the Antinous-figure, plays a far more dominant role than Penelope's suitors do in the classical tale. This is not only because he is Molteni's employer for the duration of the novel, but the change in situation is emphasized by a neat twist to the prefiguration. One of the points of friction between Molteni and his wife is his inability to afford the kind of home she would like to have. Indeed, for a long time he is unable to buy anything at all. So when Battista offers to lend Molteni his luxury flat on Capri while the film-script is being written, he successfully establishes himself as someone more effective than Molteni in Emilia's eyes. For:

> l'amore per la casa aveva in Emilia tutti i caratteri di una passione; aggiungerò che quel giorno quella passione mi apparve legata e confusa con la sensualità, come se il fatto di averle finalmente acquistato un appartamento mi avesse reso ai suoi occhi non soltanto piú amabile, ma anche, in senso tutto fisico, piú vicino e piú intimo.[97]

Since her willingness or unwillingness to respond to her husband depends in some mysterious way[98] on whether he is able to equip himself as the provider of a suitable home,

[97] *op.cit.*, p. 20; ". . . with Emilia, love of home had all the characteristics of a passion; and I must add, on this occasion, that same passion appeared to me to be bound up with, and mingled with, sensuality, as though the fact of having at least acquired a flat for her had made me, in her eyes, not merely more lovable, but also, in a wholly physical sense, closer and more intimate" (*A Ghost at Noon*, p. 16).

[98] Dominique Fernandez simply treats Emilia's reaction as "un mépris de peau" (*Le Roman italien et la crise de la conscience moderne*, Paris, 1958, p. 74). Donald Heiney, on the other hand, sees much more of a spiritual crisis underlying their relationship: "His lack of manliness, his failure for example to defend Emilia against the overtures of Battista, is connected at its very root to this failure of authenticity as an artist. It would be difficult to say which came first, but one cannot exist without the other: he is not an artist because he is not a man, and he is not a man because he is not an artist" (*Three Italian Novelists*, p. 54).

Battista has symbolically usurped Molteni's position as husband already through the offer of the villa. And if one compares Molteni's position with Odysseus', one can see how sharp the contrast is between the myth of the husband returning to his own home to claim his rights and the modern dispossessed man whose claim to his wife has been acquired by his employer. The relationship between notions of virility, wifeliness and possessions is subtly handled here,[99] for Emilia's need for a home is something much more than vulgar materialism.

The title of the English translation of the novel—*A Ghost at Noon*—refers to an enigmatic episode towards the end of the work. On the day that Emilia and Battista elope by car, Molteni goes down to the beach. He appears to meet his wife there and to row her out to a cave, but it is only when he reaches this potential love-grotto that he turns to look for Emilia in the boat and finds the whole episode to have been a vision. He returns to the villa to hear of his wife's and Battista's fatal accident. The English title is rather unfortunate, for he has his vision before their death. What he sees is quite categorically not a ghost, but an almost deliberate parody of a Freudian projection.[100] There may well be an uncanny element here, hovering between spectacle and psychology in much the same way as the film

[99] Giuliano Dego sees the situation in simple terms as "the relationship between an intellectual and a woman." The suggestion is made that "Emilia never throws any doubt on Riccardo's virility," for her to be a man "means, in accordance with the scale of bourgeois values which Emilia embodies, and which she faithfully represents, to be like Battista, a vulgar *nouveau riche* film producer, a speculator and counterfeiter of culture" (*Moravia*, Edinburgh and London, 1966, pp. 94f.). Although I find Donald Heiney's interpretation more sensitive to the complexities of their relationship than this simple notion of representation, I would stress that the problem remains open enough to invite these various different readings.

[100] "Like Molteni's other problems, the hallucination is totally inside his own head and there is nothing outside himself to blame it on" (Heiney, *op.cit.*, p. 56).

project does, but the "ghost" idea diminishes this ambiguity. And it draws our attention too much towards a piece of gothic fun, while the Italian title conjures up the disdain of Emilia for her husband, a feeling which is made even more hurtful by contrast with the idyllic ending of the *Odyssey*. Molteni's first perception of the parallels between his own marital situation and the *Odyssey* is brought about quite early on by his co-scriptwriter's reading of the epic: "Fedeltà, signor Molteni, non amore . . . Penelope è fedele a Ulisse, ma non sappiamo fino a che punto lo ami . . . e come lei sa, si può talvolta essere fedelissimi e non amare . . . In certi casi, anzi la fedeltà è una forma di vendetta, di ricatto, di rivalsa dell'amor proprio."[101] As Heiney has observed, Rheingold is a better psychoanalyst of Molteni's problems than he is an aesthetician. It is by listening to Rheingold holding forth on how to film the *Odyssey* that Molteni notices what he calls "la strana rassomiglianza dell'interpretazione omerica di Rheingold ai miei fatti personali."[102]

However, after this *aperçu*, the novel continues for some chapters without any further observations on Molteni's part about the parallels between the film he is working on and his own personal affairs. Indeed, he seems to be trying to compensate largely for his personal troubles by immersing himself in discussions of the film (as if this was not closely bound up with his own problem!). Hence, a certain ironic disparity between Molteni's perspective and the reader's

---

[101] *op.cit.*, p. 95. "Loyalty, Signor Molteni, not love . . . Penelope is loyal to Ulysses, but we do not know how far she loved him . . . and as you know, people can sometimes be absolutely loyal without loving . . . In certain cases, in fact, loyalty is a form of vengeance, of blackmail, of recovering one's self-respect. . ." (*A Ghost at Noon*, p. 78).

[102] *op.cit.*, p. 96; "the strange resemblance between Rheingold's interpretation of Homer and my own personal affairs" (*A Ghost at Noon*, p. 79).

emerges. We are aware that his odyssey has not been without its Nausicaa: a typist whom Molteni's wife catches him kissing one day, something which he tries to brush off as being of no consequence. We are able to perceive in the novel a parallel to Odysseus' return in disguise: for one evening Molteni sits unnoticed on the balcony of the villa and witnesses the tokens of affection exchanged inside between his wife and Battista. (Only later does he reveal what he has seen.) But Molteni no longer seems interested in prefigurations, he has lost the playful sense of distance that his readers may be able to maintain. So what has begun as a plot-motivated prefiguration slowly becomes independent of the characters involved and turns into an exchange between the author and the reader—the same process as Bruce Morrissette has analyzed in the case of Robbe-Grillet's *Les Gommes*.

At a much later point in the novel, when Molteni is well aware of what is going on between his wife and Battista and the situation is becoming desparate, the *Odyssey* offers him a possible solution to his problem. "Ulisse, per riconquistare l'amore di Penelope, uccide i Proci . . . In teoria tu dovresti uccidere Battista . . . ma viviamo in un mondo meno violento e assoluto di quello dell'*Odissea* . . . sarà sufficiente che rinunzi alla sceneggiatura, rompi ogni rapporto con Rheingold, riparti domani mattina per Roma. . . ."[103] But poor Molteni is not even uncompromising enough to carry out a decision of this kind. He vacillates until Fate and the lovers themselves step in to bring the action to a conclusion.

[103] *op.cit.*, p. 201. "Ulysses, in order to regain Penelope's love, killed the Suitors . . . In theory, you ought to kill Battista . . . but we live in a less violent and uncompromising world than that of the *Odyssey* . . . All you need to do is to throw up the script, break off all relations with Rheingold and leave again for Rome tomorrow morning" (*A Ghost at Noon*, p. 161). Significantly, Molteni is more concerned with cutting himself off from Rheingold, who is revealing the truth to him, than with the main protagonists.

Yet even if he is unwilling to follow in the footsteps of Odysseus, Molteni is still able to use the *Odyssey* as a measure for amateur psychoanalysis:

> Perché Battista, Rheingold ed io avevamo tre concezioni tanto diverse della figura di Ulisse? Proprio perché le nostre vite, i nostri ideali umani erano diversi. L'immagine di Battista, superficiale, volgare, retorica e insensata rassomigliava alla vita e agli ideali o meglio, agli interessi di Battista; quella più reale ma ridotta e avvilita di Rheingold era in accordo con le possibilità morali e artistiche del regista; infine la mia, senza dubbio la più alta e insieme la più naturale, la più poetica e insieme la più vera, derivava dalla mia aspirazione forse impotente ma sincera ad una vita che non fosse compromessa e svuotata dal denaro né abbassata al livello fisiologico e materiale.[104]

Il disprezzo is in some ways an over-explicit novel. Obvious images are emphasized gratuitously, symbolic relationships are stressed to a degree that would be impertinent, if this were not to draw attention to the pedestrian character of the narrator-hero. Yet Moravia manages to assign to his mythological imagery a relatively sophisticated set of tasks: through the figures of Battista and Rheingold, he can parody certain tendencies in modern films and novels, and even (as Fernandez has suggested) come to terms with his own passion for psychoanalytic fiction. He can present an ironic situation whereby Rheingold's inter-

[104] *op.cit.*, p. 240. "Why did Battista, Rheingold and I myself have three so very different conceptions of the figure of Ulysses? Precisely because our lives and our human ideals were different. Battista's image, superficial, vulgar, rhetorical and senseless, resembled the life and the ideals—or rather, the interests—of Battista; Rheingold's, more real, but diminished and degraded, was in accordance with the moral and artistic possibilities of Rheingold; and finally mine, without doubt the loftiest yet the most natural, the most poetical, yet the most true, was derived from my aspiration, impotent perhaps and yet sincere, after a life that was not tainted and crippled by money or reduced to a purely physiological and material level" (*A Ghost at Noon*, p. 192).

pretation, a travesty of the *Odyssey*, can nevertheless be a perceptive, yet incomplete analysis of Molteni's situation. And he can rely on the reader's insights into such a familiar and heavily underscored prefiguration to give a fuller interpretation of Molteni's tragic predicament than either the hero himself or Rheingold are able to give. We shall, in fact, come across this effective combination of prefigurative pattern and first-person narrative once more later, in a more complex form, in Macdonald Harris's *Trepleff*.

The Technique of Juxtaposition: John Bowen's A World Elsewhere, *Hans Erich Nossack's* Interview mit dem Tode, Ann Quin's Passages

There used to be a time when the wise old legends of the Greeks were all being written in modern terms. Nowadays, it seems, the approach is rather different; the legend is repeated as it stands more or less, while side by side with it the author unravels a contemporary net of events or emotions.[105]

In this chapter, we have moved from considering a group of individual devices, each capable of introducing a mythological analogy, to a discussion of three novels where the prefigurative motif is both a well-motivated and central feature of the action. The final type of novel to be discussed, the one described above by William Trevor, works with a less integrated mythological symbolism. John Bowen's *A World Elsewhere* and Hans Erich Nossack's *Interview mit dem Tode*, two examples of this technique of juxtaposition, both evolve a method of interpolating motifs by embodying them in whole blocks of the narrative. This method of introducing myths represents a refusal on the novelist's part to embed prefigurative imagery in the realistic narrative by using such hackneyed devices as artist-heroes creating symbolic works or characters coming across mythological

[105] "New Novels," *The Listener*, 8 March 1965, p. 345.

objective correlatives. Instead, the author leaves the prefigurations as loosely integrated entities within the work. Nevertheless, different degrees of autonomy and assimilation can be seen in the motifs used in the following two illustrations.

Gareth Payne, the fictive seagreen-incorruptible of British politics in the early sixties, retires after a scandal concerning his colleagues' dishonesty, to the Greek island of Lemnos, ostensibly to pursue his academic interests and forget the cabals and deceits of contemporary public life. Roger Turner, a young M.P., is sent out to Lemnos after a few years to try and persuade "the Honest Man" (as he is called by the press) to return to Parliament, for his party is in dire need of a figurehead. This, the central situation in *A World Elsewhere* (1965) by the English novelist John Bowen, is counterpointed with an account of the Philoctetes myth.

There are, of course, various versions of this myth. In one, Philoctetes, the marooned Greek prince, with his magic bow and festering wound, is tended by a shepherd; in another, he has some of his Meliboean troops on the island with him. But as an appropriate image for Gareth Payne the version chosen by John Bowen is that of the solitary wretch, as seen through the eyes of Neoptolemus as he arrives on the island to try to secure the bow for victory in the Trojan War:

> The old man[106] was naked like an animal or a beggar. Those parts of him on which hair would grow were concealed by it. The hair was grey and long, and tangled, and grew on him like a parasite, his body was so wasted that one might conclude that the hair sucked nourishment from it. He had begun to run to pick up the dead gull, but he stopped when he saw Neopto-

[106] Significantly, the "Old Man" is also the term Turner uses for Gareth Payne.

lemus, and now he approached more cautiously. He moved with a limp, Neoptolemus noticed, and an old rag, fellow to those drying outside the cave, was bound about one ankle.[107]

This is basically a psychological myth, for all its physicality: a myth of loneliness and despair, which for much of Bowen's novel seems a marked contrast to the world of Gareth Payne, as he lives in his Mediterranean idyll cut off from the hypocrisy he found in politics. Yet as the details of his life slowly emerge, the relevance of the myth becomes more apparent.

A World Elsewhere begins with Turner's arrival at Athens on his way to Lemnos. Here he meets Agatha Baron, an ex-girl-friend who chooses to accompany him to the island and eventually proves instrumental in persuading Payne that he ought to return to England. (Symbolically, the lengthy preamble in Athens corresponds to the deliberations of the Greeks about how to obtain Philoctetes' bow.) In many ways, Agatha seems a far better candidate for the Odysseus prefiguration, if there is to be one in the novel, than do the forces in London who send Turner out to Greece on his mission, for she has a greater share of Odysseus' guile.

The novel's correspondences are built up through a series of juxtapositions: a chapter about Turner in modern Greece is followed by a section retelling part of the Philoctetes myth. The two "plots" are synchronized, so that Turner's arrival on the island and meeting with Payne is juxtaposed with the above description of Neoptolemus' first encounter with Philoctetes. For about half the novel, the mythological passages appear to be direct authorial comment (as they are, for example, in David Stacton's *Kaliyuga*). The turning-point comes when we discover that Payne himself is the author of this new version of the myth. Until this juncture,

[107] *op.cit.*, p. 121.

we have been led to believe that Payne is engaged solely in a piece of research on Heraclitus, but then we discover that the passages from one of his manuscripts (quoted in italics) form part of the Philoctetes myth inserted into the novel.

The draft of what would be an article and might be a chapter of his book, written in pencil on yellow paper, lay in a pile of sheets under a brass paperweight.

He put the yellow sheets away into the top right-hand drawer, clipped the cards in use together, and returned them to the front of the index. He took from the top left-hand drawer of the desk another manuscript, paused to read over the last few pages, and then chose a clean sheet of paper, and began to write. *"The ship dropped anchor outside the bank of mist that hid the island, and Neoptolemus was rowed ashore alone."* Turner seemed a pleasant young fellow. The Old Man crossed out *"was rowed ashore"* and substituted *"came ashore."* Better to use an active verb, and anyway, if he was rowed, he wasn't alone. Turner was one of the new, state-educated—what was the word? meritocracy. No famous father. No Achilles, dead or living. Was there an Odysseus somewhere behind him?

"As he took his first steps on the rocky beach, the mist was pierced by a shaft of sunlight: he was like an actor, stepping into a spotlight to begin the play." The difference was that he, Gareth Payne, was not wounded, and had no wish to leave his island. As for his being armed with the bow of Heracles, why he had some gift for administration, and enjoyed the practice of it; that was all. There were plenty as good as he, and he himself had other talents, other concerns. The pursuit of scholarship was an ideal; it was the pursuit of truth itself, while government was only a going-on from one day to another. *"The beach was deserted. He must not too obviously seek the wounded man, but must happen across him, as it should seem, by accident."*

Nor could the fall of a single city be of much importance today. Just as there was no one man to be a saviour, so there was no one task. And it had always been so. Consider Troy—all the fuss about Troy, the ten years' war about Troy, which in fact fell many times, and the brace of Mycenaean Greeks who sacked it were themselves overwhelmed by the Dorians within a hundred years. The story is pointless, he thought. They might have left Philoctetes to rot on the island, and nothing very much would have been altered, except that Sophocles would not have had a subject for his play.

If now, after Turner's visit, he could see the correspondence between his own life and the story he was writing, it was because unconsciously he had always seen it, had cast himself in this role, and had made a hobby out of writing a fiction of which he was himself the hero. *"Philoctetes, if he were alive, must have found or built himself a shelter."* It did not matter. Any hobby must offer self-gratification of some kind; as long as self-gratification did not turn into self-abuse, there was no harm in it. He did not allow writing this fiction to interfere with his serious work, and worked at it only during his recreation-time. Furthermore, hobby or no, it was also a task, to be finished, and so a kind of discipline as well as a gratification.[108]

Once this turning-point has been passed and we know who composed the Philoctetes sections, much of *A World Elsewhere* is narrated more directly from Payne's perspective. He returns again and again to the limitations of the correspondences he perceives between his situation and Philoctetes'. One of his problems is inventing an ending to "his" myth. He wonders in despair whether he should not resort to some *deus ex machina*: "Sophocles in his play has Neoptolemus repeat his offer to take Philoctetes home, and Philoctetes accepts. Just as they are about to depart, the god Heracles appears from a machine, and tells Philoctetes that it is his duty to go to Troy instead. Well, if ever a *deus ex machina* were needed, it was now."[109] Chapter 16 of the

[108] *op.cit.*, pp. 116-117.
[109] *op.cit.*, p. 165.

novel consists of a series of projected endings to the myth:
"*I fall into the epic style,*" Payne observes, "*only because I
do not know what is to happen next.*"[110] The Old Man
realizes that securing an end for his myth would be tantamount to discovering how he himself should act. But his
problem is that he is unaware of any wound.

> If I am to be Philoctetes in my own drama, what is
> my wound, and what my bow? the Old Man thought.
> Well—the bow: that was obvious now. It was not his
> talent for administration; he could not preen himself
> on that. "*As for being armed with the bow of Heracles,
> why he had some gift for administration,*"—they did
> not want that gift or need it. They did not want the old
> man at all; they wanted his reputation—for one does
> not make one's own reputation; it is made by others; it
> is the sum of what is thought by others. They wanted
> an image, not the substance of the Old Man. "*He had
> some gift for administration*"—nobody in Britain wor-
> ries much if administration should be incompetent. The
> British are used to that; they prefer it. If the Party
> managers could get his reputation, his image, his
> shadow without him, they would be glad to take it, but
> his reputation was more securely attached to his per-
> son than the bow to Philoctetes.
> And the wound?
> There was no wound: he was unwounded. And he
> did not wish to leave the island.[111]

Gareth Payne's wound, although it takes him a long time to
acknowledge the fact, is his delusion of self-sufficiency and
the debilitating effect this has on those around him, especially his sister. Living on Lemnos with Payne, she "seemed
absurdly glad to see Roger" at his first visit;[112] indeed, she
later appears so lonely that she takes an almost pathological
part in mourning the death of one of the local boys. It is

---

[110] *op.cit.*, pp. 178f.   [111] *op.cit.*, pp. 157-158.
[112] *op.cit.*, p. 108.

Roger Turner's friend Agatha[113] who points out how much Payne's idyllic retirement has been bought at the expense of his sister's happiness. "Forget about helping people. Just help your sister."[114] Payne at first refuses to return to London for this flimsy reason: "I cannot go back to politics, only because my sister is unhappy. If I were to do that, I should end by hating her. You must know that."[115] However, the final version that he is eventually able to write of the myth, after this conversation—indeed the fact that he is now able to bring it to a successful conclusion—makes it clear that in all probability he will return.

> The god said, "You must return because you are a man, as I was, and as they are. Unless you die or become a god yourself, there is no escaping it; you are of that kind. By living alone you are diminished. You must know and be known or you are nothing. You must feel and inspire feeling. You must be agent and patient. All that most makes you a man requires that you should be among men. That is your obligation. It is to yourself, and to none other, and if you should end by hating yourself, it is no great matter, and better than that you should be less than yourself.
>
> "You must return for nobody's sake but your own," the god said. "Because I am your friend, I tell you this."[116]

Needless to say, Bowen avoids over-sentimentalizing the ending by transferring such insights from the modern character to the figures in the myth.

A World Elsewhere is a novel which plays skilfully throughout with the reader's expectations. The relationship

---

[113] There is a certain irony to the fact that Agatha finds herself staying at Payne's house after spraining her foot, of all things; she ostensibly has the wound, not Payne, but she points out his symbolic wound to him. Similarly, he is ironically called Payne, even though he claims to have no pain-giving wound.

[114] *op.cit.*, p. 215.   [115] *op.cit.*, p. 215.   [116] *op.cit.*, pp. 216f.

181

between mythological and modern sections is not revealed until about halfway through (although the length of the mythological pieces, dealing in detail with what is, after all, a well-known myth, could only be justified by the fact that they offer indirect information about Payne). Whether or not the prefiguration is going to be followed remains open until the final chapter of the novel, and even then the fact that Payne successfully completes his myth need not necessarily mean that he will return to British politics. The novel also has a richness of vision where other works tend to be one-sided: we are given a vivid sense of both modernity and antiquity. Modern Greece as well as the background of contemporary British politics (with overtones of the Profumo affair) come to life. And despite the author's comment in his foreword that "the myth is not bound by time," one receives a differentiated sense not only of the general parallels but also of the discrepancies between the realities of the myth and those of the modern world. This effect originates partly from having the myth narrated by a character in the work who is as much concerned with differences as anything, and partly from revealing to the reader, through dramatic irony, parallels that this figure (Payne) cannot admit to. The result is a cross between the artist-novel and the kind of juxtaposition where myth and modernity are genuinely unrelated, except symbolically.

In Hans Erich Nossack's *Interview mit dem Tode* (1948), the mythological sections are clearly distinct from the themes of the other episodes. The novel contains two mythological tales: "Kassandra" and "Orpheus und. . . ."[117] Both of these occur side by side with, and hence act as symbolic comment on, descriptions of events in Germany during the Second World War and the following period. The motivation for the Greek motifs lies not only in the individual parallels between modernity and mythology, but in a

[117] *op.cit.*, pp. 62-93 and pp. 256-258.

general conviction that things do not change much. Talking of the Sack of Troy, one of the figures in "Kassandra" says: "Das ist vor tausend Jahren so gewesen und wird in tausend Jahren nicht anders sein."[118] The juxtaposition of the story "Dorothea," an account of the aftermath of the Allies' bombing of Hamburg in 1943, with a tale about the Trojan War is intended to stress similarities between past and present. However, *Interview mit dem Tode* does not entail a simple, comparative juxtaposition of the Trojan War and World War Two. It has eleven independent stories treating the themes of death and catastrophe in various styles and within numerous settings. Two major stories give a vivid account of the bombing of Hamburg; two have mythological themes; some of the others treat fairy-tale subjects. One, "Der Jüngling aus dem Meer," includes a merman who may be the angel of death. Hanna, the narrator here, asks him if he is this and receives no direct answer.[119] Another tale, "Apassionata," is about a character who goes to the moon. And there is a telltale story entitled "Das Märchenbuch": referring to a collection of fairy-tales which is the book the narrator misses most from his bombed-out library. *Interview mit dem Tode* also acquaints us with a number of allegorical figures. In the title story, we witness an interview with Death, who appears just as overworked as his more famous embodiment in Wolfgang Borchert's *Draußen vor der Tür*. Furthermore, we are offered, in the figure of "Klonz" an image of the omnipresent, buoyant *petit bourgeois* who manages to survive and make a mockery of all catastrophes.

Amidst these various levels of fiction—*reportage*, mythology, fairy-tale, allegory, anecdote—it is not possible to discern the pattern of alternation between theme and motif

[118] *op.cit.*, p. 73. "That was so a thousand years ago and will be no different in a thousand years' time."
[119] *op.cit.*, p. 153.

which William Trevor describes in his account of the technique. The two longest sections are devoted to the bombing of Hamburg and the ensuing chaos. The position of the two mythological stories, coming after these descriptions, permits them to function as retrospective comment on the wartime ordeal. Because the stories are placed one after the other without any explanation to link them, the reader himself searches for the link and looks for common denominators. Although such juxtaposition demands more imaginative cooperation from the reader than most other types of prefiguration looked at in this chapter, various clues are left to be followed. For example, one finds a revealing etymological link between the stories "Kassandra" and "Dorothea." Dorothea tells us that her name means "divine gift" ("Gottesgeschenk")[120] and we are reminded in the mythological tale that Cassandra's foresight is also a divine gift: "die Gabe von Phöbos."[121] Although the Trojan and Hamburg disasters are compared, these two figures are possibly contrasted. Cassandra can see into the future, but Dorothea cannot. Dorothea's name may be taken as ironic, if one assumes that it indicates how different our age is from heroic antiquity, or serious, if she is meant to be a gift to the hero, who discovers her during the exodus from the city to the safety of the plain outside.

In the second mythological tale in the cycle, "Orpheus und . . . ," which closes the novel, the mood of contrast is more strongly developed. Many versions of myths purport finally to give us the truth about them, a truth which, they suggest, has long been distorted.[122] Nossack also resorts to

[120] op.cit., p. 15.
[121] op.cit., p. 84.
[122] For example, the title of Franz Kafka's "Die Wahrheit über Sancho Pansa" (*Beschreibung eines Kampfes*, New York, 1946, p. 96), or the remark in his "Das Schweigen der Sirenen" which tells us: "Es wird übrigens noch ein Anhang hierzu überliefert. . ." and proceeds to offer a new reading (*op.cit.*, p. 98). Yannis Ritsos's poem "Penelope's despair" begins with a series of denials: "Not that she

this standard technique of denigrating the tradition in order to vindicate his particular version of why Orpheus turned around on his way up from Hades. He begins: "Es wird nun immer erzählt . . ."; there follows the standard explanation that Orpheus turned around to ensure that Eurydice was still following him. "Das ist nicht der wahre Grund," we are then informed;[123] a new truth is needed in our day and age. Orpheus, it is suggested, did not turn back for Eurydice's sake, as he still does in Broch's version of the myth, but because he had fallen in love with his intercessor in Hades, Persephone. Hence the unfinished title: " 'Eurydike' möchten wir fortfahren, weil wir es so gewohnt sind."[124] But the missing name should really be Persephone. This twist gives an emblematic ending to Nossack's novel. The main preoccupation of modern man in a catastrophe, this interpretation of the myth would have us believe, is a fatal fascination with the idea of death and destruction (even with the idea of going to interview Death or falling in love with a denizen of the underworld). This morbid fascination is evident, rather than any great compassion for

---

didn't recognise him in the dim light of the fire;/it wasn't that he was disguised, wearing rags like a beggar./No. There were clear signs. . ."; there follows a new interpretation (quoted from *TLS*, 21 August 1970, p. 916). Wieland Schmid's "Bei den Sirenen" likewise says of the traditional tale: "Dies allerdings ist eine Sage und sicher erfunden. Glaubwürdig scheint uns, daß . . ." (*Deutsche Prosa*, ed. H. Bingel, Stuttgart, 1963, p. 298). Writing of "der Mythos Lear" in his Hamlet-novel, Döblin allows one of his characters to say: "darüber ist viel fabuliert worden. Hören Sie, wie es sich verhielt" (*op.cit.*, p. 226). One finds the same method in Michael Ayrton's introduction to *The Testament of Daedalus*: "You who read this testament and have known until now only the bare bones of the story will see how time alters and distorts matters" (London, 1962, p. 10). And it also occurs as a device in Wolfgang Hildesheimer's *Tynset*: "Ich bin der Junge in der Geschichte, der zu oft 'der Wolf' gerufen hat. Nur wird diese Geschichte falsch erzählt. . ." (Frankfurt a.M., 1967, p. 41).
[123] *op.cit.*, p. 257. "It is always said . . . that is not the true reason. . . ."
[124] *op.cit.*, p. 256. " 'Eurydice' we should like to continue, because we are accustomed to do so."

one's fellow sufferers. Persephone is important not only as a woman,[125] but also as a representative of the kingdom of death. There is as much of Schopenhauer as of Bachofen in Nossack's novel.

Again, collocating this new interpretation of the Orpheus myth with the modern setting of Hamburg during the Allied bombing raids leaves the reader to work out for himself the full significance of this complex of tales. It remains the least explicit of all the devices considered so far, yet it demands that the reader take account of the prefiguration. In novels where the mythological motifs are largely implicit or understated, the reader can choose to experience the novel at the realistic level only. However, it is impossible to do this in the case of a work like *Interview mit dem Tode* without neglecting a large and explicit part of the narrative.

With another mode of juxtaposition, a rarer sort, episodes are put side by side instead of one after the other. Rather than have mythology and modernity divided into separate passages, Ann Quin, for example, puts them in two columns on the page in her recent novel *Passages* (1969):

Depicted on vase: Wheels suspended in Palace of Hades/Persephone. Two kinds solid and spoked.	Decision between madness and security is imminent.
	Approach of death—madness the only way out?

[125] Karl August Horst sees this as a mother-fixation of the kind he also finds in *Nekyia*: "In Nossacks *Nekyia* verschlingt sich die Heimkehrerfabel mit dem Mutterfrevel. Odysseus kehrt nicht so sehr zur Gattin als zur Mutter heim, so wie in einer anderen Geschichte . . . Orpheus überm Anblick der Totengöttin und Mutter die Gattin Eurydike vergißt" (*Kritischer Führer durch die deutsche Literatur der Gegenwart*, Munich, 1962, p. 129).

"I feel as though I'm on loan from the underworld." Does she expect then for me to play Orpheus? The bleeding head singing always. Divinities of Orphism: demons rather than gods. Development of Orphism doctrine of eternal punishment.

Morbid habit of self-examination. Slayer of Orpheus had a little stag tattooed on upper part of her right arm.

She wore a thin green dress, her legs, thighs showed through. Green against white. She looked flushed. She expected him to ask her something, anything. She sensed his attention elsewhere, the door that opened a crack. The revolver appeared in an outstretched hand.

Later she tried lifting him from the floor, and fell on top. The light spiralled through her hair. Smell of the sea, figs from her hands, made him dizzy, contradicting the terror. The sort that waits at the crack of dawn. An empty bed, when even a cigarette tastes bitter. Waiting for that almighty sun . . .[126]

For a novel dealing with a schizophrenic, this split page proves remarkably effective. The mythological motifs on the left, acting as a kind of psychoanalytical commentary on the diary, gradually assume the dimensions of some frightening second self. The aesthetic interference generated by splitting the page—the reason why this kind of juxtaposition is seldom used—is here exploited to conjure up a sense of madness.

The juxtaposition of mythological sections with blocks of narrative concerned with the modern world has something in common with the technique of literary *montage*, even if it is not identical with it. Strictly speaking, *montage* entails a far less ordered presentation of two or (usually) more elements. Instead of separating mythology and modernity

[126] *op.cit.*, p. 32.

into different chapters or putting them on different halves of the page, a writer wishing to achieve the effect of *montage* would place them together within the same chapter or even within the same paragraph or sentence, for the strength of *montage* resides in its ability to present an unexpected clash of disparate elements.[127] Or, to use Herman Meyer's terms, there is more of a tension between assimilation and dissimilation in *montage*. One can appreciate the difference by comparing the technique of *A World Elsewhere*, where the long passage I quoted above put the mythological fragments in italics, with an extract from Alfred Döblin's *Berlin Alexanderplatz*.

In Döblin's novel a number of prefigurations, including Isaac and Abraham, Job, and Orestes are first presented by separate chapter headings,[128] and then the same symbolic figures slowly appear in *montage* elements at various points in the novel. The process becomes increasingly radical as the work progresses. At first, there is a paragraph change whenever a fresh prefiguration from the past is mounted on the Berlin canvas; but towards the end, the analogy may occur in a single sentence or an isolated clause. In the following passage, for example, the hero's wanderings through Berlin are comically interrupted to remind us of a number of prefigurations, including the mythological:

> Er schob ab. Vor Minnas Haus strolchte er herum. Mariechen saß auf einem Stein, einem Bein, ganz allein. Was geht mich die an. Er roch an dem Haus herum. Was geht mich die an. Soll die mit ihrem Ollen glücklich werden. Sauerkraut mit Rüben, die haben mich vertrieben, hätte meine Mutter Fleisch gekocht, wär ich bei ihr geblieben. Hier stinken die Katzen auch nicht anders wie woanders. Häseken, verschwinde wie

127 For the opposite viewpoint, see Hans Wysling's "Die Technik der Montage: Zu Thomas Manns *Erwähltem*," *Euphorion*, LVII, 1963, pp. 156-226.
128 E.g. "Gespräch mit Hiob," *op.cit.*, pp. 114-116.

die Wurst im Spinde. Werde ich hier bregenklütrig rumstehen und mir das Haus angucken. Und die ganze Kompagnie macht kikeriki. Kikeriki. Kikeriki. So sprach Menelaos. Und ohne es zu wollen, machte er dem Telemach das Herz so wehmütig, daß ihm die Tränen an den Wangen herabrollten und er den Purpurmantel mit beiden Händen fest vor die Augen drücken mußte.
Indessen wandelte die Fürstin Helena aus ihren Frauengemächern hervor, einer Göttin an Schönheit gleich.
Kikeriki. Es gibt viele Sorten von Hühnern . . .[129]

And so the reader is back again in the Berlin sphere, with a Baroque list of various kinds of chicken. The unexpected change of subject has a comic speed which a change of chapter—and in many cases a fresh chapter-heading or the use of italics—would only destroy. This is a very different device from the kind of ordered, neatly counterpointed juxtaposition described in the case of Bowen's and Nossack's novels.

William Trevor suggested that juxtaposition is a recent thing. It also appears to involve a more complex kind of mythological motif, making heavier demands on the read-

[129] op.cit., pp. 106f. Eugene Jolas's translation reads: "Off he went. He trailed up and down in front of Minna's house. Mary sat upon a stone, all alone, upon a stone. What do I care about her? He hung round the house. Let her be happy with her old man. Sauerkraut all day, it drove me away, if mother had only cooked beef, I wouldn't have taken my leave. The cats here don't stink any different from other places. Rabbit, good-bye, like the veal and ham pie. Am I going to stand here and give myself the blues looking at the house? And the whole bunch hollering cock-a-doodle-doo.
Cock-a-doodle-doo. Cock-a-doodle-doo. Thus spake Menelaus. And, without meaning to, he made Telemachus's heart so sad that the tears rolled down his cheeks, so that he had to draw his purple mantle with both hands firmly before his eyes.
In the meanwhile Princess Helen strolled from out of the women's apartments, like unto a goddess in beauty.
Cock-a-doodle-doo. There are many kinds of chickens . . ." (*Alexanderplatz: The Story of Franz Biberkopf*, London, 1931, p. 115).

189

er's ability to solve certain largely undeveloped analogies. There could well be a sense of typological progression from simple to more complex forms in the choice of prefigurative techniques. It may not be coincidental that works involving juxtaposition and the novels with rather more convoluted motif-structures to be looked at in the next chapter have all appeared in the last two or three decades.[130] They do not, of course, supersede the older techniques, but merely extend the range of structural possibilities.

[130] The dates are: *A World Elsewhere* (1965), *Interview mit dem Tode* (1948), *Passages* (1969), *Die Schuldlosen* (1950), *L'Emploi du Temps* (1956), *Nekyia* (1947) and *Trepleff* (1968).

Distorted Motif-Structures

Types of Patterning

"C'était comme une piste tracée à mon intention" the hero of Michel Butor's *L'Emploi du Temps* says in the section "Les Présages," which introduces the novel's main prefigurations.[1] His is a feeling of being set a task of detection, of having a trail to follow, with which the reader of most mythological novels is familiar. One comes to recognize that a certain degree of complexity, challenging one to solve much of the analogy for oneself, as Butor's hero does, is a property of many prefigurations. It was one of the suggested reasons why mythological similes have been used sparingly, and it also proved helpful to think in terms of concealed information in order to explain the predilection for fictive artists rather than real ones. This may even be a reason why one prefiguration is preferred to another.

Such a notion of complexity may also revolve around the question of how faithful the modern novel stays to its chosen prefigurations or, more often, around the degree of poetic license exercized in evolving mythological motifs. I have so far assumed that there exists in most works a single prefiguration for any given character. Hence my whole approach until now could be reduced to a simple model, its components being two lines: the line of the mythological prefiguration and that of the modern plot. With imitation, these two lines would either be superimposed upon one

[1] *op.cit.*, p. 81.

another or run parallel. A liberal handling of the prefiguration would result in only occasional parallels in course. A more elaborate diagram still could even include a series of dotted lines to represent the reader's patterns of expectation at any given point in the narrative, but it is doubtful whether these vague premonitions could always be expressed adequately by the lineaments of visual models. There is, in fact, much more to the concept of patterning than such schemes can reflect.

The kind of two-part, stratified model governing my approach so far has largely been valuable as a corrective: to avoid assuming or implying any identity between prefiguration and modern character. This dialectical paradigm obviates the common misconception of mythical identity in literature by turning to the aid of such images as *levels* of significance and generality, or by borrowing Joyce's idea that our reading of such novels ideally proceeds "on two planes" with the myth as a pattern *superimposed* upon the realistic events of the contemporary narrative. The danger involved in committing oneself to such imagery has not been too evident yet because novels where it could arise have been avoided. But talking of *layers* of fiction and separating *strata* of mythology and contemporaneity (or talking of *correspondences* between these spheres) may give the false impression that the two layers posited, both that of the modern events and of the prefiguration offered for them, represent self-contained, consistent entities. To counteract this over-simplification, I shall now look at patterns without this illusion of consistency to the prefigurative element.

If there is a one-to-one relationship of correspondences between the prefiguration and the modern circumstances of the plot, such as we saw in John Bowen's *A World Elsewhere*, the reader is furnished with enough of the analogy to be able to isolate the myth as a separate pattern or ingredient in the novel. The basic episodes of the Philoctetes myth concern the figure's bow and wound, for which symbolic counterparts would have to be found in a modern novel, and the two characters who come to try and take him and his bow away from his island: Odysseus and Neoptolemus. In *A World Elsewhere*, three characters are involved, as in the myth, one staying on a Greek island and two coming to visit him in order to obtain his symbolic bow. Hence a simple diagram of the relationship between characters and prefigurations would look like this:

PREFIGURATION	Philoctetes	Neoptolemus	Odysseus
CHARACTER	Gareth Payne	Roger Turner	Agatha Baron

In this case, the distinction between character and prefiguration is made even more evident than usual because of the technique of juxtaposition described above. This is the most straightforward mode of prefiguration through correspondences, with which most of us are familiar through our reading of Joyce's *Ulysses* and Stuart Gilbert's study of the novel, where the mythological motif is even literally charted at one point.

In the novels to be treated in this chapter, no such persistent, one-to-one relationship is present. Prefigurations all occur in more complex patterns and in greater numbers. These more complicated motifs fall into two basic categories: one I shall call "condensation," the other "fragmentation." For just as various interpreters of mythology's place in literature have with benefit borrowed the term "displacement,"[2] I find it useful to operate at this point with other

---

[2] In the *Anatomy of Criticism*, Northrop Frye argues that "the presence of a mythical structure in realistic fiction . . . poses certain technical problems of making it plausible, and the devices used in solving these problems may be given the general name of 'displacement' " (p. 138). Analyzing the advantages of such a term, G. W. Hartmann has recently pointed out that "the concept of displacement enables us to revalue what grosser histories of literature see merely as secularization" ("Ghostlier Demarcations," *Northrop Frye in Modern Criticism: Selected Papers from the English Institute*, ed. Murray Krieger, New York and London, 1966, p. 126).

terms initially applied to the patterns of distortion found in dreams. I use these as convenient labels and not with any desire to stress the parallels between literary motif-structures and the configuration of symbols in dreams, although there is obviously a great deal of similarity between the two modes of accommodation. The term "condensation" refers to a pattern where a number of separate prefigurations all relate to one modern event or a single character. In contrast, "fragmentation" describes the situation where a single prefiguration is refracted across a number of modern figures. The distinguishing characteristic of this process is the repeated use of a single motif in various contexts, the comparison of more than one character with a single figure from mythology.

Aldous Huxley's *Brave New World* offers a very simple example of condensation. The archetypal patterns in Huxley's novel consist of: 1. the return of the Savage to the "brave new world"; 2. his falling in love with one of its inhabitants; and 3. the sense of strangeness between the lovers. The Savage, who was brought up in the desert on a diet of Shakespeare's collected works, can supply prefigurative quotations from *The Tempest, Romeo and Juliet* and *Othello* to qualify his position.[3] This is a symbolic pattern of condensation, therefore, whereby the Savage is prefigured by Caliban, Romeo and Othello at different points in the narrative. While it would not be possible to pinpoint exactly how much of the narrative is described by each prefiguration, we do have a sense of transition. Thomas Mann also gives us the same sense of progression from one prefiguration to another in his Joseph tetralogy. Joseph, he writes to Kerényi, "wechselt aus der ursprünglichen Tammuz-Adonis-Rolle immer mehr in die eines Hermes

---

[3] See Robert H. Wilson, *"Brave New World* as Shakespeare Criticism," *Shakespeare Association Bulletin,* xxxi, 1946, pp. 99-107.

hinüber."[4] Apart from such a succession of images, one also sometimes finds a fusion of two prefigurations with the modern character at one point in the narrative. For example, in Joyce's *Ulysses*, when Stephen Dedalus is depicted as the (symbolically) fatherless son, this is done both by means of the Telemachus prefiguration and also, among others, by a Hamlet motif. And the two motifs intermingle; Stephen does not resemble Hamlet more at one point and Telemachus at another. Hence the prefigurative pattern differs in structure from the serial variety of condensation found in *Brave New World* and *Joseph und seine Brüder*. To show how they differ in function, I shall discuss both types of condensation in detail.

In mythology itself, there are countless examples of the fusion or condensation of two or more myths with one another, consisting either of the merging of two characters from earlier myths into a single figure in a later version or in the establishment of a new, modified family-tree.[5] Consequently, the proliferation of similar patterns in mythological fiction is hardly surprising. Yet whereas condensation arises in both mythology and literature, fragmentation remains, to all appearances, a peculiarly literary idiosyncrasy, and a modern one at that.

---

[4] *Gespräch in Briefen*, p. 98; Joseph "changes from his original Tammuz-Adonis role more and more towards that of Hermes."

[5] According to N. K. Sandars's introduction to *The Epic of Gilgamesh* (Harmondsworth, 1964), Ninki and Ninhursag were at one time separate deities in the Sumerian cosmogony. Later, they were transformed into a single figure with alternative appellations. This is the process of condensation at work. Writing of the Aristaeus myth, Robert Graves observes: "Proteus, who lived at Pharos off the Nile Delta has been dragged into the story by the heels—there was a famous Oracle of Apollo at Tempe, which Aristaeus, his son, would naturally have consulted" (*The Greek Myths*, I, p. 280). What the positivistically inclined Graves here attacks as "the irresponsible use of myth" can also be seen as the equivalent of poetic license in literature or as the condensation of two myths in a new form.

To my knowledge, only two critics have discussed in any detail complex patterns of this kind. Theodore Ziolkowski analyzes such a pattern in Hans Erich Nossack's *Nekyia*, and I shall have more to say about this novel later in the chapter. But the first extended discussion of such techniques appeared in Vernon Hall's account of "Joyce's Use of Da Ponte and Mozart's *Don Giovanni*." Hall analyzes the way in which a number of relationships in the novel are described by prefigurations from Mozart's opera. A series of parallels are accounted for: "Don Giovanni is Hugh E. (Blazes) Boylan, Zerlina is Molly Bloom; Zerlina's bridegroom, Masetto, is Leopold Bloom." This on its own would constitute a straightforward pattern of correspondences with no particular complication (of either condensation or fragmentation) to it.

> But Joyce does not stop here. He recognizes that in the love drama one man can play different parts at different times—even simultaneously. So in relation to the Zerlina of Martha Clifford, Bloom is Don Giovanni. . . . Even at times Bloom is the *Commendatore*, and once or twice, to his shame, Zerlina . . . when Bannon [Milly's young man] plays the role of Don Juan, Bloom is forced into the role of the father, the *Commendatore*.[6]

"But Joyce does not stop here." This statement seems to evade the real problem underlying a pattern of fragmentation, such as this has now become. For where does one desist from positing further extensions of the originally outlined prefiguration? This may sound an over-positivistic question to ask about a literary symbol; but in attempting to answer it, one perceives the quality of the symbolism.

Hall does admittedly try to rationalize his interpretative procedure by drawing our attention to a slight similarity between the endings of such names as Boylan, Bannon and

---

[6] *op.cit.*, pp. 79f.

Don Juan. (To do this, he has to change the name of his prefiguration from Don Giovanni to Don Juan!) True, these names are all disyllabics ending in the consonant "n," but the phonetic common denominator to the names, put forward to substantiate the suggestion that they are all Don Juan figures, remains rather tenuous. Even then, it may be intended to compare the modern characters directly with one another, not necessarily via the *tertium comparationis* of a prefiguration. In the absence of any similarity between names as a possible clue, the central dilemma concerning patterns of fragmentation—the question of how far they extend—would become still more acute. In *Ulysses* one finds numerous instances of the eternal triangle situation. Through an interpretation based largely on the "Sirens" chapter, Hall can convincingly demonstrate that in the case of Leopold Bloom, Molly and Boylan, at least, their relationship is prefigured by the opera *Don Giovanni*. A reader would miss something if he did not notice this. Nevertheless, one feels on less safe ground when pursuing the ramifications of this pattern into the rest of the novel's plot.

Patterns of fragmentation and condensation not only raise local problems of identification (of the kind looked at above in Chapter Two); they can, if recognized, also draw out rather partisan evaluations from the critics who have discovered them. Some, faced with these more complex motif-structures, have attacked them as faults in construction. Noting a typical instance of condensation in *Proserpina: Eine Kindheitsmythe*, Eva Augsburger has criticized Elisabeth Langgässer for distorting and confusing the myths with which she works:

> Der Mythus von Orpheus' Reise in die Unterwelt lagert sich an das symbolische Absinken Proserpinas zum Hades an—Proserpina erscheint dabei zugleich als die Unterweltsgöttin, die dem Sänger die Gattin gewähren will, und als Orpheus selbst, der hinab-

steigt, sie zu holen. Die Fabel ist hier nicht undichterisch aber ohne Rücksicht auf logische Eindeutigkeit
mythologisiert.[7]

The invocation of the classical norm of logical *claritas*
("logische Eindeutigkeit") with reference to a work of
modern literature, the somewhat emotive word "respect"
("Rücksicht"), and the sparing admission that the work is
not unpoetic as a result, seem to chastize the authoress
mildly for allowing her heroine to be compared with both
Persephone and Orpheus in one and the same work. Mixed
myths are tacitly put on a par with mixed metaphors.

Likewise, Gilbert Highet balks at the assimilation of
some mythological motifs in Joyce's *Ulysses*, not even ven-
turing such a disclaimer as "nicht undichterisch" for the
pattern. Wondering how anyone could recognize some of
the intended parallels between *Ulysses* and the *Odyssey*, he
remarks: "The title *Ulysses* is an indication; but it is obscured by Joyce's own pseudonym. He calls his young self
Dedalus and there is no tradition of any link between
Ulysses and the craftsman."[8] This is true, in a sense, but
then Joyce's novel now forges that missing link—a symbolic
one. It is a comparable preoccupation with sources that
makes W. J. Lucas remark about two motifs that he has
found in E. M. Forster's *A Room with a View*: "Now I
realise that it might seem far-fetched to make the old man
both Titurel *and* Parsifal, but that's what Forster does."[9]
But it is not really so far-fetched.

Opponents of these techniques often find them far-

---

[7] *Elisabeth Langgässer*, Nuremberg, 1962, p. 15. "The myth of
Orpheus' journey to the underworld merges into the symbolic descent
of Proserpina to Hades—as a result, Proserpina appears simultaneously as the goddess of the underworld, who wants to give the bard
his wife, and as Orpheus himself, who descends to fetch her. Here,
the plot is made mythological, not in an unpoetic way, but without
any respect for unambiguous logicality."

[8] *The Classical Tradition*, p. 505.

[9] "Wagner and Forster," p. 294.

fetched because they do not pause to examine how they are used. Therefore, to show the advantages of what Etienne Fuzellier once called "cet état de perpetuelle disponibilité" that myths enjoy,[10] it will be necessary to look in detail at some aspects of condensation and fragmentation. Both patterns will be found in Hermann Broch's *Die Schuldlosen*, but with the emphasis on fragmentation. In Michel Butor's *L'Emploi du Temps*, a straightforward condensation of two contradictory prefigurations will be seen to reflect the central moral ambiguity underlying the work. In the case of Nossack's *Nekyia*, a novel which Theodore Ziolkowski even described as a "unique exploitation of . . . the metamorphosis of myth,"[11] we shall unravel the pattern of serial condensation to show how much it is linked with the traditional form of the novel of psychological development (*Entwicklungsroman*). And finally, with Macdonald Harris's *Trepleff*, the interpenetration of both patterns will be discussed. In each case, one can see how the pattern chosen offers the reader an interpretation of the plot that could scarcely be elicited by the kind of prefigurations dealt with in the previous chapter.

Fragmentation: Hermann Broch's Die Schuldlosen

In his *Myths of the Greeks and Romans*, Michael Grant relates Virgil's version of the myth of Aristaeus and his bees. He then adds that, in one variant of the myth, Aristaeus has a daughter called Melissa, and in another version "he is the son of Melissa (= bee), and is fed by her upon nectar and ambrosia."[12] This is the classical prefiguration that Hermann Broch uses in his novel *Die Schuldlosen* (1950), a loose episodic account of a triangular love-hate relationship, set against the background of the rise of Fas-

[10] "Les Mythes," *CdS*, XIX, 1939, p. 2.
[11] "The Odysseus Theme in Recent German Fiction," p. 233.
[12] *op.cit.*, p. 309.

cism. Broch introduces into *Die Schuldlosen*—whether consciously or not, it is difficult to determine—elements from two lesser known versions of the Aristaeus myth than that in the *Georgics*. The link offered by these between the man and the bee, or in Broch's novel between an adoptive father and the daughter who is the central figure in the love drama, preserves a useful ambiguity in a work so much concerned with the confusion between mistresses and mother-figures.

The father-figure himself draws attention to the theme of confused roles with his rhetorical question: "steckt in dem merkwürdigen Verkriechen bei der Mutter nicht eben doch ein Hauptstück der Schuld mitsamt ihrem Eingeständnis?"[13] Earlier he had reproached the hero, A., with the guilt of immaturity in similar terms. "Du wolltest nicht Vater, du wolltest ausschließlich und für immer Sohn sein."[14] How appropriate, then, that Broch should resort to a motif where it remains unclear whether Melitta is the mother or daughter of Aristaeus! He can thus generate a mood of ambiguity which increases as the myth eventually becomes fragmented across a number of situations in the novel.

The initial case for presuming an allusion to Aristaeus rests on two indices: first, the name Melitta itself (which is simply a variant spelling of Melissa), and second, on a rather enigmatic remark which only makes sense if one accepts the historical perspective given by a covert motif. The passage occurs towards the end of *Die Schuldlosen*, when A. has withdrawn to the mountains after the death of his former mistress, Melitta. A. was to a large extent indirectly guilty of causing her suicide by his lack of concern for her, and this chapter, called "Steinerner Gast," depicts the final

[13] *op.cit.*, p. 327; ". . . doesn't a large portion of the guilt, together with an admission of it, lie very much in this abnormal attachment to your mother's apron-strings?"
[14] *op.cit.*, p. 320. "You didn't want to be a father, you wanted to be exclusively and forever a son."

judgment which the reader has been awaiting. The old man who comes is, as the chapter title proclaims, partly prefigured by the Stone Guest, Don Giovanni's punisher. On the realistic plane, he is Melitta's adoptive father and here her avenger. At one point in the ensuing conversation, however, before A. accepts his guilt and shoots himself, the old man makes a remark neither consonant with his position as Melitta's guardian nor with his symbolic role as Stone Guest:

Zweitausend Jahr um zweitausend Jahr vollendet sich der Weltenkreislauf. Und die Gewalt der Vollendung erschüttert nicht nur den Kosmos, sie erschüttert desgleichen und vielleicht noch mehr das Menschheits-Ich . . . wie könnte es anders sein! Die Zeit des Endes ist die der Geburt, und im Unveränderbaren geht die Veränderung vor sich, die Katastrophe des Wachstums. Begnadet und verflucht ist das Geschlecht der Veränderungszeit: es hat die Aufgabe zu leisten.[15]

One could well imagine this stilted, sententious remark finding a place in Broch's earlier novel, *Der Tod des Vergil,*[16] but it sounds a little out of place in *Die Schuldlosen* where we have so far only come across two spheres of history: the period of National Socialism and the time of the Don Giovanni motif, which runs through much of the novel. Neither of these has any bearing on the concept of the two-thousand-year cycle of history (indeed, Broch does not even refer to the Third Reich as a would-be millennium).

[15] *op.cit.*, p. 329. "Every two thousand years, the world's orbit of history is completed. And the power of the completion not only shakes the cosmos, it shakes the likes of it and, perhaps much more, the ego of mankind . . . how could it be otherwise! The time of the end is that of birth, and in the unchangeable the change works itself out, this catastrophe of growth. Blessed and cursed is the generation of a time of change: it has the task to perform."
[16] In fact, a similar remark about cycles of history does appear: Virgil "starrte zu den Sternen empor, deren schicksalsbestimmter, schicksalsbestimmender zweitausendjähriger Umlauf sich nun bald runden muste" (*Der Tod des Vergil,* p. 107).

If, on the other hand, one goes back two thousand years, this puts one, not by chance, in the time of Virgil, with his tales of Orpheus, Eurydice and Aristaeus. Here is a world conversant with the Virgilian myth about Melissa's death, to which there is a direct allusion in the novel. If this pointed allusion via the name were not present, then there would be little concrete evidence for presuming such a far-fetched motif was really relevant. Yet Broch is surely referring to this mythological aspect of *Die Schuldlosen* in a letter to Frau Brody, his editor's wife: "der 'Steinerne Gast' verdient Perfektheit, gerade weil er auf so viel verschiedenen Ebenen spielt, hinauf bis zu einer, die beinahe in Vergilscher Sphäre liegt."[17]

This Virgilian dimension depends to some considerable degree upon the role of the bee motif in the novel. The reader is first told of the old man's connection with bees in an earlier chapter.[18] After his wife's death, this veritable *deus ex machina*, Lebrecht Endeguth, returns to his former hobby of beekeeping. He becomes a traveling instructor in apiculture, moving from village to village to impart his skills. "Die Kinder nannten ihn Großvater, Bienengroß-vater. . . . Er war bienengefeit und weltgefeit und vielleicht sogar schon todesgefeit."[19] With these words, Broch skil-fully manages to combine a number of themes to be pursued later in the novel. Just as he eventually becomes the adoptive father of Melitta, so here Endeguth stands in a relationship to the bees which is comparable to guardian-ship. The appropriateness of bees to the subject of death, a motif common both to the Aristaeus myth and Samson's

---

[17] *Briefe*, pp. 410f.; "the 'Stone Guest' chapter needs perfecting, for the very reason that it operates on so many levels, right up to one which almost lies in the Virgilian sphere."

[18] "Ballade vom Imker," *op.cit.*, pp. 117-127.

[19] *op.cit.*, p. 125. "The children called him grandfather, bee-grandfather. . . . He was immune to the bees and to the world and perhaps already even immune to death."

riddle, becomes more understandable in this novel when set in the specific context of Roman mythology.

Aristaeus' bees perish because of his complicity in the death of Eurydice. Broch's novel offers a parallel to this. As the etymology of the name Melitta suggests, she is another of Endeguth's charges. He is her guardian: "Treu seinem vergangenen Glück und eingedenk des Imkertums, das ein Teil dieses Glückes gewesen war, ließ er das Kleine auf den Namen Melitta taufen."[20] When A. meets Melitta, he explains the meaning of her name to her. " 'Ich heiße Melitta.' 'Ein schöner Name,' sagte er, 'denn er bedeutet "das Bienchen," und das paßt vorzüglich auf Sie.' "[21] A.'s remark soon acquires something of an ironic twist, though unintentionally. She is certainly as busy as a bee, when A. first comes across her doing the laundry. But, in view of the Aristaeus motif, Melitta is also a suitable name to reveal the girl's mythological significance in the novel. For if Endeguth is coming as Stone Guest to punish A. for his guilt as a Don Giovanni, he is also coming as a beekeeper who has lost his favorite bee.[22]

[20] op.cit., p. 118. "True to his former happiness and mindful of his beekeeping, that had been a part of this happiness, he had the child baptized Melitta."
[21] op.cit., p. 174. " 'I am called Melitta.' 'A beautiful name,' he said, 'for it means "the little bee" and that suits you splendidly.' "
[22] Most of the attempts at explaining the enigmatic arrival of a beekeeper at the end of the novel remain too general. Hermann Weigand suggests a possible aspect of the bees' symbolic importance: "der göttliche Nimbus kommt 'dem Bienenvater' von Rechts wegen zu, wenn man sich der Verehrung erinnert, die der geflügelte Zellenstaat bei den Alten genoß" (introduction to Die Schuldlosen, p. 17). Karl August Horst sees the hive as symbolic of the cosmos and the beekeeper as "eine Gestalt, die den Schwarm der Phänomene einsammelt und in einem Weltgehäuse birgt" (Kritischer Führer durch die deutsche Literatur der Gegenwart, p. 347). Wolfgang Rothe at least comes closer to the mark when he talks of "Melitta, die den Namen einer antiken Liebesgöttin trägt" (Schriftsteller und totalitäre Welt, Berne, 1966, p. 95), but he fails to elucidate this point. Such interpretations do nothing to account for the puzzling quotation about the two-thousand-year cycle of history, and they remain rather unconvincing about the bee motif.

The narrator's remarks about the axe blows, heard at the beginning of the "Steinerner Gast" chapter, set the tone for the various motifs to be united in this episode: "kamen die Axtschläge und der Gesang nicht aus verschiedenen Richtungen, voneinander getrennt, dennoch aufeinander abgestimmt?"[23] The way in which the Aristaeus and Don Giovanni motifs similarly interpenetrate, although coming from very different sources, involves patterns of both fragmentation and condensation. For, arriving at the end of the novel to seek revenge, Endeguth is compared with both figures. Two motifs are condensed at this point. But the pattern of fragmentation is the dominant one in the novel. To what extent one can project these motif-patterns back across earlier parts of the narrative is a difficult question to answer satisfactorily, but the nature of the following attempt characterizes the quality of fragmentation.

In the *Georgics*, one reads that Aristaeus was guilty of causing Eurydice's death, whereas in Broch's novel Endeguth accuses A. of complicity in the death of Melitta. Already the sense of correspondence seems to have been disturbed. Aristaeus learns from Proteus, according to the myth, why his bees have been taken from him.

> This punishment, less than deserved, wretched Orpheus calls upon thee—unless Fate oppose—in mad grief for his wife torn away. She indeed, flying headlong before through the river, saw not her death upon her in the deep grass before her girlish feet, where that monstrous snake guarded the bank.[24]

Eurydice, so the myth has it, dies while fleeing from Aristaeus' amorous advances. In trying to evade him, she is bit-

[23] *op.cit.*, p. 313; ". . . did the axe blows and the singing not come from different directions, separated from one another and yet attuned to each other?"
[24] *Virgil's Works*, tr. J. W. Mackail, New York, 1950, p. 349. Having completed his Virgil-novel six years before, Broch was clearly drawing upon his great knowledge of the Roman poet's work to construct his motif.

204

ten by a rather Freudian serpent. So it is clear from even this brief account of the myth that, prior to the punishment chapter, one should compare A. with Aristaeus and even consider the possibility of correspondences between Melitta and Eurydice, and Endeguth and Orpheus. If these parallels are allowed, the Aristaeus figure becomes fragmented across two characters: A. in the earlier part of the novel and Endeguth in the chapter "Steinerner Gast." The whole analogy is further complicated by our knowledge that the Aristaeus A. resembles can only be the Aristaeus who is responsible for Eurydice's death, whereas the Aristaeus to whom Endeguth corresponds is the one who lost his bees as a punishment and now, perhaps disingenuously, wishes to know why. Two disparate myths were probably fused together by Virgil in the *Georgics*, the one giving a reason for Eurydice's death, the other motivating the loss of Aristaeus' bees and giving a religious perspective to agriculture. In *Die Schuldlosen* Broch has pulled these myths apart again and also interpolated a Don Giovanni motif.

So far this pattern of fragmentation may sound perplexing, but it can at least be defined. But how far can it plausibly be extended? Can we say: "but Broch does not stop here"? Any inclusion of the figures of Orpheus and Eurydice in the interpretation may be less justifiable, as there appear to be no direct allusions to them in *Die Schuldlosen*. It does not add much to an exegesis of the novel to compare Melitta with Eurydice, yet by implication this is a prefigurative role she could also be playing, if A. is earlier compared with both Don Giovanni and Aristaeus. Philandery, disaster and subsequent ritual punishment—the elements common to both prefigurations—are also the principal themes of *Die Schuldlosen*. Whereas guilt and punishment are clearly defined in the mythological paradigm, the issues look less transparent in Broch's novel; hence the proliferation of motifs and changing of prefigurative roles which help darkly to mirror, and even create, this obscurity. The patterns of distortion one can disentangle in Broch's novel give the motifs a more intangible, esoteric quality than they have, say, in *A World Elsewhere* or *Brave New World*. Whereas the technique of juxtaposition, the most complex of the types looked at earlier, may demand some detective work from the reader before he can ascertain the full relevance of the motif, fragmentation nearly always leaves behind some uncertainty about the exact "catchment-area" of the imagery. The references here may only point to Aristaeus and Melissa as prefigurations, or they may be extended to include Orpheus, Eurydice and Proteus.

Not unexpectedly, one is also confronted with a comparable ambiguity when the Don Giovanni motif is fragmented across parts of the novel. The reader meets three Don Giovanni figures in *Die Schuldlosen*. Towards the end of the novel comes the passage: "Schlußszene einer Oper, dachte A., sogar einer tragischen Oper, bestenfalls einer tragikomischen."[25] There are various reasons for supposing that the opera in question must be Mozart's *Don Giovanni*, even though the composer is not mentioned. Lorenzo Da Ponte's libretto for the opera was the first to use the name Zerlina for the servant,[26] a name which is also given to the maid in Broch's novel. Apart from this, *Don Giovanni* is the principal version of the Don Juan theme for the German-speaking world. Furthermore, the cipher A. is in all probability an allusion to the seducer in Kierkegaard's *Either/Or*, a work which in turn uses Mozart's opera as its prime illus-

[25] *op.cit.*, p. 285. "Finale of an opera, A. thought, even of a tragic opera, or at best a tragi-comic one."

[26] In Mozart's *Don Giovanni*, Weinstein notes, "Zerlina and Masetto are skilful combinations of the two corresponding characters in Tirso (Tisbea and Aminta; Batricio) and Molière (Charlotte, Pierrot)" (*The Metamorphosis of Don Juan*, p. 61).

tration of "The Immediate Stages of the Erotic or the Musical Erotic."[27]

The initial allusion to *Don Giovanni* and the first example of an application of the motif to one group of characters is to be found in the chapter "Mit schwacher Brise segeln." A. is brought face-to-face with a mirrored image of his own later position. Two lovers are sitting in a café, evidently afraid of being surprised by a third party, the woman's husband. A. notes that their rather melodramatic behavior seems out of place—more in keeping, he feels, with an opera than with real life:

> So ein elender Mist, was die redeten. Die Toten sollen aus den Gräbern kommen, um sie zu töten. Der Komtur. Der Steinerne Gast. Das gibt's nur in der Oper, meine Herrschaften, und da nur im Don Juan.[28]

In this café scene, A. merely overhears two people whom he does not know and who do not really interest him. As the novel progresses, though, the Don Giovanni image becomes more and more relevant to the main characters.

The next instance of this encroaching motif impinges much more upon the hero's world. It is connected with the past of the Baroness Elvira and her servant Zerlina, with whom A. has taken up lodgings upon his arrival in the anonymous town where most of the novel's action takes place. These names, recalling figures in Mozart's opera, reveal the place the two women have had in the adventures of some Don Giovanni-like character. A. learns later that they were both once mistresses of a certain Herr von Juna. In his introduction to Broch's *Gedichte*, Erich Kahler notes

[27] *Either/Or*, trans. D. F. and L. M. Swenson, New York, 1959, i, pp. 43-134.
[28] *op.cit.*, pp. 46f. "Such a miserable load of rubbish they're talking. The dead are supposed to come from their graves, to kill them. The *Commendatore*. The Stone Guest. That only happens in opera, my friends, and then only in Don Juan."

that this Herr von Juna, whom we do not meet, must have been a much more typical seducer than A. ever seems to be.[29] Yet even if A. is not a stereotype Don Giovanni like Herr von Juna—which is perhaps why he finds Mozart's opera so out of place when he recognizes its style in the café scene—he is still akin to Don Giovanni in many ways. His amorous escapades are simply less romantic, as we see in the final version of the prefiguration. For the third instance of the motif, in fact, directly concerns A., Melitta and Endeguth. This, the most essential of the three applications of the motif, is the only one not explicitly introduced, but merely mentioned in the title of the chapter "Steinerner Gast." In other words, one of the most vital prefigurations (like the Aristaeus motif) remains covert, i.e. not realized by the hero himself or the narrator who tends to share his perspective. A.'s ignorance of analogies could be interpreted as part of his unwitting guilt, in fact.

This triple fragmentation of motifs is a notable feature of Broch's style in general. It has often been observed that Broch was for much of his lifetime fascinated by triadic forms.[30] Some critics have attributed this to his dialectical view of life and particularly to the influence of Hegel,[31] but

---

[29] "Die Hauptfigur, Herr A., ist ein Erzneutraler, . . . ein sublimierter Don Juan . . . auf einer höheren, aber schwächeren Ebene, das Negativ und Passiv eines ganz leibhaftigen, sehr aktiven Don Juan, des 'Herrn von Juna,' der vor ihm zwischen der Baronin Elvira und der Magd Zerlina sein Spiel getrieben und unter seinen Opfern ein Schicksalsgespinst hintergelassen hat, in das der Herr A., mit all seiner Unbeteiligtheit hineingerät" (Zürich, 1953, p. 44).

[30] Broch's seriousness on this point contrasts strongly with the same motif at the end of Flann O'Brien's At Swim-Two-Birds: "Well known, alas, is the case of the poor German who was very fond of three and who made each aspect of his life a thing of triads. He went home one evening and drank three cups of tea with three lumps of sugar in each, cut his jugular with a razor three times and scrawled with a dying hand on a picture of his wife good-bye, good-bye, good-bye" (Harmondsworth, 1967, pp. 217f.). In the light of this addiction, it seems almost surprising that A. only takes one shot to kill himself!

[31] See E. Kahler's Die Philosophie Hermann Brochs, Tübingen, 1962, and M. Durzak's Hermann Broch. Der Dichter und seine Zeit,

for a reading of *Die Schuldlosen* the significant aspect of this addiction lies in the way it is reflected in the structure of the novel itself.

Bearing in mind the way Broch introduced many of his images retrospectively, in a rather cerebral, additive manner, one cannot help being struck by the general triadic structure of the motif-patterns, not only in *Die Schuldlosen* (a novel divided into three parts anyway), but also in *Der Tod des Vergil*. At the historical level of the Virgil-novel, one has the figures of Virgil and Plotia, counterpointed by the legend of Aeneas and Dido and the myth of Orpheus and Eurydice. At the more realistic level of contemporary history in *Die Schuldlosen*, one finds A., Melitta and Endeguth living in Nazi Germany, at the legendary level (to introduce the distinction again), Don Giovanni, Elvira and Zerlina, together with the *Commendatore*, and at the level of myth, Aristaeus, Melissa and possibly Orpheus and Eurydice. The fact that the reader is first introduced to the realistic and legendary planes of action and only later proceeds to the mythological motif offers another point of comparison between the two works. This is partly a process of deliberate intensification, but also one whereby the outlines of the plot in *Die Schuldlosen* become more intricate and make it less easy for the reader to judge the characters.

The following plan shows the confusing number of prefigurations applied to the major figures in the course of the novel. In it, the prefigurations marked (a) refer to the seduction, and those marked (b) to the punishment. For three characters we are offered as many as ten prefigurations.

Stuttgart, Berlin, Cologne and Mainz, 1968. Some illustrations of the effects this preoccupation had on Broch's fiction can be found in Kimberley Sparks's "The Geometry of Time" (diss., Princeton, 1963) and my article on *Die Schlafwandler*, GLL, xxv, January 1971.

CHARACTER	A.	MELITTA	ENDEGUTH
PREFIGURATIONS (a)	Aristaeus Kierkegaard's seducer A.	Eurydice	Orpheus
PREFIGURATIONS (b)	Don Giovanni Orpheus	Elvira "bee" (melissa)	Stone Guest Aristaeus

It is an involved scheme because of a complete change of roles, whereby both A. and Endeguth are prefigured by Aristaeus. Yet in a novel where guilt and innocence remain inextricably interwoven, this proves a very effective pattern of symbolic comment. The Don Giovanni prefiguration, attached to two other groups of characters in the novel apart from the hero's immediate circle, reinforces our impression that A. is not fundamentally different from everyone around him. His cipher-like name and the novel's title—*Die Schuldlosen* (the innocents) instead of the singular "Der Schuldlose"—also make the same point.

Despite the general ambiguity of these patterns, one can still distinguish degrees of guilt at certain junctures in the narrative, according to which prefiguration is emphasized. A.'s affair with Melitta looks like an ambiguous cross between seduction and rape when set against the Don Giovanni prefiguration; it becomes attempted rape, plain and simple, in the light of the Aristaeus myth. Similarly, Endeguth's search for justice at the end of the novel seems to be in order if he is the counterpart of the Stone Guest; the other prefiguration, in contrast, makes his position look much more dubious. Does he really play the role of Orpheus, the innocent bystander, within the Aristaeus configuration? Or is he perhaps not compared as well with Aristaeus himself, who at first appears to be the innocent victim seeking justice, but later turns out to bear a great deal of guilt himself? (At the realistic level, Endeguth can always be accused of neglecting his ward.) These motifs to a large extent offset one another, and the reader may well conclude with one reviewer of *Die Schuldlosen* that the characters are all "doubtful innocents."[32]

The confusion that obtains because of these hybrid motifs and patterns of fragmentation charges the novel with a general ambiguity. One can find a similar structure, with one motif offsetting the other, but this time in a pattern of condensation, in one of Michel Butor's novels.

Simultaneous Condensation:
Michel Butor's L'Emploi du Temps

A l'intérieur tout était calme; je me suis mis devant la grille du choeur, sous l'orgue, à travers laquelle j'apercevais la lueur d'une lampe à huile dans son verre rouge, et j'ai regardé dans la grande verrière à ma droite cette scène au sommet, inscrite dans un cercle, dont je savais déjà par la lecture du *Meurtre de Bleston*, qu'elle représente Caïn tuant son frère Abel, Caïn dans un cuirasse lui moulant le ventre avec des rubans flottant sur ses cuisses comme Thésée, presque dans la même attitude que Thésée aux prises avec le Minotaure, penché comme lui, le pied gauche posé sur la poitrine de sa victime allongée mais relevant la tête, nue, déjà blessée, si différent pourtant, brandissant un tronc aux racines échevelées sur le ciel rouge.[33]

Doomed to spend a year in England as a commercial translator, Jacques Revel, the hero and narrator of Butor's novel, soon becomes, as we saw in the previous chapter, acquainted with a series of symbolic mythological tapestries in the local museum of the fictitious city of Bleston. Then he comes across a stained-glass window in the local cathedral, depicting another figure who is to become as much a prefiguration of his situation as the Theseus tapes-

[32] *TLS*, 24 July 1953, p. 476.   [33] *L'Emploi du Temps*, p. 72.

tries are.[34] And already, in the description quoted above, these two images begin to coalesce in his mind.

The common denominator of the Theseus myth and the story of Cain and Abel is the central killing, but the two prefigurations offer very different interpretations of the act. In the Theseus myth, the slaying of the Minotaur is an act of liberation, a curse is lifted. And this positive evaluation is transferred by the prefiguration[35] to the modern events in Butor's work. There are numerous variations on the labyrinth motif in the novel; most important is the fact that Butor does not content himself with the cliché image of Man in the labyrinthine modern city. A more fundamental experience for Revel is "le labyrinthe du temps et de la mémoire"[36] through which he has to find his way as he writes down a record of his stay in the city of Bleston:

> Le cordon de phrases qui se love dans cette pile et qui me relie directement à ce moment du 1er mai où j'ai commencé à le tresser, ce cordon de phrases est un fil d'Ariane parce que je suis dans un labyrinthe, parce que j'écris pour m'y retrouver, toutes ces lignes étant les marques dont je jalonne les trajets déjà reconnus, le labyrinthe de mes jours à Bleston, incomparablement plus déroutant que le palais de Crête, puisqu'il s'augmente à mesure que je le parcoure, puisqu'il se déforme à mesure que je l'explore.[37]

One of the conceits of the novel's time-structure is that the narrator describes his exploration of the labyrinth of the city, upon his arrival there, at the same time as he experi-

---

[34] There is also an Oedipus motif in the novel, linking the detective with the Greek figure in the same way as they are compared in Robbe-Grillet's *Les Gommes*. For details, see Roudaut's *Michel Butor* (pp. 163ff.). However, Roudaut tends to overstress the Oedipus prefiguration, which is far less important than the counterbalanced images of Theseus and Cain.

[35] *L'Emploi du Temps* in fact uses the word "préfiguration" (pp. 148, 280) and talks in terms of patterns being completed (p. 258).

[36] *op.cit.*, p. 293.

[37] *op.cit.*, p. 187.

ences and discusses the later, more complex labyrinth-experience of coming to terms with his earlier, physical disorientation. Hence, words may be his "fil d'Ariane" at the later point, but there is also Ann, his earlier Ariadne, who sold him a map and acted as guide through the city to which he was a stranger. Whichever labyrinth one thinks of, whether the physical one of the oppressive city of Bleston, or the more psychological one, the man who sets out to conquer the maze becomes something of a hero because of the hazards before him. For a long time, the Theseus prefiguration in the novel gives the plot such an heroic aura. For we concentrate not so much upon the later betrayal of Ariadne, though this is alluded to at the end of Butor's work, as upon the situation of the labyrinth. It is the experience of the metropolis rather than any specific Minotaur which colors Revel's stay in Bleston. In this context, the environment seems hostile, and it is also foreign, as Crete was to Theseus. There is a passive quality to Revel's heroism, for he neither appears to kill a Minotaur, nor to desert an Ariadne—for Ann herself becomes engaged to someone else rather than being deserted. "Toute une figure s'est achevée dans cette exclusion de moi-même,"[38] Revel exclaims, upon hearing this news. Revel somehow manages to avoid the negative aspects of Theseus' heroism—his need to trample over others—and yet retains some of his grandeur. If there is no Minotaur,[39] except in the sense that the city itself is both maze and Minotaur, there is still the struggle to make sense of things. So, in general, the Theseus prefiguration appears to lend Revel a positive quality.

In contrast, the killing of Abel, a fratricide, can have none of the heroic dimension that exploring and mastering the labyrinth has. Instead of lifting a curse, it brings one down

[38] *op.cit.*, p. 258.
[39] R.-M. Albérès suggests the image of "un labyrinthe . . . dont le Minotaure est peut-être la mort" (*Michel Butor*, Paris, 1964, p. 37).

upon Cain and his descendants. Hence the stained-glass window with the Cain figure on it, leading Revel to apostrophize Bleston as Cain's town, introduces a certain ambiguity into the novel by contradicting the Theseus myth. It might be that, if Bleston is Cain's town, then the man who sets himself up against it is still being heroic. But the noticeable feature of the Cain prefiguration in this novel is that Revel tends to be compared with Cain, not contrasted with him. This is made very clear at one point in the work, where Revel is looking at the Cain Window of the cathedral and the red light from the blood depicted there is refracted onto him:

> Le sang rouge s'est mis à couler jusqu'en bas, comme une lente averse dans tout le ciel rouge de la cité, derrière les métiers de Yabal, derrière l'orchestre de Yubal, derrière la forge de Tubalcaïn, puis, débordant du Vitrail, à couler sur les murs et sur les dalles, même sur les bancs, même sur mes mains, surtout sur mes mains couvertes, teintes, imprégnées de cette épaisse couleur lumineuse, comme des mains de meurtrier, comme si j'étais condamné au meurtre, mes mains au centre de la flaque, mes mains au centre de la tache projetée par la scène d'en haut dans le silence.[40]

The image of having blood on one's hands is obviously a negative one, almost the opposite of Theseus' heroic slaughter of the Minotaur. And the way the red light is seen to travel from Cain to Yabal, Yubal and Tubalcain (his descendants) and then on to Revel is an indication that Revel becomes guilty of something through association with the city.

The Theseus prefiguration is dominant in the novel; it is introduced first and it is referred to far more frequently than the Cain motif. After all, the novel is narrated by Revel and it is obvious that he would prefer to see himself as

[40] op.cit., p. 197.

Theseus in some contemporary labyrinth, taking on the whole world, than as a Cain murdering some Abel. But the Cain motif emerges far more forcefully towards the end; "je compose, forge et tisse, fils de Caïn."[41] (The verbs used here link Revel closely with the artisans, descendants of Cain, depicted in the window of the cathedral.) What needs to be explored in a little more detail in the case of *L'Emploi du Temps* is the way in which a simple condensation of two motifs adds an immense complexity to the plot.

One reason for such an ambiguity is that there is not a murder, in the strict sense of the word, even though both prefigurations have led us to expect one. What there is, instead, is a murder motif running through the novel. The first suggestion of murder comes in the title of a detective novel which Revel uses as a guide to the city, because it is set there: "Le Meurtre de Bleston."[42] The hero later meets the author of the novel and finds his name to be George Burton; he is a local writer of detective stories who published this particular work under the *nom de plume* of J. C. Hamilton in order not to be recognized by the inhabitants of Bleston. When Burton is later knocked down by a hit-and-run driver, Revel feels certain that it is not by chance. The complications in Butor's novel arise as a result of the "accident," for this not only leads to Revel betraying the secret of Burton's *nom de plume*, but also to his growing feeling of complicity in the attack on him. It is largely in connection with this possible accident-theme that the Cain and Abel prefiguration becomes woven into the novel's imagery.

[41] *op.cit.*, p. 264. In Sturrock's interpretation of this motif, "the artist is the fratricide because the building of a new city, an imaginary one, involves the suppression of the old or real one" (*The French New Novel*, London, 1969, p. 123).

[42] For a detailed account of the complex relationship between "Le Meurtre de Bleston" and *L'Emploi du Temps*, see Sturrock, *op.cit.*, pp. 162-164.

To understand why the hero should feel so involved in the question of George Burton's (alias J. C. Hamilton's) "accident," one has to go back to the first part of the novel. Here, Revel describes the author of "Le Meurtre de Bleston" as "un complice contre la ville."[43] He is in fact, as the Cain and Abel motif later makes clearer, a brother to Revel in his wanderings through the city. At first, when he hears of the accident, Revel presumes that "la main de Bleston s'est abattue sur George Burton."[44] He even feels for some time, because of the type of car identified as having hit the author, that someone in his office has done it. But later this question of who is really responsible becomes depersonalized and the suspected driver emerges as another of the many red herrings appearing throughout the novel. Revel is subsequently less certain about this man's possible involvement in the accident, and feels himself indirectly implicated:

> ... cette vengeance que tu avais si bien commencée en m'impliquant dans ton attentat contre ton autre ennemi, George Burton, dans l' "accident" de Brown Street, qui est ton attentat, Bleston, quel que soit l'instrument dont tu t'es servi et dans lequel je conserverais une part de complicité même si James [the suspected driver] n'y était pour rien.[45]

In accepting a degree of complicity, Revel is admitting a similarity to the Cain prefiguration. But in comparison with the Theseus motif, which Revel juggles with for most of the narrative,[46] the Cain prefiguration is never admitted to directly.

---

[43] *op.cit.*, p. 57.   [44] *op.cit.*, p. 239.   [45] *op.cit.*, p. 269.

[46] A typical allusion, direct and almost deliberately escaping from the implications of the Cain motif by emphasizing the Theseus image, can be found in Revel's remark: "que pour moi désormais Ariane répresentait Ann Bailey, que Phèdre répresentait Rose, que j'étais moi-même Thésée" (*op.cit.*, p. 173).

It is logical that Revel should concentrate on the Theseus myth. He is, after all, something of a romantic, as we see from his constant escapist visits to the local cinema, watching sun-filled travelogues to avoid the ugly realities of life in Bleston. Concentrating on the Theseus myth largely involves a subconscious shift of guilt on to the suprapersonal level of the city; or on to one of the city's representatives, such as James Jenkins. The Cain and Abel tale, on the other hand, would amount to a personal admission of guilt towards a "brother," George Burton. But try as he will to suppress the Cain image by concentrating on Theseus, Revel is unable to forget the more negative image of his role in the city. What happens, as the following passages show, is a condensation of the two images, whereby a process of association leads the hero from one prefiguration to the other:

> j'ai songé aux flammes qui dévorent Athènes dans la dernière tapisserie du Musée, au ciel rouge derrière la ville de Caïn dans le Vitrail de l'Ancienne Cathédrale . . .[47]

> Nous avons pris le bus 32 dans Continent Street, traversant la Slee sur South Bridge, jusqu'à l'entrée monumentale avec ses deux tours carrées à ornementation de stuc très salie, surmontées, comme celles de l'anticathédrale (faudrait-il dire temple ou mosquée?) qui règne sur la ville de Caïn . . .[48]

> ce sondage dans ton sous-sol, Bleston, à travers les images affleurantes de la Rome des empereurs, de Pétra, Baalbeck et Timgad, même de la Crète . . .[49]

> les deux séries de villes et de périodes dont témoignent tes deux grands hiéroglyphes, Bleston . . . s'enlaçaient à l'intérieur de ma vision. . . .[50]

On the surface, what would appear to be taking place in Revel's mind is an innocent and typical merging of various

[47] op.cit., p. 124.
[49] op.cit., p. 268.
[48] op.cit., p. 141.
[50] op.cit., p. 295.

experiences into one archetype. But Cain's city and Theseus' world are really very different *topoi* because of different moral connotations. If Revel is unable to forget the appropriateness of Cain, he can at least try to weaken the image by pretending that it is on a par with the Theseus myth. (The fact that *L'Emploi du Temps* consists of a diary-narrative where the hero is unwilling to assent fully to his guilt, and where he prefers to use various prefigurations indiscriminately, should not blind us to the distinction between them.) The noun "meurtre" is rightly only used in connection with the Cain image; the Theseus myth concentrates as a prefiguration more on the idea of exploring. Bleston may be a murderous city, but the central ambiguity of the novel concerns the question of whether the individual is not himself an accomplice to this process; and for this kind of dilemma the condensation of two contradictory images draws the reader's attention to two, possibly irreconcilable, positions.

This link between an intricate prefigurative pattern and the exposition of a vexed moral problem can be seen in many other modern novels. One finds it in Hermann Broch's *Der Versucher*, where the Demeter myth is contrasted with the sacrifice motif of Isaac and Abraham. Again, the Bible is contrasted with mythology. And it is also to be seen in the mutually conflicting motifs in Macdonald Harris's *Trepleff* and Roger Zelazny's *The Dream Master*. But various myths or prefigurations need not necessarily be brought together to contradict one another; they can supplement each other or chart a character's psychological progress, as they do in Nossack's *Nekyia*.

Serial Condensation: Hans Erich Nossack's Nekyia

Nekyia: Bericht eines Überlebenden, Nossack's first major work, appeared in 1947. The novel is set at the end of an enormous catastrophe, comparable to the débâcle of 1945.

Having survived this archetypal holocaust, the anonymous hero seeks contacts with his past and tries to reorientate himself in a once-familiar world. The mythological motifs used register the progress of his search; they possess an inchoate quality because of the hero's own fundamental uncertainty at this time. At first, he cannot be sure which people from his past life he needs most in order to begin afresh. We witness in effect an *Entwicklungsroman* plot, with a starting-point fixed neither in childhood nor adolescence, as befits the tradition, but in what is usually referred to in the post-war cliché as the zero-point ("Nullpunkt").[51] The development of the central figure can be measured against the various directions his quest takes: the initial return to the destroyed city, followed by an attempt at positing an imaginary reader to address—so that his narrative may establish a relationship with something outside himself— and the ensuing decision to search first for his father and then his mother. The hero slowly realizes that he must go back to his origins and begin again, if his survival is to acquire some meaning. For the same reason, Nossack takes his reader back to the Hellenic sources of European culture to begin afresh from there and to seek some earlier harmony against which these devastating modern experiences can be placed and perhaps understood.[52]

Nossack's symbiosis of modern theme and mythological motifs is also motivated by the statement that the disaster has rendered all sense of temporal progression and order in history meaningless for the moment:

Die Zeit ist gebrochen. . . . Was sollen also die Zahlen?
. . . Oder bin ich wie ein eben geborenes Kind, das

[51] A good introduction to Nossack's work and the background to it can be found in Peter Prochnik's "Controlling Thoughts in the Works of Hans Erich Nossack," *GLL*, XIX, 1965, pp. 68-74.

[52] For a dissenting view, where the myths are seen as illusions, see Gotthard Montesi's "Nach der Sintflut," *Über Hans Erich Nossack*, ed. Christof Schmid, Frankfurt a.M., 1970, pp. 79-84.

behauptet: Ich bin schon neun Monate alt? Und noch
viel älter, da ich schon im Blute meiner Eltern und
Ahnen lebte? Ja, ich lebe von Anbeginn.[53]

At such a critical phase, the hero has been symbolically
born anew, and yet at the same time he carries all history
around with him, though not in any specifically Jungian
sense of synchronicity. The "Nullpunkt" is simply not as
total as some readings of Nossack's work imply. The remark
about temporal order being broken could well lead one to
expect in *Nekyia* a large number of allusions to various
ages, just as Joyce depicted the "oneness of the ages"[54] or
the "nightmare of history"[55] with an encyclopaedic range
of references to countless mythologies, legends and events
from history. Actually, the allusions in *Nekyia* are only to
Greek mythology.

The outset of the novel finds the hero wandering through
the dead town after the disaster; he goes into one of the
deserted houses and there falls asleep. He then dreams of
a gathering where he recognizes an old friend and a former
mistress. Encountering these people again and finding himself unable to recall their names, he hits upon a makeshift
solution:

Ich könnte ja Namen erfinden, und damit wäre alles
gut. Zu dem Freunde würde zum Beispiel der Name
Lysander recht gut passen, ich weiß nicht warum.
Lysander hieß ein Feldherr, der einige wichtige
Schlachten gewonnen hat. . . . Diese Frau . . . müßte so
ähnlich wie Iona heißen.[56]

[53] *op.cit.*, pp. 35f. "Time has been broken. . . . What is the point of
numbers, then? . . . or am I like a newborn child that maintains: I am
already nine months old? And much older, for I already lived in the
blood of my parents? Indeed, I have lived from the beginning of
things."

[54] Philip Edwards, "*Ulysses* and the Legends," p. 118.

[55] Cf. the "Nestor" chapter of *Ulysses* and S. L. Goldberg's *The
Classical Temper*, pp. 145ff.

[56] *op.cit.*, pp. 36f. "I could invent names, and that would solve
everything. For example, the name Lysander would suit my friend

Both of these names bring to mind the Hellenic world, even though they do not belong to Greek mythology. In the course of winning a few battles—the narrator's offhand attitude here implies that the present catastrophe will look like this from some distant perspective—Lysander put an end to the Peloponnesian War. Although Nossack's novel is set at the end of a comparably atrocious time of disaster, this analogy seems to suggest little more. The name Iona offers even less for anyone looking for a definite prefiguration at this point. While it is the name of an island off the west coast of Scotland, it also recalls the race of the Iones, but relates to no specific historical event connected with them. The names put forward do not themselves offer symbolic comment on modern events. Nor, once they have been mentioned, does the narrator even make use of them again. Instead, they merely serve to set the scene for the veiled mythological motifs to come later in the work. As the narrator himself says of the name Iona: "Es kommt mehr auf den Klang an. Sie hüllen sich da hinein, und wenn ihnen die Farbe gut steht, behalten sie den Namen."[57] Their function, in other words, is merely associative.

Apart from these two evocative names, only one Greek figure is specified in the novel. This happens at the point where the narrator is projecting an image of the person to whom he may tell his story. "Dieser andere sitzt mit dem Gesicht zum Fenster. . . . Er blickt auf den Orion."[58] First and foremost, of course, the constellation of stars is meant here, but this one group is also mentioned specifically for its mythological overtones.[59] The image of a hypothetical

admirably, I don't know why. Lysander was the name of a general who won a few important battles. . . . This woman . . . would have to be called something like Iona."

[57] op.cit., p. 37. "It is more a question of the sound. They are wrapped in it, and, if the color suits them, they retain the name."

[58] op.cit., p. 10. "This other person sits facing the window. . . . He looks at Orion."

[59] A similarly symbolic use of a constellation with mythological over-

listener, ostensibly looking at the Orion constellation instead of paying attention to the narrator, does not imply
that he is not listening to the tale. For this is a significant
tableau, not a piece of realistic fiction. A number of similarities between Orion and the narrator would suggest that
—symbolically—looking at his constellation and listening
to the hero's story amount to very much the same thing. The
image of the blinded Orion being led eastwards by his
guide Cedalion to the place where he would receive his
sight again is the apposite part of the myth.[60] A major disaster is over in Nossack's novel, just as the rape of Merope
is a thing of the past in the classical tale. In *Nekyia*, the hero
is guided towards his parents by his brother, as Orion is led
by Cedalion. In one case the blindness is literal, in the other
metaphorical. Furthermore, within the context of the City
of the Dead, the title image which dominates the whole of
the novel, it is worth bearing in mind that the word Hades
itself means "sightless." Hence the only prefiguration the
narrator actually reveals in the novel is the one drawing attention to his own metaphorical blindness. The fact that he
is apparently unaware of the major myths which (if secondary literature is a fair indication) most of Nossack's
readers appear to have noticed, is a further token of this
selfsame blindness.

In keeping with the unclear situation the work describes,
the prefigurations of *Nekyia* are covert. Hermann Kasack's
dust-cover introduction to the novel refers to the dreamlike
quality ("die als Traum erlebte Wirklichkeit") that makes
it so unlike Nossack's next war-novel. For the most part,
Interview mit dem Tode is set in definite locations (parts

---

tones was used in a much more famous early German novel: Friedrich
Hölderlin's *Hyperion*. At one point, Diotima says to the hero, while
looking at the stars: "dein Namensbruder, der herrliche Hyperion
des Himmels ist in dir" (*Sämtliche Werke*, ed. Fr. Beißner, Stuttgart,
1957, III, p. 73).

[60] Robert Graves gives an account of the myth in *The Greek Myths*,
I, p. 151.

of Hamburg and the Lüneburger Heide), and with a comparable explicitness it declares its prefigurations (Cassandra and Orpheus). *Nekyia*, in contrast, is set in an unnamed city where everything at first appears to be dead after a strange holocaust which has only a symbolic connection with the Second World War—a place where names, if used, have to be invented. (It is understandable that the author of *Die Stadt hinter dem Strom* should feel drawn to this work.) The reference to the eleventh book of the *Odyssey* in the title forms an exception to the work's general vagueness. According to Liddell and Scott, the Greek word νέκυια has two meanings: first "a magical rite by which ghosts were called up and questioned about the future"; second, "the common name for the eleventh book of the *Odyssey*."[61] Again, a certain ambiguity is maintained, for in Nossack's novel the connotation of the title seems to change from specific allusion to the *Odyssey* in the first half to the more general meaning towards the end, a not uncommon shift from myth to archetype.

With regard to the more specific reading of the word, Theodore Ziolkowski has pointed out some of the parallels to the relevant part of Homer's epic:

The novel begins with a number of Homeric allusions. The narrator decides to return to the destroyed city (the underworld); he recalls a conversation in which a friend had once said: "Nun wollen wir zu den Huren und uns wie die Schweine benehmen" (p. 73, a reference to the Circe episode); he meets, among the shades of his memory, an old man called *der Meister*, who bears an obvious resemblance in function and appearance to Teiresias: "Ich glaube, er sah sehr schlecht, vielleicht war er sogar blind. Doch das machte nichts aus; denn er nahm alles mit den Ohren wahr" (p. 70).[62]

---

[61] *A Greek-English Lexicon*, Oxford, 1929, p. 996.
[62] "The Odysseus Theme in Recent German Fiction," p. 232.

The last reference mentioned here possibly telescopes two ideas: the blindness of Teiresias and that of Orion.

To support Ziolkowski's reading, one finds clear allusions to the topology of Hades in the novel. At one point, the narrator recalls: "Ich wäre beinahe in den Fluß gefallen. . . . Man hat uns doch immer erzählt, es gäbe da einen bissigen Hund und einen Fährmann,"[63]—in other words, the Styx, Cerberus and Charon. On these specific references to the underworld, seen through Greek eyes, rests the case for interpreting the title *Nekyia* with its narrower connotation. All the motifs suggested above occur in the Homeric Book of the Dead. Although the figure of Orion is only mentioned twice peripherally in it,[64] the blindness he shares with Teiresias remains an important motif in both the *Odyssey* and *Nekyia*. The most relevant passage in Homer's epic reads:

> . . . where the fog-bound Cimmerians live in the City of Perpetual Mist. When the bright Sun climbs the sky and puts the stars to flight, no ray from him can penetrate to them . . . for dreadful Night has spread her mantle over the heads of that unhappy folk.[65]

The analogous setting in *Nekyia* is just as somber: "Oft liegt Nebel über der Landschaft und wenn die Sonne einmal scheint, ist es wie ein Zauber."[66] The darkness/blindness motif is repeated at another point in the *Odyssey*, in the reference to "the Earthshaker, who has by no means forgotten his resentment against you for blinding his beloved son."[67]

---

[63] *op.cit.*, p. 104. "I would almost have fallen into the river. . . . They always told us that there was a fierce dog and a ferryman there."

[64] In the *Odyssey* (Penguin ed., Harmondsworth, 1961), the references are to Otus and Ephialtes, described as "finer by far than all but the glorious Orion" (p. 179); and Odysseus briefly recalls seeing Orion in the underworld (p. 186).

[65] *op.cit.*, p. 171.

[66] *Nekyia*, p. 37. "Often mist lies across the countryside, and if the sun shines at all, it is like magic."

[67] *op.cit.*, p. 171.

The general mood of *Nekyia* certainly evokes the spirit of the underworld that Odysseus visits. However, the way the novel then develops, after signaling a marked similarity to part of the *Odyssey*, has led various critics to search elsewhere for further prefigurations. Two have been suggested: Telemachus seeking his father, and, for the final part of the novel, Orestes with his mother Clytemnestra. Ziolkowski has offered a detailed account of this possible change of myths at a certain point in the narrative:

> As in Joyce's *Ulysses* we have the story not only of Odysseus' search for him, but also Telemachus' search for his father. Here, however, the two figures are merged in the one person of the narrator: as Odysseus he descends to the underworld and invokes the shades, but it is the archetype of Telemachus that takes over when the narrator searches amongst the shades for his father. Even more striking is a second major alteration in the middle of the novel and the focus shifts gradually and the archetypal pattern becomes and remains Orestes. Odysseus is clearly the model of the first half, the journey to the underworld and the evocation of the shades. Then Telemachus pursues the search for his father.[68]

The "merging" described here is the pattern I have called "condensation." At a certain point in the narrative, the hero appears as the archetypal lost son searching for his father, and for this quest the Telemachus prefiguration is proposed. The arrival of the hero's father, who appears about a third of the way through the book,[69] has been taken by Ziolkowski to mark the beginning of the suspected Telemachus motif. Yet I can see no reason why one should assume this image to be a functional ingredient of the novel's symbolism. Only if one expects every modern event in the novel to have a mythological prefiguration is one

---

[68] "The Odysseus Theme in Recent German Fiction," p. 232.
[69] *Nekyia*, p. 57.

tempted to introduce the Telemachus episode from another part of the *Odyssey* to interpret this final part of the work.[70] Since the eleventh book of the *Odyssey* apparently cannot furnish a parallel for this one scene, there is no reason why one should delve further into the Homeric world to find a correspondence. None of the kinds of clue to a motif, outlined earlier, is offered to establish a fresh analogy of this kind. So whether or not there is a covert motif, always a vexed question, here hardly seems to become a serious issue. Nossack's novel works with only two motifs: Odysseus' descent into the underworld, and the tale of Orestes and Clytemnestra. Both motifs are mentioned in the eleventh book of the *Odyssey*, although only the former is treated at length. The meeting of the son with his father, on the other hand, belongs solely to the modern narrative, without being highlighted by any mythological motif at all.

The point at which the substituted Orestes motif becomes crucial to our understanding is marked by the hero's realization that he really seeks his mother, not his father:

> Bis dahin hatte ich mit keinem Gedanken an meine Mutter gedacht oder auch nur im Entferntesten vermutet, daß es sich um sie handelte. Doch kaum, daß mein Vater sie erwähnte, schien es mir, als hätte ich nie etwas anderes begehrt.[71]

Henceforth, the Orestes myth takes over from the Odysseus motif. Even so, granted this second motif is a force to be reckoned with in the novel, it would be unwise to forget— just because the Greek myth must be more familiar to the

---

[70] The resultant interpretation seems to be influenced by a knowledge of the way motifs are handled in Joyce's *Ulysses*, where there is a parallel prefigured search of son for father and father for son.

[71] *op.cit.*, p. 86. "Until then I had not thought at all of my mother or even had the slightest inkling that things concerned her. But scarcely had my father mentioned her, and it seemed to me as if I had never desired anything else."

reader from other sources[72]—that there are also references to it in the eleventh book of the *Odyssey*. This fact bestows upon the novel more of a unity than Ziolkowski sees: "despite many . . . parallels Nossack's novel defies a close comparison with the original."[73] If one compares the novel with Homer's eleventh book and discounts the Telemachus motif, a well-wrought pattern emerges.

Homer's account of Odysseus' meeting in Hades with a number of mythological figures from the past becomes an ideal framework for the condensation of various myths. In it, Agamemnon asks Odysseus if he has news of Orestes from the land of the living. " 'I know that my good Orestes has not yet died and come below.' 'Son of Atreus,' I answered him, 'why ask me that? I have no idea whether he is alive or dead.' "[74] It is the question, of course, which the hero of Nossack's novel seems unable to answer about himself as he wanders through the limbo in which the novel is set. But the condensation of two myths, leading the hero from one experience on to the next and showing that he is in a sense returning to some preordained order, makes it look as if he is going full-circle, back to the after-life from whence he came.

From what we have seen so far in this chapter, it is beginning to appear as if a definite relationship exists between given types of motif-structure and certain archetypal moods. Schemes of correspondences often generate a sense of inexorable fate. The unnamed, enigmatic kind of motif used in *Nekyia* creates an air of uncomprehended disaster, either impending or already past. The conflicting sets of images seen in *L'Emploi du Temps* engender a mood of ambivalence, centered usually on some intractable moral

[72] Aeschylus' *Oresteia* trilogy, Sophocles' *Electra* and Euripides' *Electra* and *Orestes* are the obvious sources of the myth.
[73] *op.cit.*, p. 232.　　　　[74] *op.cit.*, p. 183.

227

problem. The maze of fragmented and condensed prefigurations to be found in *Die Schuldlosen,* which will be examined now in Macdonald Harris's *Trepleff,* suits an age of uncertain values and indeterminate standards of guilt and innocence. This, it must be stressed, is in most cases completely the opposite function to the one usually attributed to the use of myths in modern novels. For, following Eliot's lead, interpreters have tended to associate the use of mythology in the novel with an attempt at simplifying the chaos of the modern world depicted.

Combined Patterns: Macdonald Harris's Trepleff

Typological studies of literature betray a tendency to *use* works of literature as illustrations, and in particular they are often inclined to isolate a single literary device from the complexity of any given work. It is a sin of reductionism often perpetrated in the past two chapters; so, to counteract this bias to some extent, I shall conclude by looking at a more involved use of prefigurative patterns. It occurs in a novel which chooses a motif from an earlier work of literature—not a "popular" myth (as Don Juan has been designated) nor a "literary" myth (as some have called Faust), but a familiar work of Russian drama which can be manipulated symbolically in the same way.

Macdonald Harris is the pseudonym of a Californian professor whose novel *Trepleff* appeared in 1968. The fact that this is a work set in contemporary American society with a prefiguration from Chekhov's *The Seagull* might invite certain speculations about the parallels between the twilight of late-Imperial Russia and the present condition of the United States. But this is not generally an academic work, of the kind Thomas Mann would write; it belongs rather to the picaresque tradition.

"I met my wife as a result of an amateur production of *The Seagull,*" the narrator-hero of Harris's *Trepleff* confesses at the beginning of the work.[75] Indeed, the novel begins with what seems to be a classic reenactment of Chekhov's play, with the producer of this amateur dramatization logically playing the role of Trigorin and even having an appropriate affair with the girl cast as Nina. By the time the (unnamed) narrator, playing Trepleff, comes to her, the Nina figure—Syd—has been jilted by the producer just as Trigorin abandons Nina; but Syd is even left bearing a child as a result of the encounter. The notion of imitation takes on a new nuance in *Trepleff* because of the method of acting employed. Egon, who has Trigorin's part and also produces the play, is a great believer in the Stanislavsky school of acting: "During the time the play was being rehearsed and produced he wanted them to think of themselves not as actors but as the characters they were playing."[76] There are some splendid parodies of method-acting techniques in the first chapter, but the notion is introduced for more serious effects too. The reader is encouraged to feel that the method fails: a certain tension remains between character and role, and this discrepancy the novel develops.

The first intimation of the complications to come emerges with the narrator's feeling that Syd is "badly cast" as Nina.[77] Nina's profound unhappiness contrasts with Syd's easy nature. Already the narrator has expressed misgivings about the acting technique; he is critical of the power the producer has, reducing the actors to mere puppets, and he describes the end effect as "a form of controlled schizophrenia."[78] When it comes to following the set prefiguration, the hero is particularly recalcitrant; the very fact that he marries the girl playing Nina is a sign that the *Seagull*

[75] *op.cit.*, p. 7.   [76] *op.cit.*, p. 9.   [77] *op.cit.*, p. 21.
[78] *op.cit.*, p. 12. More will be said about schizophrenia later, but it should be noted here that a puppet motif runs through the whole of the novel, characterizing the way one figure tends to dominate the other in each relationship described.

229

motif has been introduced as much to be departed from as to be followed.

The Trigorin figure leaves the modern Nina to have an affair with the actress playing Masha. And this makes Syd so angry that she rejects any previous sympathy she may have had for her role: "O, that Nina, what a fool she was."[79] What Syd here criticizes is the passivity of Chekhov's characters, showing an impatience with the way some of the Russian figures behave which emerges again and again in Harris's novel. The narrator, too, reacts against his role in the play. He even has a positive prefiguration to contrast with the ineffective role of Trepleff forced upon him. Having read Sinclair Lewis's *Arrowsmith* at a receptive point in his life, the narrator "decided that it was [his] destiny to be a scientist like the hero of Lewis's novel: dedicated, truth-seeking, idealistic, a white-clad figure moving among the sick and alleviating pain with the sure touch of [his] fingers."[80] Hence, when he refuses to become the parody of the Russian superfluous man, his concentration fixes once more on his youthful goal. "Now I saw that the thing was simple, much simpler than I had ever dreamed. I didn't have to be Trepleff, I didn't want to be Trepleff. I wanted to be Arrowsmith: cool, knowing, competent, Olympian, but sympathetic."[81] And this he succeeds in becoming by the end of the first chapter, where we find him well-established, carrying on a flourishing practice as a psychiatrist, living with all the paraphernalia of middle-class success, and with Syd now his wife. Looked at in the terms evolved in this study, the first chapter of *Trepleff* shows the same link between serial condensation and psychological development as was seen in Hans Erich Nossack's *Nekyia*. As he progresses, the central figure moves from one prefiguration (Trepleff) to another (Arrowsmith). But in *Trepleff* this

---

[79] *op.cit.*, p. 27.   [80] *op.cit.*, p. 8.   [81] *op.cit.*, p. 28.

sense of development engendered in the first chapter eventually proves illusory.

Before his marriage breaks up (he is a little too willing to "alleviate pain with the sure touch of [his] fingers") and before the prefigurations are shuffled once more, we have in a sub-plot a further veiled parallel to the course of Chekhov's drama. The narrator one day resolves to destroy his dog Ernest, a decision which in itself mars the general idyll he has constructed for himself. (Ernest has been enjoying a devastating love-life with the high pedigree bitches of the neighborhood, a motif which in fact itself prefigures the hero's path in later parts of *Trepleff*.) The ensuing attempt, involving dropping the dog overboard tied to the anchor of his cruiser, fortunately fails and the last that is seen of Ernest, he is striking out for the shore, having managed somehow to escape from his noose. This episode is described as a "vicarious suicide" by the narrator.[82] Symbolically, it is an event reminiscent of Trepleff's first suicide attempt in *The Seagull*. Or, looked at another way, the attempt at killing the dog is a parody of the killing of the seagull in Chekhov's play. The outcome of either reading of this episode is the feeling that the narrator-hero of *Trepleff* is a rather unlucky, if not downright incompetent individual.

Chapter 1 has something of the quality of an overture to the novel: it marks the calm before the storm, and even contains a play within the work, just as Trepleff's dramolette marks the overture to *The Seagull* proper. The real starting-point of *Trepleff* is the image of a successful professional man with a happy married life—a stereotype of security from which the narrator gradually escapes. The catalyst comes when the hero slips into an adulterous relationship with one of his more frustrated clients, assuming the role of lover partly to rescue her from a state of

---

[82] *op.cit.*, p. 41.

permanent, unloved insecurity. In her review of the novel, Kathleen Nott sees the hero as someone "who has grasped that psychiatry is meant to be about 'love,' "[83] but this is a rather generous interpretation of how the narrator casually becomes involved with the girl. The hero's realization that he is becoming something of a Trigorin in the way he manipulates people[84] comes closer to the turn his character is now taking. He is in the process of becoming an anti-hero, a role which reaches its nadir when the ex-psychiatrist, professionally struck from the register and deprived of all his money by his ex-wife and his "victim's" lawyers, ends up playing the part of gigolo to a rich American lady on her yearly visit to the fashion-houses of Europe. Although the novel is generally most explicit in naming prefigurations for the main protagonists, this lady is not related so openly to any Chekhovian character, yet it is clear from the outset that she is the modern equivalent of Mme Arkadina. The following passage reveals how much the two have in common:

> I knew enough about her now to see that she wasn't entirely sure of herself. In spite of her surface poise, her blasé air of assurance, she had a hidden need to reassert her authority over me constantly in little ways to be sure it was still there. This was the reason for the little tricks she was always inventing to test my obedience: getting me to light her cigarettes, making me carry packages and kittens in the streets, disrobing me in front of the chambermaid and various other little ceremonies to demonstrate exactly who was in charge. As long as I obeyed she could still be sure she existed. It proved something to herself that was very necessary to her.[85]

This figure, Nadia (an anagram of the last part of Arkadina), has all the trappings of a modern Arkadina, in

[83] *The Observer Review*, 15 December 1968, p. v.
[84] *op.cit.*, pp. 79f.   [85] *op.cit.*, p. 119.

fact. *Haute couture* is her histrionic equivalent of acting (as much a bathetic contrast as the narrator's own psychiatry is to Trepleff's creative writing). And she dominates most of the novel's action, just as Mme Arkadina looms over so much of Chekhov's play.

By the time he reaches Europe, the hero has stood in a number of different relationships to the *Seagull* prefiguration: he has resembled Trepleff by falling in love with a Nina, but he has differed from this initial prefiguration by actually gaining the girl. Then, the more he refuses to play the part of Trepleff, the closer he comes to resembling Trigorin. With the further refinement that in his eyes the opposite of Trepleff is not always Trigorin (for this is a nineteenth-century antithesis), but Arrowsmith, we find a certain schizophrenic element entering the work. It can be seen, for example, in the narrator's attitude to his "mistress," though she is this in name only: "Part of me hated her and part of me desired her, but the most intelligent part of me, the clear unemotional detached Trigorin part, admired her."[86] From this point onwards, whenever the narrator feels the urge to take stock of his demoralizing position, that of gigolo to his self-centered traveling companion, he turns to his Chekhov: "I was beginning to respect her, in at least part of my mind . . . but what happened to Trigorin? You call this manipulating people, all this carrying packages and running up and down stairs with her coat?" The narrator has difficulty in relating his present predicament to the prefiguration. "It seemed to me I had a slight problem here but not really. Trigorin was still around but he was collecting data. After a while he would figure out what to do with the data. At least that was what I told myself. It was possible that I was kidding myself but I didn't think so."[87] Psychotic overtones begin to emerge, for there is a complicated net-

---

[86] *op.cit.*, p. 99.   [87] *op.cit.*, p. 112.

work of doubts and protective motivations here which the ramifications of the motif do much to highlight.

The more wilfully his "mistress" behaves, the more difficult it becomes for the narrator to reconcile himself with the image of Trigorin which he seems to prefer at this stage in the proceedings. When he finally asserts himself, after taking a great deal of humiliating treatment from Nadia, the narrator very quickly finds himself evicted from the hotel where they had been staying together. Immediately he is conscious of an identity crisis:

> I was talking like some kind of Trepleff. If I was going to be Trigorin I had nobody to blame but myself, for playing my ace card too soon and for losing my temper. Most of all for losing my temper. I resolved to be more objective in the future in dealing with situations of this kind. It was a little hard to resemble Trigorin when you were being kicked out of an hotel, but at least you could keep your wits about you and be wary and astute.[88]

Again, there is something deranged in his reasoning, for being wary and astute is equated with returning to the hotel and "eating humble pie" before a triumphant Nadia.

The hero's revenge finally comes when he invidiously reminds Nadia of her age and plays upon her fears of growing old, and hence being no longer fashionable. He does this by taking her to see a gruesome collection of skeletons and bones in a crypt just off the Via Veneto in Rome. ("It reduced Helen of Troy, Romeo and Juliet, Petrarch's sonnets, all poetry and all human aspirations to something for a dog to gnaw on."[89]) The narrator is very proud of the fact that he has found Nadia's Achilles' heel and has been able to wound her grievously there. "On the whole I felt I was getting very successful at pulling puppet strings, even more successful than I expected. I might even qualify as a

---

[88] *op.cit.*, p. 131.   [89] *op.cit.*, p. 151.

Trigorin after all if I learned to control my temper and a few other things."[90]

At this juncture, the Chekhov prefiguration is given a new twist and applied afresh, to Nadia. With the narrator endeavoring to reestablish himself as something of a Trigorin, Nadia starts to resemble Trepleff. Once more, there are no explicit references to this effect, but her double suicide attempt—the first unsuccessful one, in Rome, leaving her with a bandaged head like Trepleff's—makes the change of prefiguration abundantly clear. That the fragmentation and condensation of prefigurative roles no longer respects sex differences, but has a woman playing the role of Trepleff, might at first sound quite radical. Very few novels have worked with female prefigurations referring to male characters or vice versa.[91] But this reversal is far from out of place in *Trepleff*, for the narrator's place as gigolo at this point in the plot is in itself an effeminate role, and the domineering behavior Nadia displays makes her suited to a man's part. (Although, of course, the Trepleff figure is something of a compromise between male part and unmanly behavior.)

If the narrator is generally well aware of the appropriate counterparts in *The Seagull* to various characters in his story, the fact that nothing is made of either of Nadia's successive prefigurations—first Mme Arkadina, and then Trepleff—becomes a significant aspect of his attitude towards her. Why he makes no reference to the Trepleff parallel is perhaps easier to answer. He was himself for a long time closely linked with this figure, and he is to return to it at the end of the novel. To admit that his treatment of Nadia has reduced her to playing the role of Trepleff in a melodrama of his own making would be tantamount to an-

[90] *op.cit.*, p. 153.
[91] There is, of course, an equivalent reversal in Joyce's *Ulysses*, where Bloom is prefigured by Elvira; cf. Hall, *op.cit.*, pp. 79f.

other "vicarious suicide," from the hero's point of view. By not mentioning the Trepleff correspondence, at the point where it becomes fragmented to include Nadia, the narrator manages to distance himself substantially from a woman with whom he in fact has dangerously much in common. He probably does not mention the Arkadina prefiguration for equally self-protective reasons. At the time when he begins to make a pass at Nadia, while crossing the Atlantic on the first-class ticket he forfeited all his remaining funds to buy, the hero likes to think of himself as Trigorin, the manipulator of people. (In other words, he has in mind the Trigorin who is capable of loving and leaving Nina.) On the other hand, Trigorin's relationship with Mme Arkadina is a more complex matter. She is on the whole far more of a manipulator than he is, and for this reason it would not be very flattering for the narrator to think of Nadia as Mme Arkadina and to start pondering what his relationship with her means in the light of the Trigorin-Arkadina analogy.[92]

So far, Nadia and her prefigurations have been considered in terms of what I have called plot-motivation. One can see that there are good psychological reasons why the hero, who is also the narrator of the novel and therefore in a position to suppress things unfavorable to his image of himself, should not want to consider what analogies exist for Nadia. But there are also good aesthetic reasons why the reader should not be constantly presented with a clear-cut analogy in this part of the narrative.[93]

[92] The situation here is comparable to that found in Broch's *Die Schuldlosen*, where different aspects of a prefiguration are emphasized at different places. There are two Trigorins, just as there are two Aristaeuses—a good one and a bad one.
[93] The only other reference to the motif is on p. 199: "Now that I thought of it I had insomnia and almost never slept. This was great. I was getting neurasthenic. I'll bet Trigorin slept. So did Nadia. . . ." There is no further allusion until the final chapter.

The hero's progress in the novel is from an integrated position in contemporary society to what at first appears to be a traditional outsider's role: that of parasite upon the more nauseating sides of the very society that he appears to reject. Nadia, with her fear of death and her constant preoccupation with preserving her fading beauty and keeping up a cosmopolitan appearance, with her Europe-fixation, her matriarchal posturing and her complex frigidity, becomes almost a parody of aspects of a society that the ex-psychiatrist has left behind. The hero seems to be, as a result, a figure from the picaresque tradition, for the picaro too lives off the society he rejects. There are passages reminiscent of *Felix Krull*, of Gide and Kerouac, to reinforce the stereotype employed.[94] We tend to identify with the narrator even, as much because of his ubiquitous humor as because of the first-person perspective maintained throughout. It therefore comes as something of a shock— and perhaps a further literary parody—to find that *Trepleff*, like so many other novels of recent years, is being narrated from a lunatic asylum.[95] (The indications of schizophrenia which I have already mentioned are largely the result of a hindsight reading of certain early episodes in the work.) The relevance of this shock revelation to the *Seagull* motif lies in the fact that the Chekhov prefiguration reappears at precisely the same juncture as we realize that the hero is more than the traditional outsider, that he is in fact already suffering from acute schizophrenia.[96] At this point

[94] Kathleen Nott criticizes the pastiche quality of parts of the novel, but this can be related to the theme of an identity crisis.

[95] *op.cit.*, p. 249.

[96] It would not be outside the picaresque tradition for the narrator to have bluffed his way into an asylum, but the fact that his entry into the institution does not appear to be an act of volition (his symptoms, furthermore, correspond very closely to the case-histories of mental illness cited by R. D. Laing in *The Divided Self*) suggests that he really is a schizophrenic.

he regresses to the *persona* which had been imposed upon him in the "controlled schizophrenia" of the amateur production of *The Seagull*. He "becomes" Trepleff once more.

Just before the end of the novel, the narrator is arrested by the police after an incident with a prostitute, during which he feels some inchoate urge to tell her what is happening to him. The terms he chooses are characteristic:

> I wanted to say something to explain to her that it was alright, perhaps "Today I was low enough to kill this seagull, I lay it at your feet," but I never had a chance to pronounce this benediction or farewell because during the time I was concerned to be precise in what I said and trying to decide on the exact wording, one cop was jerking me one way and the other the other way. . . .[97]

After this, the modern Trepleff finds himself certified and put away amongst those stock figures who believe themselves to be Napoleon or Joan of Arc. The ultimate variation on the *Seagull* motif in the novel is that the narrator claims to be looked after by a certain Dr. Dorn (the name of the doctor in Chekhov's play).[98] The final part of the novel is given over to the kind of intimate, solipsistic understandings that the mad sometimes share with their attendants:

> Dorn is the only one in whom I have confided my secret and for this reason he is careful not to let anyone overhear when he calls me by name. When he appears in the doorway, a smile already forming under his soft moustache, he glances around behind him before he greets me: "Good morning, Konstantin Gavrilovich." And we both smile, pretending it is a joke, although we both know it is not a joke but our secret. If anyone overheard us, of course, we could pretend it was a joke and in this way the secret would not be discovered. "What did you do this morning, shoot a seagull?" "No,

[97] *op.cit.*, p. 249.   [98] *op.cit.*, p. 251.

I shot at one, but missed." "If you kill one you must lay it at my feet." "I have already laid one at your feet. The one I killed because she threw my shoes out of the window."[99]

Primarily the narrator means Nadia, but he might also be talking about himself. For in his insanity he has come to identify fully with what was merely an objective correlative in *The Seagull*, and he lays himself at the feet of Dr. Dorn. The suicide is now no longer vicarious; but it is essentially a mental suicide. The schizophrenia is no longer controlled, as it was in the college dramatic production but inescapably psychotic. The *persona* has become an identity.

The link established in *Trepleff* between imitating a prefiguration and becoming fixated by the role to the point of mental aberration is also a theme in *Doktor Faustus* and *Passages*. Other novels of recent years, such as Zelazny's *The Dream Master* and Spencer's *Asylum*, use the reenactment of myths as a way out of madness: offering a therapeutic reversal of the *idée fixe* through psycho-drama. Whereas Thomas Mann could still see the reenactment of a myth as a noble goal,[100] it has been presented as a negative process in various recent novels. According to John Sturrock, "all Robbe-Grillet's novels . . . depend on myths, because they all represent the sub-tension of a private fantasy, distorting the real world to satisfy its own imperious needs."[101] The second, pejorative meaning of myth seems to be asserting itself. Nowadays characters in fiction often refuse, as the narrator of *Trepleff* at first wisely does, to follow their prefigurative roles through, seeing in them something of a straitjacket. The hero of Döblin's Hamlet-novel puts into words a typical sentiment nowadays:

[99] *op.cit.*, pp. 255-256.
[100] Notably in "Freud und die Zukunft," *Adel des Geistes*, Stockholm, 1945.
[101] *op.cit.*, pp. 174-175.

Ich stelle fest, ich bin nicht im Spiel. Wenn dies ein
Theaterstück sein soll und Schicksale darstellen,
meines ist nicht dabei. . . . Darum gehe ich jetzt aus
und entdecke mich.[102]

The extent to which myths have been shown in this chapter to confuse the outline of the plot, rather than put it into
focus, also reflects a change in attitude to myths that appears to have taken place since the beginning of the century. In his essay on Alberto Moravia, Dominique
Fernandez has argued that the use of mythology in *Il
disprezzo* is largely a reaction against the limitations of
Freudianism. And *Il disprezzo* is, as was suggested earlier,
a novel that comments very much on a whole tradition of
mythological fiction. Kingsley Amis sums up the mythoclas-
tic mood of many characters in recent novels of this kind
in a little poem entitled "Sonnet from Orpheus":

> . . . now I'm tired of being the trade-name
> on boxes of assorted junk; tired of
> conscription as the mouthpiece of your brash
> theories, of jigging to your symbol-crash.
> Speak for yourselves, or not at all: this
> game is up—your manikin has had enough.[103]

Attitudes to myths, inside or outside literature, may have
changed in recent times, with a certain anti-myth reaction
setting in. Yet this change in attitude has not led to the dis-
appearance of mythological motifs from contemporary fiction. At most, they have been more often used in a pejorative way. Such prefigurations appear to have remained part
of a standard method of telling a story and commenting on
it at the same time from a different perspective.

---

[102] *op.cit.*, p. 512. "I perceive that I am not part of the act. If this
is supposed to be a play and depict people's fates, mine is not part of
them. . . . So I'll leave now and go and discover myself."

[103] Quoted by Elizabeth Jennings in *Poetry Today*, London, 1961,
p. 10.

Select Bibliography

The first part of the bibliography offers a selection of prefigurative novels, including all those discussed in this book. The editions cited are the ones used in this study. When the prefigurations involved are not apparent from a novel's title, I have indicated them in parenthesis after an entry, whereever there have not been too many for this to be practical. Except in the case of Russian novels, the bibliography cites works in their original language. Where English translations are available, this has been pointed out in the footnotes.

The subsequent list of secondary literature on my subject is of necessity very restricted. While I have listed all the work on prefigurations and mythological correspondences in fiction with which I am familiar, the selection of works on mythology in other genres and on the subject of classical mythologies and archetypes has been limited to a handful of works which I found to be particularly useful. All material of a more general nature is referred to fully in the footnotes and does not appear in this bibliography.

Translations of passages quoted in German and Italian are given in the footnotes, but secondary material presented in support of a point explained in the text is generally confined to the footnotes and is not translated.

The following abbreviations have been used for periodicals or works of reference cited frequently in the footnotes and in the bibliography:

CdS   *Cahiers du Sud*
DVjs   *Deutsche Vierteljahrsschrift für Literaturwissenschaft und Geistesgeschichte*
GLL   *German Life and Letters*

MFS   *Modern Fiction Studies*
Novel   *Novel: A Forum on Fiction*
OED   *The Shorter Oxford English Dictionary,* Oxford, 1956³
PMLA   *Publications of the Modern Language Association*
TLS   *The Times Literary Supplement*

Mythological Novels and Novels with Other Prefigurations

Bachmann, Guido. *Gilgamesch.* Wiesbaden, 1966.

Baker, Dorothy. *Cassandra at the Wedding.* New York, 1966.

Beuchler, Klaus. *Aufenthalt auf Bornholm.* Rostock, 1969. (*Iliad*)

Blish, James. *Black Easter or Faust Aleph-Null.* London, 1969.

Bowen, John. *A World Elsewhere.* London, 1965. (Philoctetes)

Broch, Hermann. *Die Schuldlosen.* Ed. Hermann J. Weigand, Zürich, 1950. (Aristaeus; *Don Giovanni*)

——. *Der Tod des Vergil.* Zürich, 1952. (Orpheus; Aeneas)

——. *Der Versucher.* Ed. Felix Stössinger. Zürich, 1955. (Demeter; Abraham and Isaac)

Brophy, Brigid. *The Snow Ball.* London, 1964. (*Don Giovanni*)

Brown, Harry. *The Stars in their Courses.* London, 1961. (*Iliad*)

Buechner, Carl Frederick. *A Long Day's Dying.* London, 1951. (Philomela)

Bulgakov, Mikhail. *The Master and Margarita.* London, 1967. (Faust)

Burgess, Anthony. *A Vision of Battlements.* Dublin, 1965. (*Aeneid*)

——. *The Eve of Saint Venus.* London, 1968.

Butor, Michel. *L'Emploi du Temps.* Paris, 1957. (Theseus; Cain and Abel)

——. *La Modification.* Paris, 1957. (*Aeneid*)

Canetti, Elias. *Die Blendung*. Vienna, 1935. (*Odyssey*; Aphrodite, Hephaistos and Ares)

Christie, Agatha. *The Labours of Hercules*. London, 1947.

Delaney, Samuel. *The Einstein Intersection*. London, 1969. (Orpheus)

Döblin, Alfred. *Berlin Alexanderplatz: Die Geschichte vom Franz Biberkopf*. Berlin, 1960. (Orestes; Abraham and Isaac)

———. *Hamlet oder Die lange Nacht nimmt ein Ende*. Munich, 1957. (*King Lear*; Pluto and Proserpina)

Elliot, Janice. *The Singing Head*. London, 1968. (Orpheus)

Frisch, Max. *Homo Faber*. Frankfurt a.M., 1957. (Daedalus; Orestes; Oedipus)

———. *Mein Name sei Gantenbein*. Frankfurt a.M., 1964. (Hermes; Philemon and Baucis)

Gorki, Maxim. *Bystander*. London and Toronto, 1930. (Faust)

Harris, Macdonald. *Trepleff*. London, 1968. (*The Seagull*)

Härtling, Peter. *Niembsch oder der Stillstand: Eine Suite*. Stuttgart, 1964. (Don Juan)

Hartlaub, Geno. *Nicht jeder ist Odysseus*. Düsseldorf, 1967.

Hersey, John. *Too Far to Walk*. London, 1966. (Faust)

Hesse, Hermann. *Demian*. Frankfurt a.M., 1966. (Abraxas; Eve; Cain)

Hill, Pamela. *Forget not Ariadne*. London, 1965.

Huxley, Aldous. *Brave New World*. London, 1932. (*The Tempest*; *Romeo and Juliet*; *Othello*)

Jahnn, Hans Henny. *Fluß ohne Ufer: Die Niederschrift des Gustav Anias Horn*. 2 vols., Munich, 1949-1950. (Gilgamesh)

Joyce, James. *A Portrait of the Artist as a Young Man*. London, 1916. (Daedalus)

———. *Ulysses*. Paris, 1922. (Also: *Hamlet*; *Don Giovanni*)

———. *Finnegans Wake*. London, 1939.

Kirsch, Hans Christian. *Bericht für Telemachos*. Munich, 1964.

Langgässer, Elisabeth. *Triptychon des Teufels—Ein Buch*

von dem Haß, dem Börsenspiel und der Unzucht: Mars, Merkur, Venus. Dresden, 1932.

———. *Proserpina: Eine Kindheitsmythe.* Hamburg, 1948.

———. *Märkische Argonautenfahrt.* Hamburg, 1959².

Leskov, Nikolai. "Lady Macbeth of Mtsensk," *The Enchanted Wanderer and other Stories.* Moscow, 1966, pp. 9-68.

Malamud, Bernard. *The Natural.* London, 1952. (Sir Perceval)

Mann, Heinrich. *Die Göttinnen oder die drei Romane der Herzogin von Assy: Diana, Minerva, Venus.* 3 vols., Leipzig, 1916-1918.

Mann, Thomas. *Joseph und seine Brüder.* Frankfurt a.M., 1960. (Osiris; Thoth; Tammuz; Hermes)

———. *Doktor Faustus: Das Leben des deutschen Tonsetzers Adrian Leverkühn, erzählt von einem Freunde.* Oldenburg, 1960.

Melville, Hermann. *Moby Dick.* London, 1952. (Osiris)

Merrill, James. *The (Diblos) Notebook.* London, 1965. (Orestes)

Moravia, Alberto. *Il disprezzo.* Milan and Rome, 1954. (Odyssey)

———. *L'attenzione.* Milan, 1965. (Oedipus)

Nossack, Hans Erich. *Nekyia: Bericht eines Überlebenden.* Frankfurt a.M., 1961. (Odyssey)

———. *Interview mit dem Tode.* Frankfurt a.M., 1963. (Orpheus and Persephone; Cassandra)

———. *Spätestens im November.* Frankfurt a.M., 1963. (Paolo and Francesca)

Perez de Ayala, Ramon. *Luna de miel, luna de hiel.* Madrid, 1923. (Daphnis and Chloe)

———. *Los trobajos de Urbano y Simona.* Madrid, 1923. (Daphnis and Chloe)

Queneau, Raymond. *Le Vol d'Icare.* Paris, 1969.

Quin, Ann. *Passages.* London, 1969. (Centaurs)

Robbe-Grillet, Alain. *Les Gommes.* Paris, 1963. (Oedipus)

Schallück, Paul. *Don Quichotte in Köln.* Frankfurt a.M., 1967.

Schneider, Rolf. *Der Tod des Nibelungen.* Rostock, 1970.
Spencer, Colin. *Asylum.* London, 1970. (Cain and Abel; Oedipus)
Stacton, David. *Kaliyuga: A Quarrel with the Gods.* London, 1965. (Siva)
Thiess, Frank. *Die Verdammten.* Hamburg, 1962. (Plato's Double Men)
Turgenev, Ivan. "A King Lear of the Steppe," *Five Short Novels by Ivan Turgenev.* New York, 1961, pp. 225-293.
Updike, John. *The Centaur.* Harmondsworth, 1966.
Zelazny, Roger. *The Dream Master.* London, 1968. (Daedalus; Sir Perceval; Tristan and Isolde)
Zwerenz, Gerhard. *Casanova oder der Kleine Herr in Krieg und Frieden.* Munich, 1966.

Literature on Archetypes, Mythology, and Myths in Literature

Abele, Rudolph von. "*Ulysses:* The Myth of Myth." *PMLA,* LXIX, 1954, pp. 358-364.
Aler, Jan (ed.) *De Mythe in de Literatuur.* The Hague, 1964.
———. "Mythical Consciousness in Modern German Poetry," *Reality and Creative Vision in German Lyrical Poetry.* Ed. August Closs. London, 1963, pp. 183-197.
Andres, Stefan. "Mythos und Dichtung," *Die Wirklichkeit des Mythos.* Ed. Kurt Hoffmann. Munich, 1965, pp. 11-25.
Asenbaum, W. *Die griechische Mythologie im modernen französischen Drama.* Diss., Vienna, 1956.
Auerbach, Erich. *Scenes from the Drama of Contemporary Literature.* New York, 1959.
Awad, Louis. *The Theme of Prometheus in English and French Literature: A Study in Literary Influence.* Cairo, 1963.
Baacke, Dieter. "Erzähltes Engagement: Antike Mythologie in Döblins Romanen." *Text + Kritik,* 13/14, 1966, pp. 22-31.

Baisette, Gaston. "Sur le retour aux mythes." *CdS*, xix, 1939, pp. 121-131.

Bergsten, Gunilla. *Thomas Manns "Doktor Faustus": Untersuchungen zu den Quellen und zur Struktur des Romans.* Lund, 1963.

Bianquis, Geneviève. *Faust à travers quatre siècles.* Paris, 1935.

⸻. "Thomas Mann et le 'Faustbuch' de 1587." *Etudes Germaniques*, v, 1950, pp. 54-59.

Blanchot, Maurice. "Romans Mythologiques," *Faux Pas*. Paris, 1943, pp. 232-239.

⸻. "Thomas Mann et le mythe de Faust." *Critique*, vi, 1950, pp. 3-21.

Bloch, Adèle. "The Archetypal Influences on Thomas Mann's *Joseph und seine Brüder.*" *Germanic Review*, xxxviii, 1963, pp. 151-156.

Blotner, Joseph L. "Mythic Patterns in *To the Lighthouse*," *Virginia Woolf's "To the Lighthouse."* Ed. Morris Beja. Bristol, 1970, pp. 169-188.

Bodkin, Maud. *Archetypal Patterns in Poetry.* Oxford, 1950.

Booth, Wayne. *The Rhetoric of Fiction.* Chicago and London, 1961.

Bradbury, Malcolm. "Iris Murdoch's *Under the Net.*" *Critical Quarterly*, iv, 1962, pp. 47-54.

Brennan, Joseph Gerard. *Three Philosophical Novelists: James Joyce, André Gide, Thomas Mann.* New York, 1964.

Bruner, Jerome S. "Myth and Identity." *Daedalus: Journal of the American Academy of Arts and Sciences*, 1959, pp. 349-358.

Burnham, James. "William Troy's Myths." *Partisan Review*, v, 1938, pp. 66-70.

Bush, Douglas: *Mythology and the Renaissance Tradition in English Poetry.* New York, 1957.

⸻. *Mythology and the Romantic Tradition in English Poetry.* New York, 1957.

⸻. *Pagan Myth and Christian Tradition in English Poetry.* Philadelphia, 1968.

Butler, E. M. *The Tyranny of Greece over Germany.* Cambridge, 1935.

———. *The Fortunes of Faust.* Cambridge, 1952.

Calarco, N. Joseph. *Tragic Being: Apollo and Dionysus in Western Drama.* Minneapolis, 1968.

Campbell, Joseph. *The Hero with a Thousand Faces.* New York, 1965.

Cassirer, Ernst. *The Philosophy of Symbolic Forms: II. Mythical Thought.* New Haven, Conn., 1965.

Chase, Richard. *Quest for Myth.* Baton Rouge, La., 1949.

Dabezies, André. *Visages de Faust au XXᵉ Siècle: Littérature, idéologie et mythes.* Paris, 1967.

Dalziel, Margaret. "Myth in Modern English Literature," *Myth and the Modern Imagination.* Ed. Margaret Dalziel. Dunedin, 1967, pp. 27-50.

Dickinson, Hugh. *Myth on the Stage.* Urbana, Ill., Chicago and London, 1969.

Dietrich, Margaret. "Antiker Mythos im modernen Drama," *Das moderne Drama: Strömungen, Gestalten, Motive.* Stuttgart, 1961, pp. 388-426.

Díez del Corral, Luis. *La función del mito clásico en la literatura contemporánea.* Madrid, 1957.

Dornheim, Alfredo. "Goethes 'Mignon' und Thomas Manns 'Echo': Zwei Formen des 'Göttlichen Kindes' im deutschen Roman." *Euphorion,* XLVI, 1952, pp. 315-347.

Edwards, Philip. "*Ulysses* and the Legends." *Essays in Criticism,* V, 1955, pp. 118-128.

Eliot, T. S. "Ulysses, Order and Myth," *James Joyce: Two Decades of Criticism.* Ed. Seon Givens. New York, 1948, pp. 198-202.

Emrich, Wilhelm. "Symbolinterpretation und Mythenforschung," *Protest und Verheißung.* Frankfurt a.M., 1960, pp. 67-94.

Faber du Faur, Curt von. "Der Seelenhüter in Hermann Brochs *Der Tod des Vergil*," *Wächter und Hüter: Festschrift für Hermann Weigand.* Yale, 1957, pp. 147-161.

Feuerlicht, Ignace. "Thomas Manns mythische Identifikation." *German Quarterly,* XXXVI, 1963, pp. 141-151.

247

Fiedler, Leslie. *No! by Thunder: Essays on Myth and Literature.* Boston, 1960.

Fischler, Alexander. "Recent Visitors to the Fountain of Narcissus," *Proceedings of the 14th Annual Pacific Northwestern Conference of Modern Languages.* Banff, 1963, pp. 149-156.

Franklin, W. Bruce. *The Wake of the Gods: Melville's Mythology.* Stanford, 1963.

Frenzel, Elisabeth. *Stoff-, Motiv-, und Symbolforschung.* Stuttgart, 1963.

Frye, Northrop. *Anatomy of Criticism: Four Essays.* Princeton, 1957.

———. *Fables of Identity: Studies in Poetic Mythology.* New York, 1963.

Fuzellier, Etienne. "Les Mythes." *CdS*, xix, 1939, pp. 1-11.

Gilbert, Stuart. *James Joyce's "Ulysses": A Study.* New York, 1962.

Goldberg, S. L. *The Classical Temper: A Study of James Joyce's "Ulysses."* London, 1963.

Goodness, Paul. "A New Virgil Myth." *Commentary*, 1946, pp. 494-495.

Gosztonyi, Alexander. "Hermann Broch und der moderne Mythos." *Schweizerische Monatshefte*, xlii, 1962, pp. 211-219.

Grant, Marion. "The Function of Myth in the Novels of Michel Butor." *Journal of the Australasian Universities Language and Literature Association*, xxxii, 1969, pp. 214-222.

Grant, Michael. *Myths of the Greeks and Romans.* London, 1962.

Graves, Robert. *The Greek Myths.* 2 vols. Harmondsworth, 1960.

Gronicka, André von. "Myth Plus Psychology: A Stylistic Analysis of *Death in Venice*," *Thomas Mann: A Collection of Critical Essays.* Ed. Henry Hatfield. Englewood Cliffs, N.J., 1964, pp. 46-61.

Hall, Vernon. "Joyce's Use of Da Ponte and Mozart's *Don Giovanni*." *PMLA*, lxvi, 1951, pp. 78-84.

Hamburger, Käte. *Thomas Manns "Joseph und seine Brüder": Eine Einführung.* Stockholm, 1945.

———. *Von Sophokles zu Sartre: Griechische Dramenfiguren, antik und modern.* Stuttgart, 1962.

Herd, Eric W. "Myth and Modern German Literature," *Myth and the Modern Imagination.* Ed. Margaret Dalziel. Dunedin, 1967, pp. 51-76.

———. "Myth Criticism: Limitations and Possibilities." *Mosaic,* II, 1969, pp. 69-77.

Highet, Gilbert. *The Classical Tradition: Greek and Roman Influences on Western Literature.* Oxford, 1949.

Hillard, Gustav. "Thomas Manns Mythenspiel." *Merkur,* x, 1956, pp. 112-123.

Horst, Karl August. "Wandlungen des Mythos." *Merkur,* VII, 1953, pp. 489-491.

Hunger, Herbert. *Lexikon der griechischen und römischen Mythologie mit Hinweisen auf das Fortwirken antiker Stoffe und Motive in der bildenden Kunst, Literatur und Musik des Abendlandes bis zur Gegenwart.* Vienna, 1953.

Hyman, Stanley Edgar. *The Armed Vision: A Study in the Methods of Modern Literary Criticism.* New York, 1952.

Jolles, André. *Einfache Formen.* Halle, 1930.

Jouan, F. "Le Retour au mythe grèc dans le théâtre français contemporain." *Bulletin de l'Association Guillaume Budé,* June, 1952.

Jung, Carl Gustav. *"Ulysses"; Wirklichkeit der Seele: Anwendungen und Fortschritte der neueren Psychologie.* Zürich, 1934, pp. 132-169.

——— and Karl Kerényi. *Einführung in das Wesen der Mythologie.* Zürich, 1951.

Kahler, Erich. "Das Fortleben des Mythos," *Die Verantwortung des Geistes: Gesammelte Aufsätze.* Frankfurt a.M., 1952, pp. 201-213.

Kanters, Robert. "De l'Usage des Mythes." *CdS,* XIX, 1939, pp. 51-56.

Kartiganer, Donald M. "Job and Joseph K.: Myth in Kafka's *The Trial.*" *MFS,* VIII, 1962, pp. 31-43.

Kenner, Hugh. *Dublin's Joyce.* London, 1955.

Kerényi, Karl, *see* C. G. Jung.

———, *see* T. Mann.

Kermode, Frank. "The Myth-kitty," *Puzzles and Epiphanies: Essays and Reviews 1958-1961.* London, 1962, pp. 35-39.

———. *The Sense of an Ending: Studies in Fiction.* London, 1967.

Killy, Walther. "Mythologie und Lyrik." *Neue Rundschau,* LXXX, 1969, pp. 694-721.

Kirk, G. S. *Myth: Its Meaning and Functions in Ancient and Other Cultures.* Cambridge, 1970.

Kluckhohn, Clyde. "Recurrent Themes in Myth and Mythmaking." *Daedalus,* 1959, pp. 268-279.

Koopmann, Helmut. "Mythus und Psychologie," *Die Entwicklung des "intellektualen" Romans bei Thomas Mann.* Bonn, 1962, pp. 147-168.

Kreft, Jürgen. *Hamlet—Don Juan—Faustus (Vaterflucht—Mutterbindung—Disintegration): Interpretationen dreier moderner Romane.* Diss., Bonn, 1955.

Kushner, Eva. *Le Mythe d'Orphée dans la Littérature française contemporaine.* Paris, 1961.

Langbaum, Robert. "Browning and the Question of Myth." *PMLA,* LXXXI, 1966, pp. 575-584.

Langer, Susanne K. *Philosophy in a New Key: A Study in the Symbolism of Reason, Rite and Art.* Cambridge, Mass., 1951.

Larousse Encyclopedia of Mythology. Ed. Félix Guirand, trans. Richard Aldington and Delano Ames. London, 1965.

Lehnert, Herbert. *Thomas Mann: Fiktion, Mythos, Religion.* Stuttgart, Berlin, Cologne and Mainz, 1965.

Leiris, Michel. "Le Réalisme mythologique de Michel Butor." *Critique,* CXXIX, 1958, pp. 99-118.

Levin, Harry T. "Some Meanings of Myth." *Daedalus,* 1959, pp. 223-231.

Lewis, C. S. "On Myth," *An Experiment in Criticism.* Cambridge, 1961, pp. 40-49.

Lucas, W. J. "Wagner and Forster: *Parsifal* and *A Room with a View," Romantic Mythologies.* Ed. Ian Fletcher. London, 1967, pp. 271-297.

Lytle, Andrew. "The Working Novelist and the Mythmaking Process." *Daedalus*, 1959, pp. 326-338.

Malzig, Richard. *Odysseus: Studien zu antiken Stoffen in der modernen Literatur.* St. Gallen, 1949.

Mann, Thomas and Karl Kerényi. *Gespräch in Briefen.* Zürich, 1960.

Manton, G. R. "The Making of Myth," *Myth and the Modern Imagination.* Ed. Margaret Dalziel. Dunedin, 1967, pp. 9-26.

Matthews, Honor. *The Hard Journey: The Myth of Man's Rebirth.* London, 1968.

Maulnier, Thierry. "Greek Myths: A Source of Inspiration for Modern Dramatists." *World Theatre*, VI, 1957, pp. 289-293.

Mautner, Franz H. "Die griechischen Anklänge in Thomas Manns *Der Tod in Venedig.*" *Monatshefte*, XLIV, 1952, pp. 20-26.

Meinert, Dietrich. "Hermann Brochs *Der Versucher*: Versuchung und Erlösung im Bannkreis mythischen Erlebens," *Sprachkunst als Weltgestaltung: Festschrift für Herbert Seidler.* Ed. A. Haslinger. Salzburg and Munich, 1966, pp. 140-152.

Merivale, Patricia. *Pan, the Goat-God: His Myth in Modern Times.* Cambridge, Mass., 1968.

Meyer, Herman. *The Poetics of Quotation in the European Novel.* Trans. Theodore and Yetta Ziolkowski. Princeton, 1968.

Miller, James E. (ed.) *Myth and Method: Modern Theories of Fiction.* Lincoln, Nebraska, 1960.

Miller, Leslie L. "Myth and Morality: Reflections on Thomas Mann's *Doktor Faustus*," *Essays on German Literature in Honour of G. Joyce Hallamore.* Ed. M. S. Batts and M. G. Stankiewicz. Toronto, 1968, pp. 195-217.

Moeller, Hans-Bernard. "Thomas Manns venezianische Götterkunde." *DVjS*, XL, 1966, pp. 184-205.

Morrissette, Bruce A. "Oedipe ou le cercle fermé," *Les Romans de Robbe-Grillet.* Paris, 1963, pp. 37-76.

Mühlher, Robert. *Dichtung und Krise: Mythos und Psy-*

chologie in der Dichtung des 19. und 20. Jahrhunderts.
Vienna, 1951.

Murray, Henry A. "Introduction to 'Myth and Mythmaking.'" *Daedalus*, 1959, pp. 211-222.

Negus, Kenneth. *E. T. A. Hoffmann's "Other World": The Romantic Author and his "New Mythology."* Philadelphia, 1965.

Nemerov, Howard S. *The Quester Hero: Myth as Universal Symbol in the Works of Thomas Mann.* Harvard, 1940.

Nielsen, Birgit S. "Adrian Leverkühns Leben als bewußte mythische imitatio des Dr. Faustus." *Orbis litterarum*, xx, 1965, pp. 129-158.

Pellegrini, Alessandro. "Mythos und Dichtung im Werk von Cesare Pavese." *Castrum Peregrini*, xviii, 1954, pp. 7-24.

Peyre, Henri. *L'Influence des Littératures antiques sur la Littérature française moderne: Etat de Travaux.* New Haven, Conn., 1941.

Plöger, Jürgen. *Das Hermesmotiv in der Dichtung Thomas Manns.* Diss., Kiel, 1961.

Prescott, Joseph. "Homer's *Odyssey* and Joyce's *Ulysses.*" *Modern Language Quarterly*, iii, 1942, pp. 427-444.

Proffer, Carl R. "*Taras Bulba* and the *Iliad.*" *Comparative Literature*, xvii, 1965, pp. 142-150.

Reichert, D. *Der griechische Mythos im modernen deutschen und österreichischen Drama.* Diss., Vienna, 1951.

Richter, Bernt. "Der Mythosbegriff Thomas Manns und das Menschenbild der Joseph-Romane." *Euphorion*, liv, 1960, pp. 411-433.

Roudaut, Jean. *Michel Butor ou le Livre futur.* Paris, 1964, pp. 195-206.

Rose, H. J. *A Handbook of Greek Mythology, Including its Extension to Rome.* London, 1958.

Rosenfeld, Claire. *Paradise of Snakes: An Archetypal Analysis of Conrad's Political Novels.* Chicago and London, 1968.

Rothschild, Jakob. *Kain und Abel in der deutschen Dichtung.* Frankfurt a.M., 1933.

252

Rougemont, Denis de. *The Myths of Love*. Translated by Richard Howard. London, 1963.

Rutherford, Andrew. "Joyce's Use of Correspondences." *Essays in Criticism*, VI, 1956, pp. 123-125.

Saunders, F. W. "The Mythical Background to Henri Bosco's *Rameau de la Nuit*." *Miscellany*, 1969, pp. 216-229.

Schmidbauer, Wolfgang. "Mythos und Psychologie." *Studium Generale*, XXII, 1969, pp. 890-912.

Schmidt-Henkel, Gerhard. *Mythos und Dichtung: Zur Begriff- und Stilgeschichte der deutschen Literatur im 19. und 20. Jahrhundert*. Bad Homburg, 1967.

Schönbeck, Uwe. *Erzählfunktionen des Mythos bei Thomas Mann*. Diss., Kiel, 1964.

Schoolfield, George C. "Broch's Sleepwalkers: Aeneas and the Apostles." *The James Joyce Review*, II, 1958, pp. 21-38.

Schwerte, Hans. "Mythische Welt." *Zeitwende*, XXVII, 1956, pp. 127-129.

Schorer, Mark. "The Necessity of Myth." *Daedalus*, 1959, pp. 359-362.

Slochower, Harry. "The Uses of Myth in Kafka and Mann," *Spiritual Problems in Contemporary Literature*. Ed. Stanley Romaine Hopper. New York, 1957, pp. 117-126.

———. *Mythopoesis: Mythic Patterns in Literary Classics*. Detroit, 1970.

Stanford, W. B. *The Ulysses Theme: A Study in the Adaptability of a Traditional Hero*. Oxford, 1954.

Steinecke, Hartmut. "Die Aufhebung des polyhistorischen Romans im mythischen Roman," *Hermann Broch und der polyhistorische Roman*. Bonn, 1968, pp. 156-166.

Stenbock-Fermor, Elisabeth. "Bulgakov's *The Master and Margarita* and Goethe's *Faust*." *The Slavic and East European Journal*, XIII, 1969, pp. 309-325.

Stone, R. G. "Myth in Modern French Literature," *Myth and the Modern Imagination*. Ed. Margaret Dalziel. Dunedin, 1967, pp. 77-94.

Strich, Fritz. *Die Mythologie in der deutschen Dichtung: Von Klopstock bis Wagner*. 2 vols. Halle, 1910.

Tillyard, E. M. W. *Myth and the English Mind*. New York, 1962.

Traschen, Isadore. "The Use of Myth in *Death in Venice*." *MFS*, xi, 1965, pp. 165-179.

Trousson, Raymond. *Le Thème de Prométhée dans la Littérature européenne*. 2 vols. Geneva, 1964.

Troy, William. "Thomas Mann—Myth and Reason." *Partisan Review*, v, 1938, pp. 24-32 and 51-64.

———. "A Further Note on Myth." *Partisan Review*, vi, 1938, pp. 95-100.

Vivas, Eliseo. "Myth: Some Philosophical Problems." *Southern Review*, vi, 1970, pp. 89-103.

Watson-Williams, Helen. *André Gide and the Greek Myth: A Critical Study*. Oxford, 1967.

Weinstein, Leo. *The Metamorphosis of Don Juan*. Stanford, 1959.

Weisinger, Herbert. *The Agony and the Triumph: Papers on the Use and Abuse of Myth*. Michigan, 1965.

Wellek, René and Austin Warren. *Theory of Literature*. New York, 1956.

———. *Concepts of Criticism*. New Haven, Conn. and London, 1963.

Wescott, Frederick C. *Poetry and Myth*. Washington, 1927.

White, John J. "Virgil, Broch and the Cycle of History." *Germanic Review*, xli, 1966, pp. 103-110.

———. "Myths and Patterns in the Modern Novel." *Mosaic*, ii, 1969, pp. 42-55.

Wykes, David. "The *Odyssey* in *Ulysses*." *Texas Studies in Literature and Language*, x, 1968, pp. 301-316.

Ziolkowski, Theodore. "The Odysseus Theme in Recent German Fiction." *Comparative Literature*, xiv, 1962, pp. 225-241.

———. *The Novels of Hermann Hesse: A Study in Theme and Structure*. Princeton, 1965.

Index

255

5, 22; problem of definition,
32-42; etymological approach,
32, 33; return to, 3-6, 23
myth criticism, 33, 34
Mythe, contrasted with *Mythos*,
39
mythical style, 38n
mythique, ambiguities of the
adjective, 36, 37
Mythologem, 44
mythological: allusions, overt and
recondite, 74, 75; characters,
as allegories, 11, their
relationship to modern figures,
97-100; fiction, categories of,
51-54; identity, 98; motifs,
distinguished from myths
proper, 7-11; motifs, techniques
of motivation—chapter
headings, 132-33, names,
134-35, similes and metaphors,
136-39, titles, 120-30
mythology in fiction, contrasted
with its use in other genres,
14, 15, 24-27; historical
background to, 14-17;
metaphorical descriptions of,
20, 21
mythology in literature, *a priori*
judgments of, 76-91;
diachronic accounts, 91-94;
national attitudes to, vii;
"elegiac" attitude to, 85; and
regression, 77-81; and
chauvinism, 77; and the
rhetoric of fiction, 17; as
pretentiousness, 87, 88; as
anachronism, 89; as an
ennobling device, 85, 86; as a
structural principle, 113-17;
as a source of optimism or
pessimism, 17; non-aesthetic
attitudes to, 17-24
Mythos, 37, 38, 39; and *mythisch*,
37, 38
myths, narrated *in toto*, 7; new
created from old, 8n; popular
and literary, 71-73; and
archetypes, 27, 28, 35, 42,
43; substituted for archetypes,

45-51; and legends, 67-71,
209; and psychological
complexes, 47, 48
Mythus, 38n

Nabokov, Vladimir, *King, Queen,
Knave*, 125n; *Lolita*, 59; *The
Defense*, 125n
Narcissus, 23, 47
Nausicaa, 9n, 173
Negus, Kenneth, 14n
Nemerov, Howard Stanley, 25,
45, 46
Neoptolemus, 107, 175-82, 193
Nestor, 135
Nielsen, Birgit, 108, 109, 110
Nietzsche, Friedrich, 27, 48, 59n,
83, 84
Nina, a prefiguration from
Chekhov's *The Seagull* in
Macdonald Harris's *Trepleff*,
229-39
Ninhursag, 195n
Ninki, 195n
Niobe, 9n
Nossack, Hans Erich, 24n, 29, 47,
219n; *Interview mit dem
Tode*, 53n, 70, 93, 175,
182-88, 190n, 222; *Nekyia*, 70,
130, 143, 186n, 190n, 196,
199, 218-28, 230; *Spätestens
im November*, 70, 127, 147
Nott, Kathleen, 232, 237n
Novalis, *Heinrich von
Ofterdingen*, 14n

O'Brien, Flann, *At-Swim-Two-
Birds*, 208n
Odysseus, 9n, 43, 88, 166-82,
193, 224n, 226
Oedipus, 47, 49, 50, 63, 132,
212n
O'Neill, Eugene, *Mourning
Becomes Electra*, 25, 26, 82
Orestes, 89, 127, 135, 188,
225-28
Orion, 9n, 221, 222, 224
Orpheus, 38, 45, 46, 92, 93,
156-66, 182, 184, 185, 186,
187, 197, 198, 201-206, 223